MW00716747

Computational phonology is one of the newest areas of computational linguistics, and is experiencing rapid growth as its practitioners apply the wealth of theories, technologies and methodologies of computational linguistics to phonology. This book is the first to survey these developments, and it does so in a way that is accessible to computational linguists, phonologists and computer scientists alike. The interests of these diverse groups overlap in the subject area of constraints. The goal of this book is to explore the use of constraints in modern non-linear phonology and then – drawing on insights from constraint-based grammar and constraint logic programming – to formalise and implement a constraint-based phonology.

Studies in Natural Language Processing

Computational Phonology

Studies in Natural Language Processing

Series Editor: Branimir Boguraev, Apple Computers Inc.

Editorial Advisory Board
Don Hindle, AT&T Bell Laboratories
Martin Kay, Xerox PARC
David McDonald, Content Technologies
Hans Uszkoreit, University of Saarbrücken
Yorick Wilks, Sheffield University

Also in the series

Semantic Processing for Finite Domains, M.S. Palmer
Reference and Computation, A. Kronfeld
Text Generation, K.R. McKeown
Planning English Sentences, D.E. Appelt
Relational Models of the Lexicon, M.W. Evens
Systemic Text Generation as Problem Solving, T. Patten
Memory and Context for Language Interpretation, H. Alshawi
Machine Translation, edited by S. Nirenburg
Semantic Interpretation and the Resolution of Ambiguity, G. Hirst
The Linguistic Basis of Text Generation, L. Danlos
Computational Linguistics, R. Grishman
Studies in Natural Language Parsing, edited by D. Dowty, L. Karttunen and
    A. Zwicky
Language and Spatial Cognition, Annette Herskovits
Machine Translation Systems, edited by Jonathan Slocum
Challenges in Natural Language Processing, edited by M. Bates and R.M. Wei-
    schedel
Computational Linguistics and Formal Semantics, M. Rosner and R. Johnson
Inheritance, Defaults and the Lexicon, edited by E.J. Briscoe, A. Copestake and
    V. de Paiva

Computational phonology

A constraint-based approach

by
STEVEN BIRD

University of Edinburgh

 CAMBRIDGE
UNIVERSITY PRESS

Published by the Press Syndicate of the University of Cambridge
The Pitt Building, Trumpington Street, Cambridge CB2 1RP
40 West 20th Street, New York, NY 10011-4211, USA
10 Stamford Road, Oakleigh, Victoria 3166, Australia

First published 1995

Printed in Great Britain at the University Press, Cambridge

A catalogue record for this book is available from the British Library

Library of Congress cataloguing in publication data

Bird, Steven.
Computational phonology: a constraint-based approach / Steven Bird
    p.   cm. – (Studies in natural language processing)
Includes bibliographical references and indexes.
ISBN 0 521 47496 5 (hardback)
1. Grammar, Comparative and general – Phonology – Data processing.
2. Computational linguistics. 3. Constraints (Artificial intelligence)
4. Language and logic. I. Title. II. Series.
P217.3.B57   1995
414'.0285–dc20   94-30865 CIP

ISBN 0 521 47496 5 hardback

SGB

For Andrew and Alison

Contents

Preface   **xiii**

1 Introduction   **1**
    1.1   Introduction to phonology   4
    1.2   The formal adequacy of autosegmental notation   12
    1.3   Computational phonology   14
           1.3.1   Motivation   14
           1.3.2   Finite-state methods   16
           1.3.3   Connectionist methods   19
           1.3.4   Other approaches to computational phonology   25
           1.3.5   Towards declarative phonology   27
    1.4   Constraint-based phonology   27
           1.4.1   The declarative/procedural controversy   28
           1.4.2   Constraint-based grammar   29
           1.4.3   Constraints in phonology   31
           1.4.4   Intensionality   32
           1.4.5   Compositionality   34
           1.4.6   The lexicon   35
    1.5   The history of constraints in phonology   36
           1.5.1   Some reactions to generative phonology   37
           1.5.2   Categorial phonology   39
           1.5.3   Unification-based approaches   42
           1.5.4   Inheritance-based approaches   44
           1.5.5   Logic-based approaches   45
           1.5.6   A finite-state approach   46

| | | 1.5.7 | Other approaches | 48 |
| | 1.6 | Conclusion | | 49 |

2 A logical foundation for phonology **51**

	2.1	Sorts		52
		2.1.1	Prosodic sorts	52
		2.1.2	Subsegmental sorts	55
	2.2	Hierarchical organisation		57
		2.2.1	Dominance	57
		2.2.2	Appropriateness constraints	58
		2.2.3	Branching degree	61
		2.2.4	Re-entrancy	62
		2.2.5	Autosegmental licensing	63
		2.2.6	Prosodic licensing and stray erasure	64
		2.2.7	Conclusion	65
	2.3	Temporal organisation		65
		2.3.1	Sequential versus simultaneous	65
		2.3.2	Precedence and overlap	66
		2.3.3	Deriving the no-crossing constraint	68
		2.3.4	Points and intervals	69
		2.3.5	Inclusion and simultaneity	72
		2.3.6	Homogeneity and convexity	72
		2.3.7	Linear ordering and immediate precedence	73
		2.3.8	Conclusion	76
	2.4	The interaction of hierarchical and temporal structure		77
	2.5	Temporal feature logic		80
		2.5.1	The syntax of $\mathcal{L}$	80
		2.5.2	A model-theoretic semantics for $\mathcal{L}$	81
		2.5.3	Depicting models	81
		2.5.4	Validities	82
		2.5.5	Some abbreviatory conventions	83
	2.6	Phonological rules		84
		2.6.1	Phonological rules and logical implication	85
		2.6.2	Default rules	86
	2.7	Conclusion		88

3 A critique of destructive processes **91**

  3.1 Conditions on alternations 91

  3.2 Deletion as alternation with zero 93

    3.2.1 Consonant deletion in Samoan 93

    3.2.2 R-insertion/deletion in English 95

  3.3 Deletion as a phonetic process 97

    3.3.1 Acoustic hiding 97

    3.3.2 Neutralisation 98

  3.4 Resyllabification 100

  3.5 Feature changing harmony 104

    3.5.1 Vowel harmony in Montañes Spanish 104

    3.5.2 Consonant harmony in Chumash 105

  3.6 Conclusion 106

4 A theory of segmental structure **109**

  4.1 The evidence for hierarchical organisation 111

    4.1.1 The laryngeal node 111

    4.1.2 The supralaryngeal node 113

    4.1.3 The manner node 115

    4.1.4 The place node 117

    4.1.5 Sub-place groupings 118

    4.1.6 Conclusion 121

  4.2 An articulatory model 122

    4.2.1 The gestural score 123

    4.2.2 The hierarchical organisation of articulatory features 124

    4.2.3 Manner features 127

    4.2.4 Spreading constriction degree 128

  4.3 Formalising the theory 130

  4.4 Conclusion 133

5 Implementation **135**

  5.1 Model building 136

  5.2 Internal representation 137

    5.2.1 Truth values 137

    5.2.2 Predicates 138

    5.2.3 Axioms 139

    5.2.4 An example 141

    5.2.5 Complexity issues 144

5.3   Prolog/C interface   144
      5.3.1   Prolog search and backtracking   145
      5.3.2   The Prolog/C interface illustrated   147
      5.3.3   Overcoming the Schönfinkel-Bernays limitation 150
      5.3.4   Why not use Prolog directly?   151
5.4   Conclusion   152

6 Conclusion   **153**

Appendix: Logical extensions   **157**
A.1   The feature matrix   157
      A.1.1   Subsegmental structures   157
      A.1.2   Prosodic structures   160
      A.1.3   Re-entrant structures   161
A.2   A modal language for phonological description   162
      A.2.1   Logical framework   162
      A.2.2   Expressing phonological constraints   166
      A.2.3   Conclusion   169

References   **171**

Language index   **193**

Name index   **195**

Subject index   **199**

Preface

This book is an expanded and reorganised version of the author's PhD thesis 'Constraint-Based Phonology' (Edinburgh University, 1990). It has been substantially revised to take account of recent developments in computational phonology.

This book has been composed with three audiences in mind: computational linguists, phonologists and computer scientists. The interests of these diverse groups overlap in the subject area of CONSTRAINTS, a central theme of this work. In computational linguistics there is a well-established research tradition known as CONSTRAINT-BASED GRAMMAR. Phonologists are actively studying the role of constraints in the lexicon, in derivations, on rules and on surface forms. The logic programming community in computer science is concerned with developing languages for CONSTRAINT PROGRAMMING and with efficient algorithms for constraint resolution.

For all three groups, a CONSTRAINT expresses a generalisation which should be true of all candidate solutions. Constraints INTERACT in interesting and potentially complex ways, mutually constraining the solution space. Furthermore, the notion of ORDERING is largely absent: the sequence in which constraints are applied does not affect the end result.

The goal of this book is to clarify the role that constraints play in phonology and then – drawing on insights from constraint-based grammar and constraint-programming – to formalise and implement a CONSTRAINT-BASED PHONOLOGY. For practical reasons it has been necessary to restrict this exercise to the established core of practice in contemporary phonology (e.g. feature geometry, autosegmental association, prosodic hierarchy, licensing) and avoid some of the more controversial and less well-understood devices. On the computational side, it has been necessary to avoid the use of defaults in the interests of producing an implementation in the style of a constraint solver.

There are several motivations for this work. First, the practising phonologist faces severe limitations when it comes to developing and testing a sizeable theory; computerisation promises to alleviate this burden. Second, work in the field of natural language processing is limited to languages without complex phonological processes represented in the orthography; an implemented contemporary phonological model may help to overcome such a restriction and enable natural language processing technology to be applied to a much wider range of languages. Third, it is sometimes claimed that rule-based speech recognition systems exhibit poor performance as a result of employing the 1960's SPE rule system; contemporary non-linear phonological models bear a closer resemblance to the speech stream and they promise to provide a fresh source of symbolic techniques to guide speech recognition systems. Finally, it is possible to view phonology as a bridge between the speech technology community and the natural language processing community; attention to developments in phonology may help to achieve the long-term prospect of having integrated speech and language systems.

It is a pleasure to acknowledge my debt to several people who have been instrumental in helping me transform a collection of ideas into the form of a monograph: Patrick Blackburn, Jo Calder, John Coleman, Robin Cooper, Mark Ellison, Dafydd Gibbon, Mark Johnson, András Kornai, Marcus Kracht, Bob Ladd, Chris Mellish, Dick Oehrle, Geoff Pullum, Mike Reape, Jim Scobbie, Henry Thompson, Richard Weise, Pete Whitelock, and many others. The material presented here has also been used in courses at the *Second and Fifth European Summer Schools in Logic, Language and Information* (Leuven 1990, Lisbon 1993), the *32nd Annual Meeting of the ACL* (Las Cruces, 1994) and the *2nd Australian Linguistics Institute* (Melbourne, 1994), and I would like to thank the participants for helping to test the material and for providing valuable feedback. In particular I would like to thank Ewan Klein, for his careful guidance during the PhD on which this work is based, and for his clarity of thought and practical wisdom about presentation, which were nothing short of inspirational. I am indebted to my other teachers Roland Sussex, John Upton and Jean-Louis Lassez who fostered my interests in linguistics, mathematics and constraint-logic programming while I was a student at Melbourne University.

It has been a pleasure to collaborate with Bran Boguraev (the series editor) and the staff at Cambridge University Press in the production of this book. I am also grateful to the following organisations for financial support: the Overseas Research Studentship Awards Scheme, Edinburgh University, the Victoria League, the Linguistic Society of America and the Science and Engineering Research Council.

Greater debts are nearer to home. My christian friends in Scotland have been an extended family to me while I have lived in exile from Australia. My parents, by their example, taught me perseverance and dedication to the task, for which I am eternally grateful. Finally, I thank Kay for being such a rich blessing on my life throughout this work.

1   Introduction

The last two decades have witnessed a vigorous growth of new descriptive notational devices in phonology. These devices have had enormous heuristic value in helping practitioners to see and intuitively understand complex phenomena. However, linguistic notations should be 'perfectly explicit' and ought not 'rely on the intelligence of the understanding reader' (Chomsky, 1965, 4). It is not clear that modern non-linear phonology, to any great extent, meets these fundamental requirements of generative grammar. If current work in computational phonology and speech technology is focused on the outdated SPE model (Chomsky and Halle, 1968) it is because nothing more recent has surpassed SPE's formal explicitness. Therefore, it is time for these new phonological frameworks to be placed on a formal footing.

Those who are suspicious of formalism may cry foul at this point. After all, many a good linguistic insight has been buried under a barrage of definitions and theorems, and a preoccupation with technical hygiene may blinker one's vision of what is really going on. However, the solution is not to retreat to a position where *formulating* a description is synonymous with *formalising* a description. Rather, we need to recognise that formalisation has considerable heuristic value of its own. After all, linguistic theorising in this century has been characterised – possibly even driven – by a tension between attempts at rigorous theories of linguistic structure and attempts to formulate intuitively sensible descriptions of linguistic phenomena.

Beyond this, formalisation is fundamental to the empirical basis of the field. The widespread practice of testing an empirical generalisation on isolated examples leads to unstable theories which are restricted to small fragments of a language. If, as noted with regret by Anderson (1989,

1

803), outside observers do not always take phonology seriously, then an important reason is different notions of what a scientific theory is and does. As we shall see below, a phonological theory which can be implemented on a computer can meet the dual requirements of rigour and non-trivial empirical content which much current work has unsuccessfully striven to achieve.

Underlying these concerns is the goal of constructing grammars which do not favour generation at the expense of recognition, or vice versa. This connects with the familiar debate about the metatheoretical undesirability of extrinsically ordered rules (Koutsoudas, Sanders and Noll, 1974; Hooper, 1976), and with earlier complaints that the derivational stance of generative phonology was inherently process-oriented. Despite claims to the contrary, many current phonological theories remain performance models. They enumerate the steps which must be taken in moving from a lexical form to a surface form, borrowing heavily on the now dated flowchart model of computation. Crucially, there is no guarantee that such rule systems work in reverse.[1] If we accept that linguistics is the study of that knowledge which is independent of processing tasks, then the statements of a linguistic theory ought to have a declarative semantics: an interpretation which is expressed solely in terms of the utterances which are licensed by theory. Of course, if a theory is going to be useful its statements should also have one or more procedural interpretations, but these ought not to be mistaken for the linguistic theory itself.

Readers with a background in computational syntax and semantics will be wondering how this computational phonology could fit into an overarching computational grammar framework. Here, our starting point is provided by the work of Deirdre Wheeler and Emmon Bach,[2] who showed how the principles of Montague grammar can be applied to phonology. However, the aim here is not to perform this integration of phonology and grammar, but rather to do phonology in such a way that this integration is possible. Therefore, a monostratal approach[3] to phonological description

---

[1] This non-reversibility is a general result, which Bear (1990) has demonstrated for Klamath (Halle and Clements, 1983, 113).

[2] Wheeler (1981, 1988); Bach and Wheeler (1981); Bach (1983).

[3] See §1.4.5 for an explanation of the term 'monostratal'.

has been adopted since this is a requirement for a phonological framework to be integrated into existing constraint-based grammar frameworks.[4]

In this connection it is necessary to introduce two distinctions. The first is the DESCRIPTION/OBJECT distinction: an expression of a linguistic theory DENOTES the class of utterance tokens which SATISFY that expression. These expressions are combined using familiar logical connectives. While there is a fundamental difference in kind between descriptions and objects, and so one might imagine that this configuration is actually polystratal, there remains only a single level of linguistic description. This state of affairs contrasts with the procedural model of traditional generative phonology in which there is no principled upper bound on the number of intermediate levels of description. Frameworks which build in this distinction are sometimes called CONSTRAINT-BASED because their linguistic descriptions act in concert to mutually constrain the solution space.

A second distinction is that of FRAMEWORK versus THEORY. A linguistic framework is essentially a formal notation in which linguistic theories can be stated. As such, a framework makes no empirical claims of its own, though a good framework should facilitate the expression and evaluation of such claims. Just as two theories which make contradictory claims can be expressed in the same framework, a given theory can potentially be encoded in a variety of different frameworks. A computational benefit of frameworks is that once a framework is implemented, a whole family of theories can be easily expressed within it, and it is not necessary to write whole implementations from scratch for each new theory.

These are the essential ingredients of what I shall call CONSTRAINT-BASED PHONOLOGY, a term derived from the established fields of constraint-based grammar and constraint logic programming. It is hoped that the eventual payoff of work in this vein will be the construction of rigorous and empirical phonological theories along with the construction of integrated systems for speech and language processing. However, in the light of this aspiration the immediate goals are more humble. After providing the necessary background material in chapter 1, a logical foundation for phonology cast in a language of classical first-order predicate logic is presented along with

---

[4]For example, Generalised Phrase Structure Grammar (Gazdar et al., 1985), Categorial Unification Grammar (Uszkoreit, 1986), Head-Driven Phrase Structure Grammar (Pollard and Sag, 1987), and Unification Categorial Grammar (Calder, Klein and Zeevat, 1988). Some evidence of initial progress in this direction can be found in Bird (1992); Bird and Klein (1994).

a model-theoretic semantics (chapter 2). This constitutes the framework in which subsequent theorising is couched. In chapter 3 this is applied to a sampler of frequently cited phenomena which might be thought to present obstacles to a monostratal approach. Chapter 4 consists of an investigation of recent proposals in the theory of feature geometry, followed by the formalising and interfacing of Sagey (1986) and Browman and Goldstein (1989). These two chapters exemplify the framework by showing how theories can be expressed. The implementation of the model used throughout this work is presented in chapter 5, in the form of a temporal constraint-solver.

The remainder of chapter 1 is structured as follows. First, an intuitive introduction to generative phonology is presented in §1.1, focusing on the progression from linear to non-linear phonology (the autosegmental version). In §1.2 the formal adequacy of the autosegmental notation is discussed and found to be deficient. This deficiency is a stumbling block for any attempt to provide a computational interpretation of the autosegmental framework. Section 1.3 presents an overview of current work in computational phonology and §1.4 is a discussion of constraint-based phonology. The history of constraints in phonology is surveyed in §1.5.

1.1 Introduction to phonology

Segmental phonology derives its name from the fundamental hypothesis that – for linguistic purposes – speech can be sliced into a linear sequence of events, like beads on a string, known as SEGMENTS. Although we will have good reason to challenge this hypothesis later, its initial appeal comes from the existence of alphabetic writing systems, which involve more or less discrete tokens arranged in sequence.

The first illustration of segmental phonology will be based on the formation of regular plural in English. The following table shows various English plural nouns, and alongside each noun is the letter *s* or *z*, indicating how the plural is actually pronounced.

word	suffix	word	suffix
caps	s	cabs	z
mats	s	pads	z
backs	s	bags	z

Observe that for words ending in *p*, *t* and *k* the plural is *s*, while for words ending in *b*, *d* and *g* the plural is *z*. In fact, this observation holds for most English nouns ending in these consonants. The question is, how do speakers know when to use *s* and when to use *z*? The answer given by traditional segmental phonology is to provide the following rule:

(1.1)   s → z / {b, d, g}___

This means that an *s* becomes a *z* in the context '{b, d, g}___'. To understand the context, imagine the *s* being in the position of the underline. In other words, an *s* is only affected if it follows a *b*, *d* or *g*. Rules like (1.1) have a transformational character, and generative phonology has sometimes been referred to, somewhat pejoratively, as 'transformational phonetics' (Foley, 1977). Rule (1.1) is not an entirely satisfactory explanation of the phenomenon. Could we arbitrarily modify some details of this rule and get an equally plausible rule? The answer is no.

To see how to proceed from here we must return to the beads-on-a-string analogy. Imagine we have a colourful necklace, as shown below. Colours are denoted by two-letter abbreviations. What is the colour of the fifth bead?

—(bk)—(gr)—(pu)—(bl)—(?)—(ye)—(re)—(wh)—

The sequence looks completely random, yet if we decompose the colours into their primary components, as shown below, it is possible to guess the pattern and discover that the fifth bead must be orange.

(1.2)

	bk	gr	pu	bl	or	ye	re	wh
R	+	−	+	−	+	−	+	−
Y	+	+	−	−	+	+	−	−
B	+	+	+	+	−	−	−	−

This technique of resolving colours into their components also works well in the discovery of patterns in sequences of phonological segments.

Let us return to the English plural. Here we have a collection of segments, like *s* and *b*, but how should they be decomposed? Consider *s* and *z*. They are identical except for the property of VOICING. The segment *z* involves a periodic vibration of the glottis, while *s* does not. English has several pairs of voiceless/voiced consonants, as shown in the following table:[5]

		lips	tongue	tongue body
		teeth	tip	palate
plosives		p/b	t/d	k/g
fricatives		f/v	s/z	ʃ/ʒ

So words ending in voiceless plosives take the plural form *s*, which is the voiceless member of the {*s*, *z*} pair, while words ending in voiced plosives take the plural form *z*, the voiced member of {*s*, *z*}. We call this an ALTERNATION involving *s* and *z*, and write *s*~*z*, '*s* alternates with *z*'. Here, we can observe that the consonant cluster must *agree* in voicing; *i.e.* a voicing ASSIMILATION has taken place. In segmental phonology, this observation can be expressed as the rule in (1.3) below.

(1.3)   s → [+voice] / [+voice] ___

This still does not quite capture the idea of assimilation, since we could just as easily have had a version of the above rule where the context was [−voice], which would be implausible. So instead the following notation is used, employing a Greek variable α which ranges over the values + and −, and a symbol S to represent a segment like *s* and *z* which is unspecified for voicing.

(1.4)   S → [αvoice] / [αvoice] ___

For the next innovation, it is necessary to return to the coloured beads. Consider again the strand of beads we saw above, repeated as (1.5a). Suppose we were to view these beads through tinted glasses. The strand in (1.5b) corresponds to yellow glasses, while that in (1.5c) corresponds to red glasses.

---

[5] The ʃ and ʒ consonants are the middle consonants of the English words *machine* and *regime* respectively.

(1.5) a.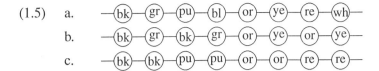
       b.
       c.

Observe that the black bead in (1.5a) remains black in (1.5b,c) regardless of which glasses are used, while the other beads are affected in different ways. For example, the blue bead in (1.5a) appears green in (1.5b) and purple in (1.5c).

Returning to phonology, let us consider the vowels of Turkish. These vowels are tabulated below,[6] along with a decomposition into DISTINCTIVE FEATURES. Notice that this table is the same as the colour chart in (1.2) but with different labels. We have already met the distinctive feature [voice]. Here we meet the features [high], [back] and [round]. The features [high] and [back] relate to the position of the tongue body in the oral cavity. The feature [round] relates to the rounding of the lips.

(1.6)

	u	o	ü	ö	ı	a	i	e
high	+	−	+	−	+	−	+	−
back	+	+	−	−	+	+	−	−
round	+	+	+	+	−	−	−	−

The analogy with beads and tinted glasses will help us to understand the vowel patterns of Turkish words. Think of each word as a strand of beads, but where each word also supplies a different pair of tinted glasses to use. Now, look at the following Turkish words. Pay particular attention to the four versions of the possessive suffix.

ip	*rope*	ipin	*rope's*
kız	*girl*	kızın	*girl's*
yüz	*face*	yüzün	*face's*
pul	*stamp*	pulun	*stamp's*

The suffix has the forms *in*, *ın*, *ün* and *un*. Observe that the vowel of the suffix agrees with the vowel of the stem, and observe that the consonants do not change (cf. the black beads). Now although the possessive nouns (in the third column) have two vowels, it is appealing to imagine that there

---

[6]Note that there is a distinction made in the Turkish alphabet between the dotted *i* and the dotless *ı*. This *ı* is a high, back, unrounded vowel that does not occur in English.

is just the one vowel which 'colours' the whole word, just as coloured glasses tint an entire view. As we have seen, Turkish actually has eight vowels, but only *four* forms of the possessive suffix. Thus, the suffix vowel is not always identical to the stem vowel, as the above data may lead one to suspect. As an example of the situation where the suffix vowel differs from the stem vowel, consider the word *el* 'hand' which has the possessive form *elin*, rather than **elen*. With the help of table (1.6) the reader should be able to determine which forms of the suffix are used for the words *çan* 'bell', *köy* 'village' and *son* 'end'. Consult the footnote for the solution.[7]

Let us see how segmental phonology might express this vowel patterning. We begin by supposing that the vowel of the possessive affix is only specified as [+high] and not specified for the features [back] and [round]. *C* denotes any consonant.

$$(1.7) \quad [+\text{high}] \longrightarrow \begin{bmatrix} \alpha\text{back} \\ \beta\text{round} \end{bmatrix} / \begin{bmatrix} \alpha\text{back} \\ \beta\text{round} \end{bmatrix} C\_\_$$

So long as the stem vowel is specified for the properties [high] and [back], this rule will make sure that they are copied on to the affix vowel. However, this approach misses out on the idea that there is just one property that is spread over the whole word. It also allows nonsense rules where the Greek variables are switched around:

$$[+\text{high}] \longrightarrow \begin{bmatrix} \alpha\text{back} \\ \beta\text{round} \end{bmatrix} / \begin{bmatrix} \beta\text{back} \\ \alpha\text{round} \end{bmatrix} C\_\_$$

Another approach available to segmental phonology, which avoids the use of Greek variables, is to suppose that the DEFAULT values for [back] and [round] are [−back] and [−round] respectively. Then we can have independent rules for [round] and [back] and these only refer to the non-default − or MARKED − values:

$$[+\text{high}] \longrightarrow [+\text{round}] / [+\text{round}] C\_\_$$

$$[+\text{high}] \longrightarrow [+\text{high}] / [+\text{high}] C\_\_$$

---

[7]

el	hand	elin	hand's
çan	bell	çanın	bell's
köy	village	köyün	village's
son	end	sonun	end's

Here we are starting to see the breakdown of the fundamental hypothesis of segmental phonology, introduced at the beginning of this section, which states that speech can be segmented into a linear sequence of discrete events. Let us suppose for a moment that speech *cannot* be sliced up in this way. In other words, suppose that picking boundaries between segments based on a feature like [back] gives different results to picking boundaries based on [voiced]. If we cut the speech stream into slices we would expect to find that adjacent slices are not independent of each other but share many properties. It is plausible that we might be able to come up with rules to express the relationship between adjacent slices. Crucially though, the more rules we had to come up with, the less plausible would be our starting assumption that slicing up the speech stream in this way helps to understand what is going on. Now, segmental phonology is sometimes assumed to have been a success because of the elaborate systems of rules and derivations that it inspired. However, the existence of such a rich armoury of constraints, rules and processes is simply an epiphenomenon. Paradoxically, the 'success' of segmental phonology is actually evidence that the segmental hypothesis is untenable.

Let us now abandon segmental phonology and try to give some content to our intuition that Turkish words are coloured with certain properties like [+back] or [–round]. Consider the words *çanın* and *köyün*. We could depict them thus:

(1.8)   a.

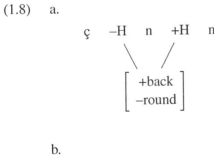

   b.

   k   +H   y   –H   n
   $\diagdown$ $\diagup$
   $\begin{bmatrix} -\text{back} \\ +\text{round} \end{bmatrix}$

Entities like [+back,–round] that function over extended regions are known as PROSODIES, and this kind of picture is called a NON-LINEAR represent-ation.

The notion of prosodies dates back to the mid-century work of Harris (1944), Pike and Pike (1947), Firth (1948) and Hockett (1954). Today this notion is present in a wide range of phonological frameworks.[8] Here we shall see the fundamentals of just one of these models, known as AUTOSEGMENTAL PHONOLOGY, so called because it views the prosodies as autonomous segments, or simply AUTOSEGMENTS.

In autosegmental phonology, diagrams like those we saw above are known as CHARTS. A chart consists of two TIERS, along with some ASSOCIATION LINES drawn between the autosegments on those tiers. The NO-CROSSING CONSTRAINT is a stipulation that association lines are not allowed to cross.[9] AUTOSEGMENTAL RULES are procedures for converting one diagram into another, by adding or removing association lines and autosegments. A rule for Turkish vowel harmony might look like the following, where V denotes any vowel:

(1.9)

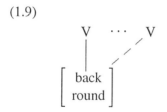

Rule (1.9) applies to any diagram containing (1.10a) and produces a similar diagram with an additional line (1.10b), which is the same as (1.8a).

---

[8] Dynamic Phonology (Griffin, 1985), Dependency Phonology (Anderson and Durand, 1987), Autosegmental and Metrical Phonology (Goldsmith, 1990) and Government Phono-logy (Kaye, Lowenstamm and Vergnaud, 1990).

[9] As we shall see in §2.3.3, this constraint is a consequence of the temporal nature of autosegmental diagrams.

(1.10) a.

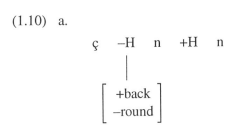

   b.

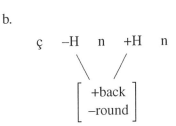

Notice that there is nothing to stop us from constructing an equivalent representation for *çanın* in (1.11) which gets us back to segmental phonology.

(1.11)

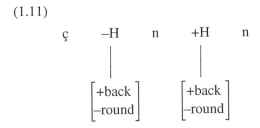

In fact there is a constraint, called the OBLIGATORY CONTOUR PRINCIPLE (Leben, 1973), which rules out such diagrams. It requires that two autosegments must be distinct if they are adjacent on the same tier.[10]

This concludes the introduction to segmental and autosegmental phonology. Now we shall move on to look at some technical problems with autosegmental phonology.

---

[10] See Yip (1988) for a survey of the obligatory contour principle.

1.2   The formal adequacy of autosegmental notation

Autosegmental phonology is fundamentally a collection of descriptive notational devices, along with conventions about their application and interpretation. Goldsmith states:

> It would not be wrong, in fact, to summarise the entire goal of autosegmental analysis as being the reduction of natural phonological processes to changes that can be expressed in the minimal autosegmental notation... (Goldsmith, 1990, 73f)

Given the central status of notation in autosegmental theory, the imprecise definition and widespread abuse of notation in the literature is somewhat disconcerting. The reader seeking a *precise* understanding of the basic elements of autosegmental representations and rules will often be left floundering. Is the association relation reflexive, symmetric or transitive?[11] What does the no-crossing constraint really mean? What does the *absence* of an association line mean? Are diagrams to be thought of as descriptions or as objects?

Here we shall consider just the no-crossing constraint. One interpretation is that the no-crossing constraint blocks the application of a rule which would result in crossing lines (Goldsmith, 1990, 30). Another view is that the no-crossing constraint *repairs* ill-formed representations by causing the deletion of the line crossed by the new line (Goldsmith, 1990, 47,79).[12] For example, consider the effect of a rule like (1.9), which spreads the initial tone of a word to subsequent vowels, as applied to (1.12).

---

[11] These properties are explained in §2.3.3.

[12] This ambiguity between blocking versus repair views has arisen in other areas of phonology, most notably in connection with the obligatory contour principle, which requires that two adjacent tier elements must not be identical (Goldsmith, 1976, 36). Leben's (1973) original definition of the obligatory contour principle clearly views it as a repair strategy which alters a representation containing adjacent identical elements by fusing them into one. However, McCarthy (1986, 222) has advocated the opposite view, where the OCP simply blocks a derivation. Yip (1988), on the other hand, advocates both views.

(1.12)

On the first application, a line from the *L* to the second *a* is added:

(1.13)

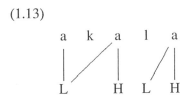

Under the 'blocking' view of the no-crossing constraint, the rule could not re-apply, since linking the *L* to the third *a* would cause a line crossing. Under the 'repair' view, there are two further steps. In (1.14a) a line which violates the no-crossing constraint is added (the asterisk indicates this ill-formedness), and in (1.14b), the old line is automatically deleted leaving the first *H* tone unassociated.

(1.14) a.

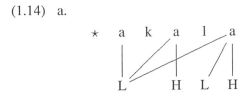

   b.

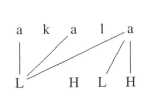

This ambiguity between the blocking and repair interpretations arises because there is only an informal connection between the well-formedness condition and a derivation it is understood to license. Therefore, the question of interpreting the no-crossing constraint needs to be addressed (see §2.3.3). Since derivations are understood to be deterministic, both interpretations cannot co-exist.

This concludes our discussion of the formal adequacy of the autosegmental notation. There are several other technical problems with current notational practice in autosegmental phonology; Bird and Ladd (1991) give a detailed critique. Once these problems are solved, the way is open for the computational implementation of autosegmental phonology. In the next section an overview of current developments in computational phonology is presented.

1.3   Computational phonology

1.3.1   Motivation

The practising phonologist is frequently beset by two problems regarding data and analysis. First, a realistically sized corpus of data is difficult to maintain and access if it is stored on paper. Putting such a corpus online is a solution, but some difficult technical problems need to be solved first.[13] Second, a realistically sized analysis is virtually impossible to check by hand. The widespread practice of testing a few interesting cases is unreliable and is no substitute for an exhaustive check. Here again, automation promises to provide a solution, provided that phonological analyses can be represented on computer. These considerations motivated some of the earliest work on computational phonology, such as Bobrow and Fraser's *Phonological Rule Tester*:[14]

> Although the theory [of SPE] has been designed and modified to enable the
> linguist to state generalizations about a language in a simple and revealing
> way, an account of some significant portion of a language often results
> in a complex and interdependent set of rules. Consequently, it becomes

[13] Griswold (1992) describes the following classic problems of multilingual computing: character rendering (character shapes, context sensitivity, diacritic placement), line rendering, data entry, internal storage, alphabetising, searching, word demarcation.

[14] Other early SPE implementations are Friedman and Morin (1971); Roosen-Runge and Kaye (1973).

more difficult for the linguist to evaluate the work he has done. In fact, linguists have reached the point today where the detail of analysis makes it impracticable to evaluate by hand even a small set of rules. In this paper the design and implementation of a system to alleviate the problem of rule evaluation for the linguist in the area of phonology are presented... (Bobrow and Fraser, 1968, 766)

Another source of motivation for computational phonology comes from the field of speech technology. If speech recognition systems incorporate a rule-based model, it is almost invariably the SPE model (e.g. Allen et al., 1987). Some have argued that this approach has foundered and that speech technologists should look to phonology for new conceptual machinery (Kaye, 1989; Kornai, 1991). In a similar way, the field of natural language processing is currently limited to a small group of languages which lack morphophonological alternations in the orthography. Gazdar made a similar observation:

Until recently there has been relatively little computational linguistic work on morphology or phonology, in contrast to the large amount of work on syntax and speech. The explanation for this state of affairs is not hard to find: most computational linguistics has dealt with English, and the latter's inflectional morphology is impoverished. Consequently, the English lexicon can be treated, for many practical purposes, simply as a list with the spelling and phonetics already encoded. Derivational morphology can be ignored ('if it occurs, list it!'), and inflectional morphology can be reduced to a few ad hoc devices to realise -S and -ED. This kind of strategy collapses completely, of course, when confronted with a language like Finnish or Turkish. (Gazdar, 1985, 604)

This is a challenge to develop a computational phonology which can be applied to the full diversity of the world's languages. Once this is done, the achievements of the field of natural language processing will have far greater applicability.

A final area of motivation comes from the long-term prospect of having integrated speech and language systems. Phonology is a potential link between the speech technology community and the natural language processing community. However, as we have seen, contemporary phonology is inadequately formalised to play this mediating role. Perhaps computational phonology will ultimately bridge the gap between these two independent areas of technological development.

In the rest of this section, the recent developments in computational phonology are surveyed.[15] We begin by considering finite-state methods, one of the earliest approaches.

1.3.2   Finite-state methods

The idea of employing FINITE-STATE TRANSDUCERS (FSTs) to represent the rule systems of generative phonology was proposed in the early 1980s by Kaplan and Kay in unpublished work[16] (though now published as Kaplan and Kay 1994), which connected with Johnson's demonstration that the relations described by generative phonological rules are REGULAR (Johnson, 1972). Koskenniemi (1983a, 1983b, 1984) proposed an FST model where rules could refer to *both* surface and lexical contexts, but that these were the only levels of representation, and so there could be no feeding or bleeding relationships between rules.[17] Koskenniemi also proposed a high-level notation for rules which could be compiled into transducer specifications (Koskenniemi, 1985). Antworth (1990) gives a detailed exposition of the rule notation, the transducer specifications and the compilation process. Ritchie et al. (1992) and Sproat (1992) also give expositions of the two-level model, while Pulman and Hepple (1993) present a two-level system incorporating a unification-based representation of segments. Here we shall see the rule notation and its application to Turkish vowel harmony.

The rule notation employs pairs of symbols, consisting of a LEXICAL symbol and a SURFACE symbol. Rules express constraints on the distribution of these pairs. There are three types of rule, as shown in (1.15).

---

[15] See Bird (1994b) for a differently structured survey.

[16] See Kay (1983, 100–4).

[17] Two rules r_1 and r_2 are in a FEEDING (resp. BLEEDING) relationship if the application of r_1 creates (resp. destroys) the context necessary for r_2 to apply (Kiparsky, 1968, 196ff).

(1.15) a. **Context restriction rule:**
$$L : S \Rightarrow A\_\_B$$
Lexical symbol L corresponds to surface symbol S only when preceded by A and followed by B.

b. **Surface coercion rule:**
$$L : S \Leftarrow A\_\_B$$
If the lexical symbol L occurs and is preceded by A and followed by B, then the surface symbol must be S.

c. **Composite rule:**
$$L : S \Leftrightarrow A\_\_B$$
This is an abbreviation for two separate rules, one involving $\Rightarrow$ and the other involving $\Leftarrow$.

Recall the constraint on sequences of vowels in Turkish that was discussed in §1.1. It is possible to give an analysis of this vowel harmony using the two-level rules in (1.16). Here, the H is a lexical symbol indicating a high vowel and @ is a wildcard symbol.

(1.16) a. $H : u \Leftrightarrow @ : \{u, o\}C^{\star}\_\_$

b. $H : ü \Leftrightarrow @ : \{ü, ö\}C^{\star}\_\_$

c. $H : i \Leftrightarrow @ : \{i, e\}C^{\star}\_\_$

d. $H : ı \Leftrightarrow @ : \{ı, a\}C^{\star}\_\_$

Rule (1.16a) states that a lexical H corresponds to a surface u if and only if (iff) the immediately preceding vowel on the surface tape is either u or o. Rule (1.16d) licenses the correspondence between lexical *çanHn* and surface *çanın* shown in (1.17).

(1.17)

ç	a	n	H	n
			↕	
ç	a	n	ı	n

The two-level model has been used in the analysis of a variety of phonological phenomena. Antworth (1990, §6) gives a sampler of two-level rules for such processes as assimilation, deletion, insertion, gemination, metathesis, infixation and reduplication.

One shortcoming of the two-level model is that there are no generally available techniques for the effcent compilation of realistically sized rule sets into efficient transducers. Naïve compilation methods may be very slow and may result in fantastically large transducers (cf. Withgott and Chen, 1993, 38f; Liberman, 1994).[18] A further shortcoming of the two-level model is that it is purely linear and cannot be applied to non-linear models such as autosegmental phonology. In response to this, Kay (1987) proposed an n-way transducer model in which each autosegmental tier corresponds to a different tape. However, this model can only be used where there is a one-to-one correspondence between morphemes and tiers, as claimed for some aspects of the morphology of Arabic and a handful of other languages. Kornai (1991) proposed a linear encoding of non-linear representations which can then be trivially represented on a tape for the purposes of transduction. However, transducing between encodings is a non-trivial matter, and Bird and Ellison (1994) show that there is no principled upper limit on the amount of state information required by the transducer. In other words, using the linear encoding, certain phonological processes cannot be modelled using a regular relation. Wiebe (1992) synthesises and extends the proposals of Kay and Kornai. He defines a non-linear encoding of tiers and association lines and employs a new kind of transducer (more powerful than an FST) for manipulating encodings to simulate the operation of autosegmental rules.

These three proposals for remedying the linearity of the two-level approach all resort to non-regular manipulations of structures (or encodings) in order to express phonological derivations. Another approach is to eschew the idea of a derivation and adopt a monostratal perspective, while remaining within the confines of regular grammar. Under this view, a surface tape must be nothing more than a filled-out (or further specified) version of a lexical tape. Equivalently, we can think of a lexical tape (or automaton) as a *partial description* of a surface tape. Autosegmental tiers are viewed as descriptions which act in concert to mutually constrain surface forms. This model has been elaborated by Bird and Ellison (1994) and will be discussed in §1.5.6.

---

[18] Penn and Thomason (1994) propose an extension to finite state machines which addresses this problem.

1.3.3 Connectionist methods

Recently, the view of computation as neural processing has gained popularity amongst some phonologists. The appeal of this metaphor lies in the fact that it permits gradient behaviour to be modelled and it comes supplied with learning techniques. Gradient behaviour and *degrees* of well-formedness have frequently been advocated:

> My conception of preference laws differs from most approaches to linguistic naturalness by characterising linguistic structure not as good or bad (natural or unnatural, unmarked or marked) but as better or worse. (Vennemann, 1988, 1)

> If we think of well-formedness – or its opposite, ill-formedness – as a matter of degree, then the path that the representation takes as it moves, so to speak, from [a lexical representation] to [a surface representation] may be conveniently thought of as a downhill path towards a 'local minimum' of ill-formedness... We may capture significant 'soft' cross-linguistic universals which formerly eluded formal capture. (Goldsmith, 1990, 323,327)

> We assume that there is a substantial class of rules whose mode of operation is to increase the well-formedness of representations. Given a representational space ... the natural way to navigate around this space is to move upward in relative well-formedness. (Prince, 1990, 356)

One approach, based on the notion of spreading activation in a simple linear model, is that of Goldsmith and Larson.[19] The network proposed for modelling the metrical grid is given in (1.18) (Goldsmith, 1993c).

(1.18)

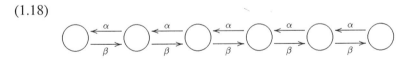

This model consists of a sequence of units, each corresponding to a syllable (or some other phonological entity). Each unit has an activation level, lying in the range $[-1, 1]$. The arcs represent inhibitory relationships between neighbouring units. At each time step the activation x_i of some unit i is computed using the following function:

$$x_i^{t+1} = K(i) + \alpha.x_{i+1}^t + \beta.x_{i-1}^t$$

---

[19] Goldsmith (1989, 1991, 1992, 1993a,b,c); Goldsmith and Larson (1990, 1992); Larson (1990, 1992). See also Laks (1995).

where the characteristic function $K(i)$ is the 'inherent activation' of unit i, and α and β are constants. Once the system has stabilised, those units with an activation greater than their neighbours correspond to stressed syllables, while all other syllables are unstressed.[20] As an example of the operation of this model, suppose that $\alpha = -0.5$, $\beta = 0$, and that for a sequence of n units, K is defined as follows:

$$K(i) = \begin{cases} 0.7, i = 1 \\ 1.0, i = n - 1 \\ 0, \text{otherwise} \end{cases}$$

Here are the results after running this network with 3–6 units.

number of syllables	stress pattern	Values					
3	σ*ό*σ	0.20	1.0	0.0			
4	*ó*σσ*ό*σ	0.95	-0.5	1.0	0.0		
5	*ó*σσσ*ó*σ	0.58	0.25	-0.5	1.0	0.0	
6	*ó*σσ*ó*σσ*ó*σ	0.76	-0.13	0.25	-0.5	1.0	0.0

One of the claimed merits of this approach is that it achieves the required stress patterns for Indonesian words with less machinery than required by Cohn's (1989) analysis, which was set in the framework of lexical phonology. This result is adduced as evidence in support of Goldsmith's opening claim that 'recent work in connectionist modelling suggests the possibility of formal models of phonological representation which will offer *deeper explanations* of basic phonological properties than our current models allow us' (1993c, *emphasis added*). However, given that the architecture of the model, along with the values of the parameters α, β and K, are to some extent arbitrary and could have been chosen differently, it is not obvious that the resulting explanation is deeper than the explanation it is intended to replace. And, as Gasser (1992a) also notes, it is not specified how a language learner accesses the derived activation levels in order to learn the parameters. One response to this would be to say that the derived activation levels correspond to a measurable phonetic parameter; in the

---

[20] It is not possible to set a global threshold value which marks the boundary between stressed and unstressed syllables: an activation of 0.25 in the five syllable version in the following table corresponds to an *unstressed* syllable, while the same activation in the six syllable version corresponds to a *stressed* syllable.

case of stress it would be some combination of pitch, amplitude and length. This would be rather appealing, since the model would then be relating phonological prominence (inherent activation) to phonetic prominence (derived activation), and theories couched in the model would have to be more accountable to the data.[21] In eschewing this approach, Goldsmith and Larson are forced to stipulate the parameters for each new analysis.

Note that Goldsmith and Larson's function for computing the activation level can be expressed as the following matrix equation. Here, the t superscripts are omitted; this equation describes the system in a state of equilibrium.

$$
\begin{bmatrix} x_1 \\ \vdots \\ x_n \end{bmatrix} = \begin{bmatrix} K(1) \\ \vdots \\ K(n) \end{bmatrix} + \begin{bmatrix} 0 & \alpha & & \\ \beta & 0 & \ddots & \\ & \ddots & \ddots & \alpha \\ & & \beta & 0 \end{bmatrix} \begin{bmatrix} x_1 \\ \vdots \\ x_n \end{bmatrix}
$$

Goldsmith and Larson are committed to their iterative procedure for computing approximations to the most desirable activation levels, describing it as the 'essence' of their model (Goldsmith and Larson, 1992, 130). However, Prince (1993) has shown how this matrix equation can be solved to give exact solutions, rather than the approximate solutions provided by Goldsmith and Larson's procedure.[22] Furthermore, Mark Ellison (*pers. comm.*) has demonstrated that computing exact solutions requires less computation time than just *four* iterations of Goldsmith and Larson's formula. Therefore, while one might wish to employ the model for the linguistic insights it gives, a more attractive operational characterisation is available.

Goldsmith and Larson's model is static in the sense that only the vector of inherent activations K (the input) and the vector of derived activations (the output) are the objects of study, as opposed to any of the intermediate stages. The behaviour of the system *through time* is not considered to be of *linguistic* interest. In comparison to this other connectionist models are more genuinely dynamic. We turn to these next.

---

[21] For example, we would expect the two syllables in the above table with the stress value of 0.25 to have the same phonetic stress.

[22] Prince (1993) has also provided a detailed mathematical analysis of Goldsmith and Larson's model along with a constraint on α and β which guarantees convergent behaviour.

Lathroum, Gasser, Lee, Hare and Corina[23] have all proposed models that use RECURRENT NETWORKS. Shillcock et al. (1992, 1993) model psycholinguistic data with a recurrent network built on Government Phonology (Kaye et al., 1990). Gasser (1992a) gives another application of recurrent networks to phonology, and this will be reviewed in detail here. His aim is to get a network to learn distributed representations of syllable structure that can be used for phonologically meaningful operations. Segments are encoded using ten binary-valued distinctive features plus an eleventh, scalar-valued SONORITY feature.[24] Segments are presented to the network in sequence, as shown in (1.19). The segment stream is given at the bottom of this diagram.

(1.19)

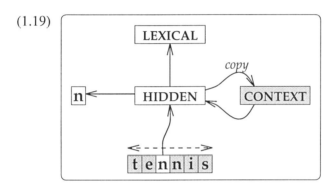

At each step the network inspects the next segment and the 'context' units, and reproduces the current segment on its output (shown on the left) while copying the hidden layer to the context buffer (shown on the right). By the time the end of the word has been reached the network has identified a lexical item, and just one of the units in the lexical layer is active.

Once trained on a set of words, the network is presented with individual *syllables*, each terminated with a boundary marker. Once the boundary marker is reached, the hidden layer is recorded as the representation of the corresponding syllable. This is illustrated in (1.20).

---

[23] Lathroum (1989); Gasser and Lee (1989, 1990, 1991); Hare (1990); Corina (1991); Gasser (1992a,b) .

[24] The SONORITY of a segment in a language is its relative inclination to be the nucleus of a syllable. A segment's sonority correlates with its proximity to the syllable nucleus, and it also correlates with the degree of openness of the vocal tract required for producing the segment.

(1.20)

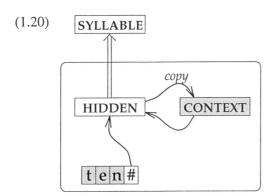

A production network can then be trained which reproduces the segment sequence given just the syllable representation as input, with a 93% success rate. Once trained on legal syllables, the production network is able to 'repair' illegal input (syllable representations produced by the network in (1.20) from illegal syllables). The network produces corrected output by inserting, deleting or modifying segments, with a 68% success rate. The syllable representation therefore captures generalisations about syllable well-formedness, although it does need to be plied with sonority information as part of the segmental representation in order to do this.

The syllable representation is also amenable to phonologically meaning-ful operations. It is possible to train a simple FEEDFORWARD NETWORK to do the following operations: (i) replace the vowel of a syllable with *u*, so that *ten* becomes *tun*, (ii) change the syllable coda to *s*, so that *ten* becomes *tes*, and (iii) spirantise the onset (changing stops to fricatives with the same place of articulation), so that *ten* becomes *sen*. This is illustrated in (1.21), where the feedforward network is shown in the shaded rectangle on the left.

(1.21)
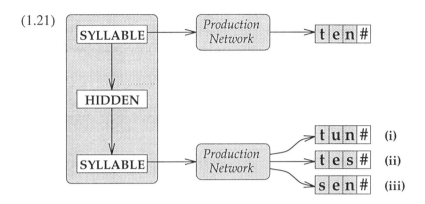

The performance of the network was better than 95% for each of the three rules. So, it seems plausible to conclude that the process of word recognition (shown in (1.19)) gives rise to distributed representations of syllable structure, supporting Gasser's claim that phonology is a byproduct of learning to recognise and produce words.

Several other connectionist approaches to phonology have been investigated which can only be touched on here. For example, Touretzky, Wheeler and Elvgren[25] simulate conventional segmental rules using a connectionist network. Unusually for a connectionist approach, theirs is a competence model employing abstract levels of representation, and is not as obviously connectionist as many of the other models, although they would dispute this (Wheeler and Touretzky, 1993, 169f). Gupta and Touretzky (1991, 1992, 1994) develop a perceptron model of stress, applied to a typologically diverse range of languages. Bellgard (1993) employs a Boltzmann machine to learn Turkish vowel harmony.

A popular *connectionist-inspired* model is known as 'optimality theory' which, Prince and Smolensky (1993, 200) claim, can be approximated by a connectionist network. However, since the focus in this section is on implemented systems, this model will not be discussed in any detail. It stands to reason that optimality theory could be interpreted within a system of prioritised default rules (Lifschitz, 1984). It also bears mentioning that some recent studies have sought to clarify the relationship between optimality theory and the constraint-based view of phonology presented in §1.4 (Scobbie, 1993a; Orgun, 1993; Ellison, 1994a,b). The common theme

---

[25] Touretzky (1989), Touretzky and Wheeler (1990, 1991), Wheeler and Touretzky (1990, 1993), and Touretzky, Wheeler and Elvgren (1990a, 1990b).

underlying both strands of research is that phonological analysis ought to result in characterisations of well-formedness instead of a collection of operations which conspire to produce well-formed output given certain inputs.

These connectionist and connectionist-inspired approaches to phonology hold out a great deal of promise, and it is clear that we are observing a paradigm shift in theoretical phonology. This is already producing new views on central matters like learning and linguistic explanation. It is too early to say what will happen to theoretical notions such as prosodic hierarchy, feature geometry, licensing, structure preservation, integrity, inalterability and so on, notions which have contributed significantly to our understanding of sound patterns over the last decade. Perhaps they can all be done away with, or perhaps they will resurface in other ways:

> If this direction of research is correct, then the picture of phonology that emerges is one in which our notions of phonological structure, including autosegmental, metrical, and prosodic components, will *rearise as the scaffolding in a network* of phonological elements whose well-formedness is calculated on the basis of an interaction of neighbouring units. (Goldsmith, 1993b, 56, *emphasis added*)

1.3.4   Other approaches to computational phonology

There have been several other applications of computational techniques to phonology, which can only be touched on here.

Learning. Ellison (1992a, 1992b) presents a model for automatic learning of phonological generalisations, exemplified for vowel harmony in a range of languages. As the system searches for new generalisations, each candidate generalisation is evaluated as to its restrictiveness on a list of words. If a generalisation is too restrictive, the number of exceptions will be high and this will detract from the overall evaluation of the generalisation. On the other hand, if a generalisation is too unrestrictive, it will not make useful predictions about which segment is coming next in a given context and this will increase the cost of storing the word list. An information-theoretic evaluation measure can be used to measure the cost, in bits, of storing a list of words in the presence of different generalisations. Accordingly, the relative simplicity of different analyses can be measured in a mathematically principled manner, something which has not been possible in generative phonology until now.

Cartwright and Brent (1994) also use an information-theoretic measure, in a system which learns to segment speech. Bird (1994a) describes a program for transcribing instrumentally obtained pitch data from tone languages. Both Ellison's and Bird's work on learning involves solving combinatorial optimisation problems using non-deterministic search methods.

Others who have investigated symbolic learning in phonology are Johnson (1984, 1993) , Powers (1991) and Stethem (1991). Daelemans et al. (1994) present a rather striking demonstration that an empiricist learning model which uses INSTANCE-BASED LEARNING actually performs better than the nativist 'Principles and Parameters' approach (cf. Dresher and Kaye, 1990), concerning the task of assigning primary stress to a corpus of around 5,000 Dutch words.

Speech. Church (1987) presents a chart parser for phonological parsing in speech recognition. Kornai (1991) presents a formalisation of autosegmental phonology (already mentioned in §1.3.2) which is designed to inform a new class of speech recognition devices called structured Markov models. To my knowledge this system has not been implemented. Phonologically well-informed approaches to speech synthesis which *have* been implemented include Hertz (1990); Coleman (1992b) .

Formal Language Theory. By and large, this area has attracted little attention in phonology. Phonological frameworks are not well studied from the perspective of formal language theory, especially those which trade in objects which are not directly related to formal languages. Ristad (1990, 1992), Ritchie (1992) and Kaplan and Kay (1994) all deal with formal models of segmental phonology. Kornai (1991) and Wiebe (1992) give language theoretic results that relate to autosegmental phonology, while Bird and Ellison (1994) try to obviate the need for this by mapping autosegmental phonology back onto finite state automata (see §1.5.6).

Other Implementations. Another application of computational phonology has been to the study of diachronic phonology.[26] Williams[27] has implemented a version of Lexical Phonology (Kiparsky, 1982). Brandon

---

[26] Hewson (1974, 1989); Eastlack (1977); Hartman (1981); Lowe and Mazaudon (1989, 1994).

[27] Williams et al. (1989); Williams (1991, 1993, 1994) .

(1991) has implemented a programming language which simulates rules of standard generative phonology, incorporating input and output filters and cyclic rule application. Maxwell (1991, 1994) has also implemented a system for generative phonology which includes a scheme for recognition that does not involve reversing rules and the concomitant ambiguity problems. Albro (1994) has implemented a system for autosegmental phonology that supports many of the standard autosegmental operations, and uses textual representations of autosegmental structures and rules. Gilbers (1992) and Tjong Kim Sang (1993) reconstruct underspecification phonology (Archangeli, 1988) using a circuit network consisting of interconnected switches. Bouma (1991) has shown how Gilbers' model can itself be reconstructed in first-order logic.

1.3.5 Towards declarative phonology

The tradition of generative phonology has been built on a computational metaphor known as SYMBOL PROCESSING. This model involves the fundamental division between data and process, which phonologists employ as their representations and rules respectively. For example, in the two-level model (§1.3.2), phonological representations reside on tapes (the data) and phonological rules are simulated using transducers (the processors). More recently other computational metaphors have been developed. For example, the view of computation as NEURAL PROCESSING has recently been advocated in the phonology literature (see §1.3.3). How, then, is one to come up with a theory of phonology which makes no commitment to any of these computational issues, while remaining computationally interpretable? This issue is the subject of the next section.

1.4 Constraint-based phonology

In the last three sections we have been introduced to phonology (§1.1), some of its problems (§1.2) and to computational phonology (§1.3). Now we are ready to take a first look at constraint-based phonology, an intensional, compositional, monostratal and lexicalist phonological framework. However, before discussing what all these terms mean, we shall briefly consider some important developments in computer science and computational linguistics that give the necessary background for the particular approach to constraints being taken here.

1.4.1   *The declarative/procedural controversy*

In the computer science literature it has long been maintained that the statement of a problem and the description of its solution should be expressed in a way that is not sensitive to implementation-specific details. For example, a Pascal programmer using a PC should not have to change her program to make it run on a Unix workstation. Similarly, the definition of the relation: 'x is the square of y' should not depend on whether squares are to be computed using a Turing machine or a neural network. In an analogous way, then, *the statement of a phonological theory should not be tied to a particular strategy for computing phonological well-formedness.* Rather, we need to adopt the distinction between DENOTATIONAL and OPERATIONAL semantics, as widely practised in the literature on the principles of programming languages.

A program can be interpreted as an abstract specification of the solution to a certain problem. Under this interpretation, a program denotes a space of solutions. A specification of the interpretation of a program solely in terms of the solution space it describes is called a denotational semantics. In contrast, the operational semantics of a program specifies how it can be interpreted as an algorithm for computing one or more solutions. There can be more than one operational semantics for a program, possibly depending upon the kind of computing machinery to be used for the computation. For example, the interpretation of a program as a set of instructions for a Turing machine is rather different from the interpretation of the same program for a neural network, even though the solutions which are computed will be the same. Therefore, in order to avoid any bias towards a particular computational metaphor, it is best that programming languages be first endowed with a denotational semantics, and a variety of operational semantics can follow later. This distinction in interpretation is sometimes called the declarative/procedural distinction. This distinction led to a famous controversy in computer science (Winograd, 1975), and the ramifications of this can still be seen today in the two largely independent communities of object-oriented programming and constraint logic programming (Boley, 1991). The controversy was fundamentally an issue of programming style; no-one ever suggested that certain kinds of functions could be computed in a procedural paradigm and not in a declarative paradigm. However, exactly this kind of spurious argumentation can be found in the phonology literature. For example, Bromberger and Halle (1989) adduce empirical evidence in favour of a procedural paradigm over a declarative one (chapter 3 is a detailed response to this kind of argument). As if to buttress their claim against the kind of argument presented here, they state in a footnote that '[This declarative/procedural] terminology, which carries a number of associations from the domain of computational linguistics, strikes us as unhelpful' (p. 51). In stark contrast to this position, the proposals advanced in later chapters will demonstrate the merits of *endorsing* the declarative/procedural distinction.

1.4.2 Constraint-based grammar

Over at least the last decade, the notion of unification has come to play a central role in the field of computational linguistics. Several linguistic frameworks employ unification as their fundamental operation (Shieber, 1986). This operation, whose technical details will not detain us here, is essentially a method for combining descriptions expressed in the feature structure notation (Johnson, 1988; Carpenter, 1992). If D_1 describes a set S_1, while D_2 describes S_2, then the unification of D_1 and D_2, written $D_1 \sqcap D_2$, describes the set $S_1 \cap S_2$. In this way, the D_i can be viewed as constraints, hence the name CONSTRAINT-BASED GRAMMAR.[28]

One variety of constraint-based grammar, namely Head-Driven Phrase Structure Grammar (Pollard and Sag, 1987), employs Saussure's notion of

---

[28] Examples of constraint-based grammar frameworks are Generalised Phrase Structure Grammar (Gazdar et al., 1985), Categorial Unification Grammar (Uszkoreit, 1986), Head-Driven Phrase Structure Grammar (Pollard and Sag, 1987), and Unification Categorial Grammar (Calder, Klein and Zeevat, 1988).

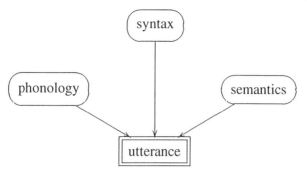

Figure 1.1: The constraint pool

a linguistic sign. In its most general sense, a sign is a pairing between a form and a meaning. In HPSG, it takes the following form.

$$\begin{bmatrix} \text{PHONOLOGY} \\ \text{SYNTAX} \\ \text{SEMANTICS} \end{bmatrix}$$

Unlike the traditional model of grammatical organisation, here the different linguistic modules operate in parallel to provide a pool of constraints which independently ensure the phonological, syntactic and semantic well-formedness of an utterance (Fenstad et al., 1987, 16), as depicted in Figure 1.1. A consequence of this view is that hierarchical structure in phonology is completely orthogonal to syntactic structure. In the traditional view, there is just the one hierarchy, with phonological units such as distinctive features at the bottom, morphemes and words in the middle reaches, and phrases and sentences towards the top. The associated processing model is serial: recognition involves a phonological component, which passes its output to the morphological or syntactic component, and so on. Hockett describes this view and proposes a radical alternative:

> There is a traditional view which sees phonologic and grammatic units as differing primarily as to size-level, so that the whole design of language involves but a single hierarchy: a morpheme consists of one or more phonemes; a word consists of one or more morphemes; a phrase of one or more words; and so on. The present view is radically different. Morphemes are not *composed* of phonemes at all. Morphemes are indivisible units.

> A given morpheme is *represented by* a certain more or less compact
> arrangement of phonologic material, or, indeed, sometimes by one such
> arrangement and sometimes by another. If we call any such representation
> a *morph*, then it becomes correct to say that a morph has a phonologic
> structure – that it consists of an arrangement of phonemes. (Hockett, 1955,
> 15)

This view leads naturally to the idea of having independent prosodic and
lexical hierarchies (cf. Inkelas, 1989; Bird, 1992).

This, then, is a constraint-based view of grammar. Next, we turn to the
question of constraints in phonology itself.

1.4.3 Constraints in phonology

In this section we ask the question: what does the conception of
constraint as used in constraint logic programming and in constraint-based
grammar tell us about constraints in phonology? First, a CONSTRAINT
is an empirical generalisation about a collection of objects. Second,
constraints interact to mutually restrict a solution space. Finally, the order
of application of constraints is immaterial to the end result.[29]

Constraints of the kind we are interested in here are familiar to phonologists in the form of morpheme structure constraints and surface structure constraints (see §1.5.1). The latter are essentially statements about
the distribution of phonological primes. Since the advent of generative
phonology, many have wanted to avoid stating distributional regularities
directly, preferring to express them implicitly through the conspiracy of
phonological rules. Although the problems with this stance have long
been recognised (Kisseberth, 1970; Shibatani, 1973), it is still an accepted
approach to the analysis of distributional regularities.

Since constraints describe occurring forms rather than abstract underlying forms, they directly express distributional facts. The theoretical
interest in an analysis will be in how it structures and relates the paradigmatic and syntagmatic information about distribution. A constraint-based
phonological analysis is to be evaluated along the same dimensions of

---

[29]This rules out the use of such procedural notions as violable constraints and repair
strategies (Paradis, 1988).

empirical and explanatory adequacy as standard generative analyses. In this connection, Pierrehumbert has observed:

> In many ways, declarative phonology is in the best tradition of Chomsky and Halle (1968). It uses a mathematically coherent formalism, and has the aim of building grammars which describe all and only the possible forms of a language. These grammars can be empirically evaluated. They can support the transfer of linguistic results to speech and language technology. In these respects, declarative phonology surpasses most current work in generative phonology. (Pierrehumbert, in Bird, Coleman, Pierrehumbert and Scobbie, 1992)

Recall that at the beginning of this section, constraint-based phonology was described as an intensional, compositional, monostratal and lexicalist phonological framework. In the remainder of this section these terms will be explicated.

1.4.4   *Intensionality*

In philosophy, artificial intelligence and cognitive science, it has often been found useful to distinguish between intension and extension (or DESCRIPTION and OBJECT).[30] This is an old idea (Frege, 1892) which continues to have impact today (see van Benthem, 1988 for a survey). The distinction between descriptions and objects introduces a degree of flexibility into linguistic notation that is unavailable without this distinction. For example, it is possible for different descriptions to denote the same object (e.g. 'morning star'/'evening star'), while some descriptions are satisfied by no objects (e.g. 'unicorn'). Also, it is possible for the description 'morning star' to be interpreted in various ways; it might denote the planet Venus, a brand of dishwashing detergent, or – most relevant here – a particular speech event. If we incorporate the distinction into phonology, we get a fundamentally different view of the relationship between phonology and phonetics from the traditional view, as also noted by Wheeler (1981), Bach (1983), Pierrehumbert (1990) and Coleman and Local (1991). Phonological representations are *descriptions* of real-world utterances (the *objects*). To see how much this view differs from the traditional generative view, consider the following remarks by Keating:

---

[30] Other equivalent terms are sense/reference and type/token.

The SPE model represents lexical items as matrices of binary-valued phonetic features; each row is a feature, and each column a segment. Phonological rules may change the values of features, or may add or delete segments... By contrast, phonetic rules *convert* the binary values into quantitative values along continuous phonetic scales... A further universal phonetic component ... will *convert* these scalar values into a representation of articulations that are continuous in time. (Keating, 1984, 286f)

It is as if abstract theoretical constructs (such as phonological represent-ations) are successively *converted* into the real objects of the domain itself (*i.e.* utterances).[31] This view has striking similarities with the view of natu-ral language semantics in 'Government and Binding Theory' (Chomsky, 1981), where syntactic structures and meanings (*i.e.* the 'Logical Form') are related to each other derivationally. It is natural to wonder whether such views are based on a category mistake (Dennett, 1987; Ryle, 1949, 213ff).

In general, a description denotes a collection of objects. Such descrip-tions are called PARTIAL, since they do not give all the detail required in order to pick out a single object. This is a convenient property of descriptions, since in phonology we never wish to pick out a single utterance; a phonological representation describes certain properties held in common by many (perhaps infinitely many) utterances. We can combine descriptions using standard operations like conjunction and disjunction. For example, if [+back] describes the set of back vowels and [+high] describes the set of high vowels, then the conjunction of these descriptions – written [+back,+high] – describes the set of high back vowels, which is just the intersection of the set of back vowels with the set of high vowels. Thus, conjoining descriptions corresponds to intersecting the sets of objects. In a similar way, disjunction of descriptions corresponds to union, while negation of descriptions corresponds to complement.

A further consequence of adopting the description/object distinction is that there can be no rule ordering. Rules are just descriptions. Although a rule might be stated in the form of a rewrite rule $a \rightarrow b$, this rule is interpreted as a logical implication, equivalent to the expression $\neg a \vee b$. This contrasts with the standard interpretation of these rules, evident from rules like [+voice] $\rightarrow$ [−voice], where the objects satisfying the description

---

[31] Keating (1990) further elaborates her model above with three procedurally related levels of phonetic representation.

on the left side of the arrow are *modified* (minimally) so that they now satisfy the description on the right side of the arrow instead.

As if to counterbalance the introduction of the new distinction, we drop an old distinction, namely the rule/representation distinction. Both rules and representations are just descriptions, perhaps differing in their level of detail but not fundamentally different in kind. A (possibly underspecified) lexical representation is a description of various forms which can be taken as instances of that representation; it denotes a set. Similarly, a phonological rule such as homorganic nasal assimilation describes the set of all forms which are compatible with the rule, excluding any forms containing unassimilated nasal-obstruent clusters. Thus, rules and representations alike denote sets and act as constraints.

1.4.5   Compositionality

The PRINCIPLE OF COMPOSITIONALITY requires that the form and inter-pretation of an expression be a function of the form and interpretation of its parts. This principle motivated Bach's (1976) RULE-TO-RULE HYPOTHESIS which requires that linguistic modules (such as syntax, semantics and phonology) be organised in parallel rather than in series (where the output of one module is the input of the next). An application of this hypothesis to phonology was developed by Wheeler (1981), and is discussed in §1.5.2. The principle of compositionality entails Partee's well-formedness constraint:

> *The well-formedness constraint:* Each syntactic rule operates on well-formed expressions of specified categories to produce a well-formed expres-sion of a specified category. (Partee, 1979, 276)

In any theoretical framework which invokes this constraint, there can be no phonological repair strategies which operate on ill-formed structures, converting them into well-formed structures, as has been advocated by some phonologists (Paradis, 1988).

An even stronger constraint than those mentioned above is the require-ment that a linguistic framework be MONOSTRATAL. This means that there is only a single level of linguistic description; descriptions pertain to occurring surface forms and not to artificially constructed abstract representations. As we shall see in §1.5.1, the requirement that a linguistic framework be monostratal is equivalent to the true generalisation condition from Natural Generative Phonology.

1.4.6 The lexicon

The LEXICALIST PROGRAMME grew out of Chomsky's *Remarks on Nominalization* (Chomsky, 1970), where he proposed to relate verbs to their corresponding derived nominals by using rules that relate lexical entries rather than by using transformations. Through the work of Bresnan, Gazdar, Jackendoff, Oehrle and others (see Hoekstra et al., 1980 for a survey) the transformational component and syntactic deep structure were eliminated entirely. A number of linguistic formalisms grew out of this programme, including Lexical Functional Grammar (Kaplan and Bresnan, 1982), PATR-II (Shieber et al., 1983) and Generalised Phrase Structure Grammar (Gazdar et al., 1985). A radical form of this lexicalism involved the elimination of not only transformations and deep structures but phrase structure rules as well, drawing on insights from categorial grammar (Karttunen, 1986; Pollard and Sag, 1987). 'This simplification of the grammar is made possible by an enrichment of the structure and content of lexical entries, using both inheritance mechanisms and lexical rules to represent the linguistic information in a general and efficient form' (Flickenger, Pollard and Wasow, 1986). In Head-Driven Phrase Structure Grammar, inheritance mechanisms and lexical rules are structured into a taxonomic system of lexical types, known as a HIERARCHICAL LEXICON (Pollard and Sag, 1987, 191–218):[32]

> Lexical information is organised on the basis of relatively few – perhaps several dozen – word types arranged in cross-cutting hierarchies which serve to classify all words on the basis of shared syntactic, semantic, and morphological properties. By factoring out information about words which can be predicted from their membership in types (whose properties can be stated in a single place once and for all), the amount of idiosyncratic inform-ation that needs to be stipulated in individual lexical signs is dramatically reduced. (Pollard and Sag, 1987, 192f)

---

[32]This view of the lexicon is closely related to knowledge representation schemes in artificial intelligence such as KL-ONE (Bobrow and Webber, 1980), deductive databases (Minker, 1987) and the object-oriented programming paradigm.

Under this view, the lexicon is the place where most – if not all – linguistic generalisations reside. This differs fundamentally from the traditional view whereby 'the lexicon is really an appendix of the grammar, a list of basic irregularities' (Bloomfield, 1933, 274), which Hoeksema (1985, 2) aptly caricatures as the 'junk yard' view of the lexicon.

As we shall see in §1.5.4, the question of how phonology should be incorporated into this model of the lexicon is still under investigation. Morpheme structure constraints, which state regularities about certain classes of morpheme, fit naturally into this model. For example, the vowel harmony in Yoruba is restricted to nouns (Archangeli and Pulleyblank, 1989, 175), and so the required constraint on vowel sequences might be formulated as a property of the noun type in the lexicon. This model of the lexicon also connects with work in phonology that has called for the partial specification of lexical entries and the use of lexical redundancy rules (e.g. Natural Generative Phonology §1.5.1, Montague Phonology §1.5.2). Wheeler (1981, 183) observed that there are two equivalent ways of viewing the relationship between lexical redundancy rules and lexical entries. One can consider the entries to be partially specified, with unspecified features being filled in during the course of a derivation by redundancy rules. Alternatively, one can consider the entries to be fully specified, where the redundancy rules are not involved in derivations but are involved in the computation of the information content (or simplicity) of the lexicon.[33]

1.5   The history of constraints in phonology

The use of constraints in phonology has taken many different forms over recent decades. The allophonic rules (or phonetic redundancy rules) and phonotactics of American structuralist phonemic phonology can be viewed as a system of surface structure constraints: phonemes are cast as

---

[33] Jackendoff (1975) discusses these alternatives in more detail, referring to them as the 'impoverished-entry theory' and the 'full-entry theory'. Ellison (1992b) shows how an information measure can be applied to a lexicon with fully specified entries and redundancy rules, so that it is not necessary to use underspecification in order to see which of two analyses stipulates less information.

(possibly overlapping) sets of allophones[34] and the contextually appropriate allophone is selected by the action of phonotactic constraints. When no one allophone is singled out as basic, or 'underlying', then it is possible to regard such phonemes as partial descriptions, a defining property of constraints, as we saw in §1.4.4. A similar position was adopted in the tradition of Firthian prosodic analysis:

> The general principle of treating any one form as basic, or as a norm, the remaining variants having only the status of derived forms, is repugnant to prosodic analysis. (Sprigg, 1965, 62)

Furthermore, the Firthian analysts eschewed any notion of ordering, thereby conforming to another central property of constraint systems (§1.4.4).

> The essential content of the statement that 'rule A precedes rule B' is that information supplied by the operation of rule A is necessary to the correct application of rule B (and on the other hand, information which may be *destroyed* by the application of rule A is not available to rule B). If all rules are represented by prosodies, and these are defined as relations between a uniform level of structure and its phonetic instantiations, there is no analogue of the notion of ordering ... it is quite clear that the Firthian prosodic analysis is entirely a theory of representations. (Anderson, 1985, 188f, *emphasis in original*)

The advent of generative phonology and the SPE model (Chomsky and Halle, 1968), with its highly procedural model of phonology, drew attention away from constraints. Properties of surface forms were not to be expressed directly but arose out of the combined action of lexical specifications, morpheme structure rules and derivations. No rule could be said to act like a constraint, since the effect of the rule could always be undone by later rules. Although this view has survived to the present intact, it has also been challenged right from the start, as we shall see in the next section.

1.5.1 Some reactions to generative phonology

Complaints about the abstractness of generative analyses[35] led to new models which retained the earlier notions about constraints. For example,

---

[34] Similarly, archiphonemes were viewed as sets of phonemes.

[35] Many of these complaints have been gathered together in the volume of papers from the Chicago Linguistic Society parasession on Natural Phonology (Bruck et al., 1974).

Shibatani (1973) advocated 'surface phonetic constraints', which 'state possible and impossible combinations of phonetic features at the phonetic level, *i.e.* represent true generalisations about the phonetic pattern of a language'. This connects with earlier work by Stanley who advocated 'rules which state redundancies at the phonetic level' (Stanley, 1967, 397). To illustrate Shibatani's approach, we shall consider his analysis of Turkish vowel harmony.[36]   Shibatani views vowel harmony as 'cooccurrence restrictions on vowel features in successive syllables'. Alternating vowels are expressed as archiphonemes (*i.e.* sets of vowels) in the lexicon, and the selection of the appropriate vowel is done automatically by the surface phonetic constraint for harmony. Here is one such constraint:

(1.22)

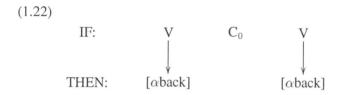

The Turkish word *kızlar* 'girls' is represented morphophonemically as /kız + lEr/, where /E/ = {/e/, /a/}. The stem vowel is fully specified because it does not alternate, while the suffix vowel is not fully specified. The surface value of the suffix vowel is determined by rule (1.22) which instantiates /E/ as /a/. If no other constraints reject the phonetic form [kızlar] then this is the allowed form. Note that rule (1.22) is rather different to the generative version in (1.7). Rule (1.7) could take a form like **kızler* and *convert* it into the required form *kızlar*. In contrast, rule (1.22) would simply rule *kızler* out as illformed.

Calls for the re-introduction of surface structure constraints comprised one strand of objections to the SPE model. Another complaint about generative phonology was its use of extrinsic rule ordering. Koutsoudas (1972), Ringen (1972), Vennemann (1972), Koutsoudas et al. (1974) and Pullum (1976) provided a battery of empirical and metatheoretical arguments for the undesirability of extrinsic rule ordering, in favour of models where rule ordering is determined by universal principles.

These two independent objections to the SPE model were drawn together in a collection of work known as NATURAL GENERATIVE PHONOLOGY

---

[36] Turkish vowel harmony has already been discussed in §1.1 and §1.3.2.

(Vennemann, 1974; Hooper, 1976; Hudson, 1980). Fundamental to this approach were two principles: the TRUE GENERALISATION CONDITION,[37] which states that all generalisations should be 'surface true' and the NO ORDERING CONDITION which requires that there be no rule ordering (whether extrinsic or governed by universal principles). Consequently, derivations can add (but not alter) information. Furthermore, what was previously a derivational rule becomes lexicalised as a lexical redundancy rule:

> [In Natural Generative Phonology] phonological relations must be encoded simply as more or less systematic connections between fully-specified lexical entries. Both [rajt] (*write*) and [raːjd] (*ride*) are entered in the lexicon as such; and the 'rule' of vowel lengthening is reduced to the status of a lexical redundancy rule... The great bulk of the descriptive burden on this view is borne by conditions of well-formedness imposed on lexical representations; but even these can only be stated insofar as they are completely exceptionless and 'surface true'. (Anderson, 1985, 340)

Thus, Natural Generative Phonology has much in common with constraint-based grammar and, I would claim, represents an enlightened reaction to the procedural thinking of the day. However, the model did not survive, mainly because it predicted that there is no neutralisation, a claim which was anathema to phonologists at that time.[38] Remarkably, the prediction regarding neutralisation has been confirmed by several recent phonetic studies, reviewed in §3.3.2. There are now signs that the true generalisation condition is re-emerging in current theoretical phonology (see §1.5.7).

1.5.2   Categorial phonology

Categorial grammar is a style of grammatical analysis dating back to the 1930s, in which words and phrases are assigned to one or more categories which determine their combinatorial properties (Oehrle et al.,

---

[37]This term was also employed by Stanley (1967, 421ff).

[38]For reviews of Natural Generative Phonology, see Harris (1978); Jensen (1978); Gussmann (1980); Piggott (1980); Dresher (1981). An explanation of neutralisation is given in §3.3.2.

1988). Bach and Wheeler have proposed a phonological application of categorial grammar called MONTAGUE PHONOLOGY (Bach and Wheeler, 1981; Wheeler, 1981; Bach, 1983) which shares several assumptions with the constraint-based approach to grammatical description.[39] Wheeler proposed two classes of rule: phonotactic rules and phonetic interpretation rules. The phonotactic rules 'characterise the set of well-formed syllables, feet, words and phonological phrases' (Wheeler, 1981, 39). Example (1.23) gives two rules for the construction of well-formed syllables, where the symbol '$\frown$' denotes concatenation:

(1.23) a. PR_i: if $\alpha \in S/R$ and $\beta \in R$ then $\gamma \in S$ where $\gamma = \alpha \frown \beta$.

       b. PR_j: if $\alpha \in V$ and $\beta \in V\backslash R$ then $\gamma \in R$ where $\gamma = \alpha \frown \beta$.

Here, terms like S/R, R and S are CATEGORIES. R and S are basic categories denoting the sets of segment strings which are possible rhymes and syllables respectively. The derived category S/R denotes those strings of segments which would be syllables if a string of category R appeared to the right, in other words S/R denotes the set of onsets. The derived category $V\backslash R$ denotes those segment strings which would be rhymes if a string of category V (*i.e.* a vowel or sequence of vowels) appeared to the left. To see how this notation works, consider the following derivation for the word *cat*.

(1.24)

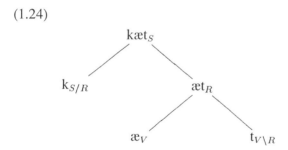

The phonotactic rules generate strings of segments which correspond to the underlying representations of standard generative phonology. These rules

---

[39]The name 'Montague Phonology' is modelled on the name 'Montague Grammar', a theory of syntax and semantics (Dowty, Wall and Peters, 1981). Some advocates of Montague Phonology have viewed it as a formalisation of Hockett's (1954) item-and-process paradigm (Schmerling, 1983; Hoeksema and Janda, 1988).

operate alongside the phonetic interpretation rules, in conformity with the rule-to-rule hypothesis (see §1.4.5). Consider the following pair of rules:

(1.25)   a. PR_i: if $\alpha \in S/R$ and $\beta \in R$ then $\gamma \in S$ where $\gamma = \alpha \frown \beta$.

      b. RI_i: /s/ → [ʃ] / __i

In (1.25) we see the phonotactic rule from (1.23a) repeated, alongside an interpretation rule for palatalisation. The interpretation rule applies simultaneously with the phonotactic rule to generate the phonetic segment [ʃ] corresponding to the underlying /s/. Although rule (1.25b) has the appearance of an SPE rule, it does not function in a derivation in the traditional way; rule (1.25b) cannot feed other rules since there is a difference in kind between rule inputs and outputs, a state of affairs summed up by the maxim 'don't reinterpret interpretations' (Bach and Wheeler, 1981, 35). Consequently, extrinsic rule ordering is not permitted in Montague Phonology; the application of interpretation rules is driven by the application of the phonotactic rules. Wheeler contrasts this approach to the standard view:

> In the standard theory, the input to the phonology is a string generated by the syntax. The domain of application of the phonological rules is the entire string. Boundary symbols are required to restrict the application of phonological rules between certain domains. I am claiming that the rules of phonetic interpretation apply in conjunction with the phonotactic rules. The domain of application of the phonetic rules is the string derived by combining the expressions of the appropriate categories. If a rule of phonetic interpretation is associated with the phonotactic rule which combines onsets and rimes to form syllables, then no information above the level of the syllable is available to the rule. That is, by assuming that the rules of phonetic interpretation are associated with particular phonotactic rules, we can account for the fact that certain rules apply within restricted domains. (Wheeler, 1981, 48f)

An additional restriction on interpretation rules is that they may only further specify a phonetic representation by filling in values which have not already been interpreted (Wheeler, 1981, 66, 182). These restrictions on the behaviour of rules is compensated for by a greater degree of flexibility in the lexicon than was traditionally countenanced. In particular, segments could be incompletely specified in lexical forms (Bach and Wheeler, 1981, 35), with the unspecified features to be filled in during a derivation or else interpreted as the unmarked value. Alternations which involve the conversion of marked feature values into unmarked ones are described by lexical rules.

In proposing lexical underspecification and prosodically conditioned rule application, Montague Phonology was well before its time. The framework is more powerful than Natural Generative Phonology (see §1.5.1) by virtue of having an underlying level of representation. Consequently, such phenomena as neutralisation are expressible in Montague Phonology (Wheeler, 1981, 64ff, §3) but not in Natural Generative Phonology. The conception of phonetic interpretation rules in Montague Phonology is compatible with the rules of the two-level model (see §1.3.2), although no-one has attempted to integrate the two models.

Following on from the seminal work of Bach and Wheeler, several others have presented models using this general framework. The linguistic applications of this body of work have been numerous, including English stress and segmental alternations (Wheeler, 1981), consonant alternations in Korean (Bach and Wheeler, 1981), metrical phonology (Dogil, 1984; Moortgat and Morrill, 1993), Russian devoicing (Wheeler, 1988), infixation, reduplication and metathesis in a variety of languages (Hoeksema and Janda, 1988), intonation, accent placement and focus (Steedman, 1990; Steedman, 1991; Bird, 1991b; van der Linden, 1991) and prosodic phrasing (Moortgat, 1988; Oehrle, 1991).

1.5.3   Unification-based approaches

The success of unification-based grammar for natural language syntax and semantics has inspired a number of researchers to investigate similar ideas in phonology. The recurrent theme which underlies all these approaches is the idea that representations can become increasingly specified during the course of a derivation but they cannot be destructively modified, and that linguistic rules are unordered, functioning like a pool of constraints. This section surveys some of the developments in this area.

Scobbie (1991a, 1993b, 1993c) presents a model which he terms ATTRIBUTE VALUE PHONOLOGY (AVP). An AVP representation consists of a sequence of attribute-value structures, each describing roughly segment-sized units. Each structure consists of a melody (MEL) and a syllable

(SYL) attribute. Consider the following autosegmental representation for the word *Andy*, where PoA represents place of articulation specifications.

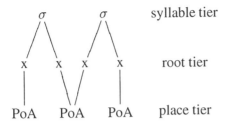

This representation is expressed in the following rather complex-looking structure (Scobbie, 1991a, 32). Here we shall be primarily concerned with the coindexing.

(1.26)

$$
\left\langle
\begin{bmatrix}
\text{MEL} & \boxed{1}\, a \\
\text{SYL} & \boxed{2}\begin{bmatrix} \text{NUC} & \boxed{1} \\ \text{E-SYL|NUC} & \boxed{3} \end{bmatrix}
\end{bmatrix},
\begin{bmatrix}
\text{MEL} & \boxed{3}\begin{bmatrix} \text{NASAL} & + \\ \text{PLACE} & \boxed{4}\, cor \end{bmatrix} \\
\text{SYL} & \boxed{2}
\end{bmatrix},
\right.
$$

$$
\left.
\begin{bmatrix}
\text{MEL} & \boxed{5}\begin{bmatrix} \text{PLACE} & \boxed{4} \end{bmatrix} \\
\text{SYL} & \boxed{6}
\end{bmatrix},
\begin{bmatrix}
\text{MEL} & \boxed{7} \\
\text{SYL} & \boxed{6}\begin{bmatrix} \text{CONS} & \{\boxed{5}\} \\ \text{NUC} & \boxed{7}\, i \end{bmatrix}
\end{bmatrix}
\right\rangle
$$

Observe that this structure consists of a sequence of four attribute-value structures, where each structure corresponds to one of the x-slots of the root tier in the autosegmental diagram. Structure below the root tier is represented in the MEL attribute, while structure above the root tier is in the SYL attribute. The fact that the first two segments are in the same syllable is represented by the index $\boxed{2}$, and the sharing of place of articulation for the second and third segments is represented by the index $\boxed{4}$.

In AVP, tiers other than the root tier are not directly accessible. The notion of a tier is reconstructed as a sequence of paths. For example, if $R = \langle i, j, k \rangle$ is an AVP representation, then $\langle i|\text{SYL}, j|\text{SYL}, k|\text{SYL}\rangle$ is the syllable tier of R. The sequencing of the syllable tier is thereby inherited from the sequencing of R itself. Along with tiers, association is also given a novel definition in AVP, whereby x is associated to y iff x is dominated by y in the attribute-value representation.[40]   Thus, syllables and place specifications are associated to the root tier, but not vice versa.

An interesting restriction on the coindexing of structures like (1.26) is proposed, called the 'sharing constraint'. This requires that any index must be assigned to a contiguous subsequence of attribute-value structures in an AVP representation. This constraint, plus the requirement that attributes be single-valued, gives rise to the no-crossing constraint (discussed in §2.3.3). Coindexing is used for the kind of structure sharing required to represent geminates (doubled consonants or vowels). Scobbie uses the fact that coindexed structures cannot subsequently be broken apart in order to fashion an account of geminate integrity (Schein and Steriade, 1986) and inalterability (Hayes, 1986b).

There have been several other proposals for the employment of unification in phonology. Broe and Coleman have both noted the similarities between unification-based phonology and Firthian prosodic phonology. Broe (1991b, 1991a, 1993) provides prosodic analyses of several complex phenomena (including aspiration in Hārautī and Grassmann's law) using unification and attribute-value structures. Coleman (1990, 1991, 1992a, 1993a, 1993b) has presented a unification-based phonology with special attention paid to the lexicon and such phenomena as the Great Vowel Shift, and phonetic interpretation for driving speech synthesis. Others who have employed a unification-based or declarative approach to phonology include Carson (1988), Chung (1990), Dirksen (1992, 1993), Pulman and Hepple (1993), Waksler (1990), Wiese (1990) and Walther (1992, 1993).

1.5.4   Inheritance-based approaches

Another strand of work in computational phonology comes under the general heading of inheritance. Lexical and prosodic classes are interrelated by way of inheritance networks, which allow linguistic observations to be stated in a maximally general way and possibly overridden by more specific generalisations (cf. Kiparsky's ELSEWHERE PRINCIPLE (1973)). Linguistic

---

[40] This is similar to the proposal by Wiese (1990) to equate association with dominance in an attribute-value structure.

data at one level of a hierarchy inherit all the attributes of data higher up in the hierarchy. For example, if we suppose that heavy syllables are a subclass of syllables, then properties of syllables (such as having an onset) are automatically inherited by heavy syllables.

There have been several implementations of inheritance models for phonology to date. Daelemans (1987) used an object-oriented programming paradigm for Dutch phonology. A number of researchers have applied the DATR system of Evans and Gazdar (1989a,b, 1990) to phonology: Gibbon (1990) for Kikuyu tonology, Gibbon (Evans and Gazdar, 1990, 99f) for Archangeli's version of underspecification phonology (Archangeli, 1988), Cahill (1989, 1990) for syllable-based morphological processing for a variety of languages, and Reinhard and Gibbon (1991) for German umlaut and Arabic morphology. Calder and Bird (1991) applied default logic to underspecification phonology. Klein (1991, 1992) used the OBJ language for defining metrical trees and feature geometries as abstract data types. Mastroianni (1993), Bird and Klein (1994) and Mastroianni and Carpenter (1994) have expressed phonological information using typed feature structures and cast phonological operations in terms of typed inference mechanisms.

1.5.5   *Logic-based approaches*

Another area of recent investigation has been applications of logic to phonology. The present study, along with work by Bouma (1991) and Russell (1993), is an application of first-order predicate logic. Bouma has investigated underspecification phonology (and its incarnation as 'digital phonology'; see §1.3.4), while Russell has investigated Government Phonology. Applications of modal logic to phonology have been proposed by Calder and Bird (1991) and Bird and Blackburn (1991).[41] Finally, several people have studied applications of categorial logic to phonology (Moortgat and Morrill, 1993; van der Linden, 1991; Oehrle, 1991), as already discussed in §1.5.2.

---

[41]See §A.2 for some details of the approach taken by Bird and Blackburn (1991).

1.5.6   *A finite-state approach*

Until recently, all finite-state approaches to phonology have employed transducers, following on from Koskenniemi's two-level model (see §1.3.2). This approach is tailored to the SPE system and it is natural to wonder if there is any possibility of defining a finite-state model which is compatible with the principles of constraint-based grammar. Recently, Bird and Ellison (1994) have done just this. They begin by considering automata as descriptions of tape 'objects', and observing that there is a natural algebraic structure on the class of automata, involving the operations of intersection (∩), union (⊔) and complement (¬). Such automata can then be seen as representing the phonology attribute in a sign-based grammar (Bird, 1992).

Bird and Ellison construct an automaton-based semantics for the representations and rules of autosegmental phonology, based on the temporal semantics of Bird and Klein (1990), to be discussed in §2.3. Their approach will be briefly presented here. Suppose we have a simple autosegmental diagram as shown on the left in (1.27). This is translated into the encoding on the right.

(1.27) A   B   *encoding*   A:1 B:2

                                                             C:2 D:1

          C   D

The encoding, inspired by Wiebe (1992), lists the autosegments followed by a number showing how many associations each autosegment has. Each tier is represented on a separate line.

The next step is to write each autosegment with a Kleene plus, to allow autosegments to 'denote' extended intervals of tape. Each association is written as 0^*10^*, a regular expression for a sequence of any number of 0s, followed by a 1, followed again by any number of 0s. This captures the idea that, while an autosegment denotes an interval, an association corresponds to some point *during* an interval where there is an overlap with another interval (see §2.3.4). So the encoding in (1.27) is converted into the following regular expressions:

$$A^+ \sqcap (0^*10^*) \quad B^+ \sqcap (0^*10^*\,0^*10^*)$$
$$C^+ \sqcap (0^*10^*\,0^*10^*) \quad D^+ \sqcap (0^*10^*)$$

Observe that adjacent instances of 0^* can be collapsed, so the two associations for autosegment B are encoded as $0^*10^*10^*$, an interval with *two* special points rather than just one. We can now evaluate the intersections in these regular expressions, and express the autosegments and associations as triples, as shown in (1.28). Here, the triples with an association mark are shaded.

(1.28)

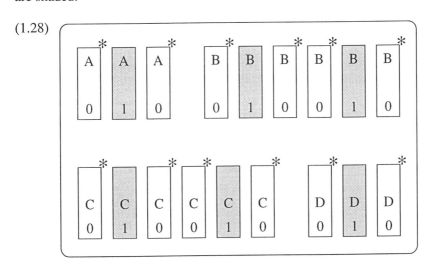

The next step is to intersect the two tiers, which results in the structure shown in (1.29). The shaded blocks serve to synchronise the segmental information.

(1.29)

Now we can ignore the zeros and ones and inspect the segmental content. We can observe a period where A and C are present, followed by B and

C, followed by B and D. The output of the system is then ⟨[A,C], [B,C], [B,D]⟩, which, it is claimed, is the intended interpretation of the diagram in (1.27). Notably, this entire 'compilation' process is fully automated, with graphical input and string-based output. The reader is referred to Bird and Ellison (1994) for the details of this process, and for a demonstration of how it can be generalised to representations with an arbitrary number of tiers, and to autosegmental rules.

1.5.7   Other approaches

There have been a number of signs that generative phonology has become more declarative in its outlook over recent years, and one can even discern a re-appearance of the *true generalisation condition* (defined in §1.5.1). For example, Rice (1989, 331) writes that 'a general goal in recent phonological work has been the elimination of structure-changing processes from the grammar'. Steriade (1988) rejects the feature-changing approach required by Kiparsky's Strict Cycle Condition (Kiparsky, 1982) in favour of Prince's free element condition (Prince, 1985), which states that the rules of primary metrical analysis are 'feature-filling' only. Kaye et al. (1990, 221) write: 'Governing relations are defined at the level of lexical representation and remain constant throughout a phonological derivation.' Lodge (1992, 13) writes that 'underspecification of lexical-entry forms enables us to restrict phonological theory to declarative statements about the structure of lexical items, and to avoid having recourse to feature-changing and deletion rules'.

Certain approaches to prosodic structure have a declarative flavour. For example, in unpublished work McCarthy and Prince have claimed that many languages exhibit a lower bound on the size of major category words of two moras; Kanerva (1989, 38ff) presents an example of this phenomenon for Chicheŵa. Goldsmith has made the following observation in connection with an analysis of Sierra Miwok verbs:

> This analysis, with all its morphologically governed phonological rules, arbitrary rule ordering, and, frankly, its mind-boggling inelegance, ironically misses the most basic point of the formation of the past tense in Sierra Miwok. As we have informally noted, all the second stem forms are of the shape CVCVCC, with the last consonant a geminate, and the rules that we have hypothetically posited so far all endeavour to achieve that end without ever directly acknowledging it. (Goldsmith, 1990, 87)

Scobbie (1991b) has surveyed other indications of the trend towards declarative phonology.

1.6 Conclusion

This chapter has presented the defining properties of constraint-based phonology: intensionality, compositionality, monostratality and lexicalism. The approach has been situated with respect to current and past developments in phonology, computer science and computational linguistics. In the next chapter a formalisation of constraint-based phonology is presented in the setting of first-order predicate calculus, a universal language for formal specification.

2   A logical foundation for phonology

The phonological literature is rich with conventions for representing linguistic structures in graphical form. The aim of this chapter is to present a simple logical framework in which notational proposals can be expressed, evaluated and applied.[1]   A central concern will be to provide existing notational conventions with a formal syntax and a formal semantics in this setting. Phonological representations depict various linguistic 'objects', such as syllables, segments, place nodes and so on, along with various temporal and structural relations between them. Rather than defining the syntax of a graphical language, I employ a formal language – in the non-graphical sense of the term – and adopt certain conventions for depicting logical descriptions, following Johnson (1988, 28).

Fundamental to the approach described in this chapter is the notion of an EVENT. An event is a period of time during which a certain property holds (van Benthem, 1983, 113). Events are generally structured out of smaller events, and correspond to such phonological entities as gestures, features, syllables and phrases. More precisely, events will be taken to be the denotation of terms in the description language.

The approach taken in this chapter is axiomatic. The reasons for stating axioms are numerous. For example, given a collection of phonological units and certain information about the relations existing between various units, it is possible to deduce further information. Thus, if we know that a segment p precedes a segment i and that i precedes n, we can infer that p precedes n using (13e), equating x and y. Put slightly differently, the composite statement '$p \prec i$, $i \prec n$ and $p \prec n$' contains redundant information, given

---

[1]The work presented here has grown out of Bird and Klein (1990).

the transitivity of the relation $\prec$, and so we can abbreviate it by omitting '$p \prec n$'.

In addition, it is possible to tell if a description is consistent; we use the axioms and inference rules to derive all that can be derived and check that no contradictory statements are present. To summarise then, the axiomatic approach admits *inference*, *abbreviation* and *consistency checking*. The axiomatic approach is not new to phonology,[2] but there are no recorded attempts to axiomatise autosegmental phonology.

This chapter is organised as follows. In §2.1 a classification of phonological entities into sorts is presented. In §2.2 and §2.3 we investigate the hierarchical and temporal relations between these entities. The interaction of temporal and hierarchical relations is explored in §2.4. The development in the first four sections culminates in the formal definition of a phonological description language in §2.5. Finally, it is shown how phonological rules fit into the framework in §2.6.

2.1   Sorts

2.1.1   Prosodic sorts

Consider the prosodic structure in Figure 2.1 (Pierrehumbert and Beckman, 1988, 118). It consists of a collection of labelled nodes and a collection of lines between those nodes. For now we shall concentrate on the nodes and leave the lines until later. The interpretation of the node labels is as follows: υ = utterance, ι = intermediate phrase, α = accentual phrase, ω = word, σ = syllable and μ = mora. Notice that the labels are not unique. For example, there are thirteen σ nodes, expressing the fact that the utterance contains thirteen syllables. (Lines between syllables and consonants have been omitted from this diagram.) Our description language will have variables ranging over the nodes of graphs like that in Figure 2.1. These variables are represented using the symbols x, y and z (possibly subscripted). We can restrict the range of a variable by giving it a SORT. For example, we shall say x is a syllable iff *syl*(x) is true. Similarly

---

[2] Others who have employed an axiomatic approach in phonology include Bloomfield (1926), Bloch (1948), Greenberg (1959) and Batóg (1967).

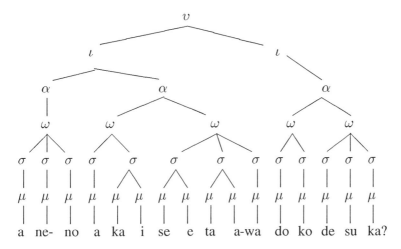

Figure 2.1: Prosodic structure for a Japanese utterance

for moras: the predicate *mora*(x) is true iff x is a mora.[3] We can do this for each level of the hierarchy in Figure 2.1.

Notice also that each node of Figure 2.1 has only one label. It would not be possible for a node to be simultaneously labelled σ and μ since syllables and moras are distinct entities. In other words, the expression *syl*(x) $\wedge$ *mora*(x) is always false, regardless of which node x denotes. Another way of writing this is given in (2.1a). A logically equivalent formulation appears in (2.1b).

(2.1)   a. $\forall x, syl(x) \rightarrow \neg mora(x)$

   b. $\forall x, mora(x) \rightarrow \neg syl(x)$

The lowest level of the above prosodic structure is the 'segment tier'. Each element of this tier is a segment. However, unlike the other levels of prosodic structure, it is not the case that all nodes on this level have the same label. For example, there are seven 'a' labels and four 'e' labels. Continuing with the sort predicates, *a*(x) could pick out just those nodes which are labelled with an 'a', and *e*(x) could pick out those nodes labelled 'e', and so on. Moreover, a predicate *segment*(x) could pick out all and

---

[3]This sort system concerns the nodes of a tree. It is not intended to give us a way of saying, for example, that the English word 'a' is simultaneously a segment, a mora and a syllable.

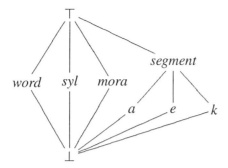

Figure 2.2: A partial sort lattice for prosodic structures

only those nodes in the segment tier. The situation can be expressed using the following (partial) formula:

(2.2) $\forall x, segment(x) \equiv a(x) \vee e(x) \vee k(x) \vee \cdots$

This formula states that something is a segment if and only if it is also an *a* or an *e* or a *k* etc. These relationships between sorts may be expressed graphically using a LATTICE; an example is given in Figure 2.2. The top-most node in the lattice is labelled $\top$ (top). By convention, $\top$ is the most general description and in the present context it describes all prosodic structure nodes. The downwards branching arcs can be thought of as expressing disjunctions. For example, a node described by $\top$ (*i.e.* all nodes) can be also described as a segment or a mora or a syllable etc. In turn, a segment can also be described as an *a* or an *e* etc. The bottom-most element in the lattice is labelled $\bot$ (bottom). By convention, $\bot$ represents inconsistent information; it describes nothing. The lattice expresses the constraint that if a node is both a syllable and a mora, then it is also described by $\bot$. In other words, no node can be both a syllable and a mora. Similarly, no node can be both an *a* and an *e*, and no node can be both a *word* and a *k*.

Each line in Figure 2.2 corresponds to an implication. For example, the line between the *a* and segment nodes corresponds to the following:

(2.3) $\forall x, a(x) \rightarrow segment(x)$

More specifically, the lattice in Figure 2.2 corresponds to the following collection of formulas, universally quantified over x.

CV tier:

root tier:
laryngeal tier:
[spread]:
[constricted]:
[voiced]:
supralaryngeal tier:
manner tier:
[nasal]:
[continuant]:
[strident]:
place tier:
[coronal]:
[anterior]:
[distributed]:

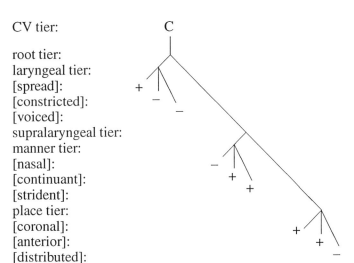

Figure 2.3: Hierarchical representation for [s]

(2.4)

$$
\begin{aligned}
\top(x) &\equiv word(x) \lor syl(x) \lor mora(x) \lor segment(x) \\
word(x) &\rightarrow \neg syl(x) \land \neg mora(x) \land \neg segment(x) \\
syl(x) &\rightarrow \neg mora(x) \land \neg segment(x) \\
mora(x) &\rightarrow \neg segment(x) \\
segment(x) &\equiv a(x) \lor e(x) \lor k(x) \\
a(x) &\rightarrow \neg e(x) \land \neg k(x) \\
e(x) &\rightarrow \neg k(x)
\end{aligned}
$$

2.1.2   Subsegmental sorts

As a second example, consider the kinds of diagrams which have been proposed for representing hierarchical sub-segmental structures. An example of such a structure is given in Figure 2.3 (Clements, 1985, 248). In this diagram only some of the nodes are labelled. However, we can think of the column of words to the left of the tree as being a collection of node labels. The highest unlabelled node will be considered to have

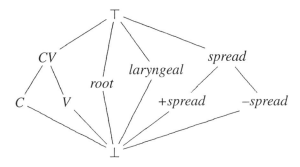

Figure 2.4: A partial sort lattice for sub-segmental structures

the label 'root', the next 'laryngeal', the next 'spread' and so on. (Sagey
(1986), Hayes (1990) and others label all nodes in this way.) The sort
lattice for these nodes is given in Figure 2.4. The *CV* sort picks out all
CV-tier elements, the *C* sort picks out the consonants (a subset of the set
picked out by *CV*) and so on. Note that *spread* picks out the objects which
can have a specification for the [spread] feature. The sorts *+spread* and
−spread pick out (mutually exclusive) subsets of *spread*. So, we can see
that the purpose of sorts is to pick out various subsets of a given set of
nodes.[4]

In this section we have seen a technique for classifying the nodes
of a hierarchical structure through the use of a sort system. However,
this is only a fragment of the overall picture. For example, as things
stand at present, there is nothing to stop a vowel in this CV-tier from
dominating sub-segmental structure containing a [−continuant] feature,
which is impossible as all vowels are [+continuant]. In order to solve this
problem it is necessary to postpone further discussion of sorts until after the
hierarchical organisation of phonological structures has been discussed.[5]

---

[4] The reason for not employing + and − as sorts directly is because we never want to
refer to the class of nodes that have a + value as opposed to a − value of an arbitrary feature.
For example, Clements' representation for [s] above has five nodes with a '+' label: spread,
continuant, strident, coronal and anterior. These nodes have no more in common with each
other than any other subset of nodes. Note also that the use of sorts *spread*, *+spread* and
−spread implements an internal view of negation: $\neg +spread(x) \not\equiv -spread(x)$.

[5] A constraint which prevents vowel nodes from dominating [−continuant] appears in
(2.10).

2.2 Hierarchical organisation

2.2.1 Dominance

In the previous section we saw two kinds of hierarchical structure, one for prosodic structure and one for sub-segmental structure. The nodes of these trees are related to each other by dominance (Clements, 1985, 248; Pierrehumbert and Beckman, 1988, 145f). Clements' definition is as follows:

(2.5) Given any two nodes M, N such that M lies on the path between N and the root of the tree, M is said to DOMINATE N; if no node intervenes between M and N, M IMMEDIATELY DOMINATES N.

The lines in Figures 2.1 and 2.3 represent the immediate dominance relation. This relation is asymmetric: if M immediately dominates N then it is not possible for N to immediately dominate M. If the vertical orientation of these diagrams on the page were not significant then it would be necessary to employ arrows instead of lines in order to capture this directionality. Note also that immediate dominance is irreflexive: it is not possible for a node to dominate itself. More generally, it is not possible to follow dominance lines and end up where we began. These three properties are expressed in the following axiom, where δ is the immediate dominance relation.[6]

(2.6) $\forall x_0 x_1 \cdots x_n, \neg x_0 \, \delta \, x_1 \, \delta \, \cdots \, \delta \, x_n \, \delta \, x_0, (n \geq 0)$
Dominance is acyclic

The dominance relation $\delta^\star$ is defined as the transitive closure of the immediate dominance relation. It is therefore irreflexive, asymmetric and transitive.

---

[6]Note that axiom (2.6) expresses the irreflexivity of dominance ($n = 0$) and the asymmetry of dominance ($n = 1$). The notion of dominance as employed in phonology corresponds closely to the use of the term in feature logics. However, dominance will be treated here as a relation rather than as a collection of partial functions, for two reasons. First, in phonological structures, it is the nodes and not the arcs which are labelled. Second, there can be multiple arcs emanating from a node.

2.2.2   *Appropriateness constraints*

Now that sorts and the δ relation have been defined, it is reasonable to wonder if there is any significant interaction between the two. As it happens, there are some tight constraints on the sorts of nodes which can be related by dominance. Perhaps the best known constraint of this kind is the STRICT LAYER HYPOTHESIS (Selkirk, 1984, 26). Selkirk proposes a strict ordering of prosodic categories, where a category at level i in the ordering immediately dominates a sequence of categories at level $i - 1$. Sagey (1986, 33) adopts a similar constraint on subsegmental structures. Recall the prosodic structure in Figure 2.1, part of which is reproduced in (2.7) below.[7]

(2.7)

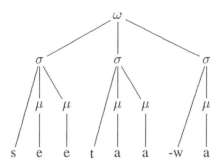

For Figure 2.1 and (2.7) we employ the APPROPRIATENESS CONSTRAINT in (2.8).

(2.8)

$$
\begin{aligned}
\forall xy, x\,\delta\,y \;\;\rightarrow\;\; & (\textit{utterance}(x) \wedge \textit{intermediate-phrase}(y) \\
\vee\;\; & \textit{intermediate-phrase}(x) \wedge \textit{accentual-phrase}(y) \\
\vee\;\; & \textit{accentual-phrase}(x) \wedge \textit{word}(y) \\
\vee\;\; & \textit{word}(x) \wedge \textit{syllable}(y) \\
\vee\;\; & \textit{syllable}(x) \wedge (\textit{mora}(y) \vee \textit{segment}(y)) \\
\vee\;\; & \textit{mora}(x) \wedge \textit{segment}(y))
\end{aligned}
$$

---

[7] Note that this structure violates the Strict Layer Hypothesis since it contains syllables that dominate segments directly.

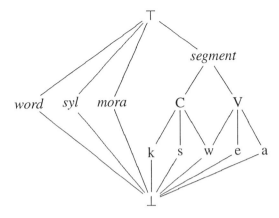

Figure 2.5: Revised sort lattice for prosodic structures

This constraint says of any pair of nodes x and y where x immediately dominates y that either x is an utterance and y is an intermediate phrase, or x is an intermediate phrase and y is an accentual phrase, and so on. Note that the fifth line of (2.8) is more complex than the others. If x is a syllable then y is either a mora or a segment. This is necessary in order to allow syllables to dominate either moras or segments.

Notice that in (2.7) the only kind of segments which are immediately dominated by a mora are vowels and the only kind immediately dominated by a syllable are consonants. The former is simply a coincidence and there are many situations where we shall want to permit moras to dominate consonants. However, the fact that syllables can immediately dominate consonants (and not vowels) is part of the definition of syllable structure in this version of the moraic theory (Hayes, 1989).

In order to express this constraint succinctly we first enrich the lattice in Figure 2.2 to include the C and V sorts, as shown in Figure 2.5. Note the ambivalent status of the glide w. Given this revised sort lattice, we state in (2.9) the constraint that segments which are immediately dominated by syllables must be consonants.

(2.9) $\forall xy, x \; \delta \; y \wedge syl(x) \wedge segment(y) \rightarrow c(y)$

So far we have seen a range of appropriateness constraints stated as logical formulas. It is convenient to have a graphical representation of these

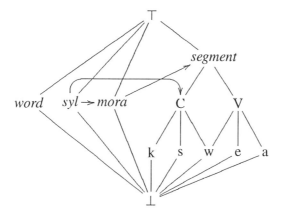

Figure 2.6: Appropriateness graph for prosodic structure

constraints. One way to achieve this is to view δ as a binary relation on
sorts.[8] If it is possible for a node of sort s to immediately dominate a node of
sort t, then we enter an arrow between s and t into the sort lattice, as shown
in Figure 2.6. The arrow represents the immediate dominance relation δ.
Two arrows emanate from the sort *syl*, since it can immediately dominate
two different sorts of node. If a syllable immediately dominates a segment
then that segment must also be a consonant. A similar representation can
be provided for Clements' tree in Figure 2.3.

However, this general approach does not go quite far enough. As was
observed at the end of §2.1.2, it is necessary to prevent a vowel on the
CV-tier from dominating a [–continuant] specification. Indeed, this is
just one of many similar dependencies which cannot be expressed directly
using appropriateness constraints on immediate dominance. Instead, it is
necessary to employ the transitive version of this relation $\delta^\star$. The statement
of the constraint appears in (2.10).

(2.10) $\forall xy,\ v(x) \wedge x\ \delta^\star\ y \wedge continuant(y) \rightarrow +continuant(y)$

---

[8] Carpenter has developed a similar approach to appropriateness (Carpenter, 1992, 86).

2.2.3 *Branching degree*

We have seen that appropriateness constraints restrict the sorts of nodes which can be immediately dominated by a particular node. For example, if a root node immediately dominates another node, then that node must be either a laryngeal node or a manner node. However, this has nothing to do with the total number of nodes which a node can dominate. Given the formalism so far, the situation where a root node dominates a thousand laryngeal nodes is as acceptable as the situation where a root node dominates only one laryngeal node. In some situations, we shall want to place some restrictions on the amount of branching which can occur.[9] The most common situation in sub-segmental structures is for there to be at most one occurrence of a given sort of node dominated by any node. This constraint is expressed in (2.11) for the laryngeal node.

(2.11) $\forall xyz, x \, \delta \, y \wedge x \, \delta \, z \wedge laryngeal(y) \wedge laryngeal(z) \rightarrow y = z$

This kind of restriction can be generalised. Suppose that nodes of sort t can occur at most n times as constituents of a node of sort s. Then if some node x dominates nodes $y_1, \ldots, y_{n+1}$, where each y_i is of sort t, then at least two of these nodes must be identical. This constraint is expressed in (2.12), where i ranges from 1 to $n + 1$.

(2.12) $max(s, t, n) =_{\text{def}}$
$\forall x \, y_i, s(x) \wedge x \, \delta \, y_i \wedge t(y_i) \rightarrow y_j = y_k$ for some j, k.

Constraints like (2.12) impose an upper limit on the degree of branching. In certain situations it may also be desirable to be able to impose a lower limit on branching. Suppose some sort s must occur at least m times as a label on the constituents of a node. This is expressed as follows:

(2.13) $min(s, t, m) =_{\text{def}}$
$\forall x, s(x) \rightarrow (\exists y_i, x \, \delta \, y_i \wedge t(y_i) \wedge y_j \neq y_k)$ for all j, k.

---

[9]Of course, there are situations where it may not be possible to impose a principled upper bound on the degree of branching. Indeed, this is a direct consequence of the Strict Layer Hypothesis (see §2.2.2): structures are depth-bounded and so successively larger utterances require greater branching degrees. Goldsmith (1990, 18f) has proposed constraints on the number of associations allowed per segment, and the proposals advanced here for δ might conceivably be carried over to $\circ$, the overlap relation to be defined in §2.3 for modelling association.

An abbreviatory notation for these constraints will be given in §2.5.5 and exemplification can be found in §4.3.

2.2.4   Re-entrancy

So far we have seen prosodic and sub-segmental structure represented using trees. However, it is widely recognised that phonological structures are not trees, as the following example illustrates for the word *Jennifer* (Clements and Keyser, 1983, 3).

(2.14)

In this structure there are nodes which are dominated by more than one node. For example, the *n* and *f* consonants are AMBISYLLABIC (*i.e.* shared by two syllables) and both are dominated by two σ nodes. Structures containing nodes like these are called RE-ENTRANT. If re-entrant structures like (2.14) need to be excluded, we can adopt constraint (2.15). This states that if nodes x and y dominate node z then $x = y$.

(2.15) $\forall xyz, x \, \delta \, z \wedge y \, \delta \, z \rightarrow x = y$

This constraint may be required for certain grammars; it is not proposed as a universal constraint. It may be that we wish to state the above constraint for particular kinds of nodes only, and on a language-specific basis. For example, consider the parameters proposed by Paradis and Prunet (1989, 323) for the Fula language:

(2.16)   Parameters: nodes allowed to spread:
      i.   articulator nodes?   Fula: *no*
     ii. place nodes?   Fula: *yes*

It is only necessary to add a constraint for (2.16i), as the default situation is for spreading to be allowed. A constraint which prevents articulator nodes from spreading is given in (2.17).

(2.17) $\forall xyz, x\ \delta\ z \wedge y\ \delta\ z \wedge$ articulator$(z) \rightarrow x = y$

If we want to state such a constraint for individual nodes we could write:

(2.18)   *not-shared*$(z) =_{\text{def}} \forall xy, x\ \delta\ z \wedge y\ \delta\ z \rightarrow x = y$

An application of (2.18) is discussed in §3.2.2. More discussion of re-entrancy in phonology can be found in Bird (1991a); Scobbie (1991a); Coleman (1992a).

2.2.5   Autosegmental licensing

Further constraints on hierarchical structure comes under the heading of AUTOSEGMENTAL LICENSING (Goldsmith, 1990). We shall begin by briefly discussing Itô's Coda Filter (Itô, 1989, 224). Itô adopts the constraint in (2.19) to prevent a place of articulation specification from appearing in a syllable coda unless it simultaneously appears in the following syllable onset.

(2.19)   **Itô's Coda Filter:**

Itô argues that this filter does not apply to a representation where a place specification is shared between a coda and a following onset, even though such a representation would appear to match the structure in (2.19). This additional stipulation is known as the linking constraint (Hayes, 1986b), which requires that association lines mentioned in structural descriptions be exhaustive. The force of the linking constraint is to prevent the coda filter from applying if the place node is linked to more than one consonant. So, a place node linked to *two* coda consonants is not ruled out by (2.19). Notwithstanding this shortcoming, the coda filter is intended to encode the constraint that, regardless of what else a place node is linked to, it must be linked to a syllable onset. This amounts to a circuitous version of the expression in (2.20), where $s_1 = onset$ and $s_2 = place$.

(2.20) **Autosegmental Licensing:**

s_1 licenses $s_2 =_{\text{def}} \forall x, s_2(x) \rightarrow \exists y, (s_1(y) \wedge y \, \delta^\star \, x)$

s_1 *licenses* s_2 *if for all nodes of sort* s_2 *there is a node of sort* s_1
dominating s_2

2.2.6 Prosodic licensing and stray erasure

Prosodic licensing 'requires that all phonological units belong to higher
prosodic structure: segments to syllables, syllables to metrical feet, and
metrical feet to phonological words or phrases' (Itô, 1989, 220). Presuma-
bly the prosodic hierarchy is finite, and so there must be some level which
is not required to be prosodically licensed. We shall take this to be the
phrase level. Now prosodic licensing may be defined as follows.

(2.21) *licensed*$(x) =_{\text{def}} \exists y, phrase(x) \vee phrase(y) \wedge y \, \delta^\star \, x$
For all nodes x, *either* x *is a phrase or there is a phrase* y *where* y
dominates x.

This states that all phonological units are either phrases or are dominated
by phrases. The appropriateness constraints will ensure that, for example,
syllables are dominated by feet and not moras or anything else. It is only
necessary to state that *everything* is ultimately dominated by a phrase.[10]

Closely connected to the idea of prosodic licensing is STRAY ERASURE
(Steriade, 1982). This is a mechanism whereby phonological units which
cannot be incorporated into prosodic structure without the structure beco-
ming ill-formed are deleted. As we shall see in §3.2.2, stray erasure can
be modelled using alternation with zero. Independent well-formedness
constraints on prosodic structure will occasionally force the zero alternant
to be selected.

---

[10] Note that Scobbie (1991a, 40, 45) has argued against the view of association as
temporal overlap, arguing that prosodic licensing (or anchoring) cannot be expressed under
this view of association. However, as we have seen here, prosodic licensing is indeed
achievable in this model by using the dominance relation (and not the association relation).

2.2.7 Conclusion

In this section the hierarchical organisation of phonological diagrams has been investigated. Two dominance relations δ and δ^* have been introduced, and it has been shown how these may be used to represent hierarchical structure. Appropriateness constraints and licensing constraints have been expressed through various interactions between the dominance relations and the sort system.

At this point we must ask if a dominance relation alone is sufficient for representing hierarchical phonological structures. Some have claimed that it is (Coleman, 1991; Scobbie, 1991a). Others, like Broe, are less certain:

> I am not optimistic that the interdependencies among features can be adequately representation by *any* network that posits a simple, asymmetric, transitive, dependency relationship between features. (Broe, 1992, 178f)

In the next section we turn to the issues which concern the interpretation of temporal organisation in phonology, and we discover that another *two* relations are necessary.

2.3 Temporal organisation

2.3.1 Sequential versus simultaneous

Let us re-examine the two running examples. A small subpart of each is reproduced below. (2.22a) depicts a syllable containing an onset and two moras, taken from (2.7). (2.22b) depicts the place subtree for the segment [s], taken from Figure 2.3.

(2.22)

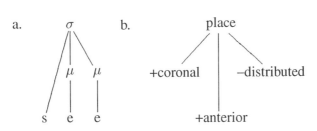

Now consider the same trees with the horizontal arrangement permuted. (2.23a) is nonsensical because the onset is in the middle of the syllable, an impossible situation. However, (2.23b) is perfectly well-formed. Moreover, (2.23b) describes the same class of linguistic objects as (2.22b).

(2.23)

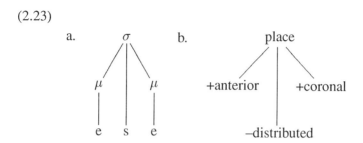

a. σ   b.   place

μ   μ   +anterior   +coronal

e   s   e   –distributed

Therefore, the temporal organisation of (2.22a) is different from the temporal organisation of (2.22b). Clements (1985, 226) calls the former kind of interpretation *sequential* and the second kind *simultaneous*. In (2.22a), left-to-right ordering on the page corresponds to temporal ordering. The onset is placed to the left of the moras because the onset is always the first part of a syllable. In (2.22b) left-to-right ordering is insignificant. An |s| segment is only created when the three daughters of the place subtree are temporally coincident.

One way to signal this difference formally is to introduce two new binary relations in addition to the δ relation. These relations are precedence, $\prec$, and overlap, $\circ$. They are the subject of the next section.

2.3.2   *Precedence and overlap*

Temporal overlap is a two-place relation which is reflexive, symmetric and nontransitive. If we employ the notation $x \circ y$ for the statement 'x overlaps y' then these facts about overlap can be stated as follows:

(2.24)   a. $\forall x, x \circ x$
                overlap is reflexive

         b. $\forall xy, x \circ y \rightarrow y \circ x$
                overlap is symmetric

If overlap were transitive, a third statement would be necessary:

(2.25) $\forall xyz, x \circ y \wedge y \circ z \rightarrow x \circ z$

However, if this were the case then $\circ$ would correspond to simultaneity. As Sagey (1988) has pointed out, such a view of association is inadequate for representations involving multiple association, like (2.26), where a temporally precedes b.

(2.26)

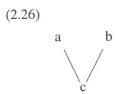

Since overlap is nontransitive, we simply omit (2.25). Members of a tier are related by 'temporal precedence'. By this we mean strict linear precedence, which is an irreflexive, asymmetric and transitive relation.[11] We adopt the notation $x \prec y$ to express the statement 'x precedes y', and write the following expressions (where negation ($\neg$) is taken to have wider scope than $\prec$ and $\circ$):

(2.27) a. $\forall x, \neg x \prec x$
             precedence is irreflexive

        b. $\forall xy, x \prec y \rightarrow \neg y \prec x$
             precedence is asymmetric

        c. $\forall xyz, x \prec y \wedge y \prec z \rightarrow x \prec z$
             precedence is transitive

Perhaps surprisingly, the properties expressed above about overlap and precedence are inadequate in a crucial way. Consider the statement: '$x \prec y$ and $x \circ y$'. Clearly, this is inconsistent given the intended interpretations of $\prec$ and $\circ$. However, we cannot demonstrate this from the above axioms. Thus, to express the mutual exclusiveness of overlap and precedence, a further statement is necessary:

---

[11]In fact, these properties only give us a strict partial ordering; to get a linear ordering, we also need an additional statement of connectedness: $\forall xy, x \prec y \vee x = y \vee x \succ y$. We will return to this in §2.3.7.

(2.28) $\forall xy, x \prec y \rightarrow \neg x \circ y$
         precedence and overlap are disjoint

At this point, we seem to have enough machinery to interpret an autosegmental diagram such as (2.29).

(2.29)

A line which connects two points, say those labeled a and c, is interpreted as claiming that there is an overlap relation holding between events a and c, while horizontal alignment of two points on the page, say a appearing to the left of b, is interpreted as claiming that a relation of precedence holds between a and b. That is, (2.29) depicts a situation which we can describe in our notation as follows:

(2.30) $a \prec b, c \prec d, a \circ c$ and $b \circ d$

It is an open question as to which further temporal relations should be adopted. Several other temporal relations have been discussed in the literature (van Benthem, 1983; Allen, 1983; Schmiedel, 1988).

2.3.3   Deriving the no-crossing constraint

Consider the situation shown in (2.31), where two association lines cross:

(2.31)

Diagram (2.31) violates the no-crossing constraint (already discussed in §1.1). We interpret this as shown in (2.32):

(2.32) $a \prec b, c \prec d, a \circ d$ and $b \circ c$

However, none of the facts about overlap and precedence stated in §2.3.2 rule out (2.32) as ill-formed. A further statement about the relationship between overlap and precedence is therefore necessary, as given in (2.33).

(2.33) $\forall wxyz, w \prec x \wedge x \circ y \wedge y \prec z \rightarrow w \prec z$

In order to help visualise constraint (2.33), we adopt Sagey's graphical conventions for representing intervals as labeled time-line segments:

(2.34)

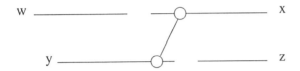

Given the statements in (2.28) and (2.33) about the relationship between overlap and precedence, the no-crossing constraint can be derived. Suppose we have $w \prec x$ and $y \prec z$. From (2.33) we know that $w \prec z$ and then from (2.28) that $\neg w \circ z$. The key point here is that the no-crossing constraint does not follow from the definitions of overlap and precedence alone, but from additional statements about their interrelationship.

2.3.4 *Points and intervals*

One virtue of Sagey's approach is that all of the properties of overlap, precedence and their inter-relationship stated above follow from the conception of an interval as a collection of points. The definitions in (2.35) are revised versions of those given by Sagey:

(2.35) a. For two intervals x and y, we write $x \prec y$ iff
$\forall p \in x, q \in y, p < q$.

 b. For two intervals x and y, we write $x \circ y$ iff
$\exists p \in x, q \in y$ such that $p = q$.

Given that $<$ is a strict linear ordering on points, it is a relatively straightforward matter to show that (2.24), (2.27), (2.28) and (2.33) follow from these
definitions and therefore do not require independent statement. This would
appear to be a desirable state of affairs, given the economy of statement
and simplicity of (2.35). However, defining intervals in terms of points is
questionable from philosophical, cognitive and phonetic viewpoints.

Although it is a deeply rooted part of our current scientific outlook to
regard time as being composed of instants and collections of instants, it
has nevertheless been argued by philosophers such as Russell that viewing
time as consisting of extended periods which admit ever-finer subdivisions
is closer to our pretheoretic intuitions. Furthermore, the suggestion that
phonological processing involves a point-based ontology (Sagey, 1988,
110) is cognitively implausible. The definitions in (2.35) suggest that in
order for an agent to verify a statement of precedence between two intervals
containing an infinity of points, she would have to spend forever comparing
the points in a pairwise manner; a similarly non-terminating procedure
would be required to falsify a statement of overlap between two intervals.
Even if one argued that such intervals contained only a finite number of
points, the cognitive processing required would be dependent upon the size
of the intervals. This is contrary to the seemingly uncontroversial claim
that it should take constant time to judge the precedence or overlap of
arbitrarily sized intervals.

The point-based approach could be rescued from this criticism by
referring to the *endpoints* of intervals. This is the approach adopted by
Hertz (1990), Coleman (1992a, 33) and Walther (1992). Let us assume, as
before, that $<$ is a strict linear ordering on points, and also that '$max(x)$'
denotes the least upper bound of interval x with respect to $<$, and that
'$min(x)$' denotes the greatest lower bound of x.

(2.36)   a. $x \prec y$ iff $max(x) < min(y)$

         b. $x \circ y$ iff $max(x) > min(y)$ and $max(y) > min(x)$

For the interval endpoints to be specifiable in a way that is independent
of the size of the interval (*i.e.* the number of points it contains, whether
finite or infinite), they must be basic to the definition of the interval. In
other words, the interval must be defined in terms of its endpoints, rather
than as the set of points it contains – for example, as $[3.42, 3.96]$, where
the numbers represent seconds since the beginning of the utterance. Given

the endpoints, it is then a simple matter to determine whether a point is contained in the interval, using (2.36).

However, this position also runs into difficulties. First, it is usually difficult to assign a determinate boundary (either perceptually or instrumentally) to the phonetic instantiation of a phonological event. We can be certain about the 'central area' of, say, an interval of nasality or friction in an utterance, but as we near either extremity of such an interval it becomes less certain whether or not a particular point is included in the interval. Consequently, it would seem desirable to allow for a degree of indeterminacy in the location of interval endpoints.

Moreover, even if it were possible from a phonetic point of view to demarcate precisely the endpoints of some particular event such as voicing, it is highly implausible that one would want to treat such boundaries as part of the phonological specification of a feature or autosegment. This is partially acknowledged by Sagey's claim that 'the points of time within a feature or x-slot are accessible only at the late level of phonetic implementation, . . ., they are not manipulable or accessible by phonological rules' (1986, 294). Yet, as also pointed out by Hammond (1988, 323), this is difficult to reconcile with the fact that points are fundamental to Sagey's ontology.

Note also that the phonetic properties of a given point can only be specified in terms of an interval (possibly very small) which contains that point. Thus on Sagey's approach, one first has to construct intervals from points, and only then attach certain properties to these intervals, a two-stage process.

Here we shall eschew the point-based ontology because of its philosophical, cognitive and phonetic problems, opting for intervals (or events) instead.[12] We can still have intervals which behave like points, by virtue of definition (2.37).

(2.37) $point(x) =_{\text{def}} \forall y, (x \circ y \rightarrow x \subseteq y)$

This definition states that x is a point iff x is included in every interval that x overlaps. The inclusion relation used in (2.37) is defined in the next section.

---

[12]It is perhaps interesting to note that the ontological shift from points to intervals is not new to linguistics; for example, a similar move was made in linguistic semantics by Bennett and Partee (1972).

2.3.5   Inclusion and simultaneity

Now that axioms for overlap have been provided, it is possible to define temporal inclusion. In fact, inclusion and overlap are interdefinable (van Benthem, 1988, 59), as shown in the following definitions. (The statement '$x \subseteq y$' should be read: x is included in y.)

(2.38)   a. $\forall xy, x \subseteq y$ iff $\forall z, z \circ x \rightarrow z \circ y$

       b. $\forall xy, x \circ y$ iff $\exists z, z \subseteq x \wedge z \subseteq y$

From this it follows that inclusion is a reflexive and transitive relation. This relation may also be useful to express constraints on the spreading of autosegments: if $x \subseteq y$ then x cannot 'spread' beyond the limits of y. Additionally, if $x \subseteq y$ and $x \supseteq y$ we shall write $x \rightleftharpoons y$ to indicate that x and y are simultaneous (or coterminous). Simultaneity is an equivalence relation, *i.e.* it is reflexive, symmetric and transitive.

2.3.6   Homogeneity and convexity

Now that we have introduced the notion of inclusion, we can ask about the subevents which might be included within a given event. Take, for example, a [+nasal] event e. It is plausible to suppose that all the phonologically relevant subevents of e also have the property of being nasal; that is, the property of nasality is uniformly spread over the whole of e. In this case, we say that the event is HOMOGENEOUS.

By contrast, we might want to claim that a *stop* event e can be further analyzed as a *closure* event e_1 followed by a *release* event e_2. We can now do so simply by stating that e includes both e_1 and e_2. Events which contain distinct subparts in this way will be termed HETEROGENEOUS.[13]

A related issue arises when we consider a phenomenon such as vowel harmony. We would like to be able to say that the distinctive features common to harmonising vowels come from a single source, namely the properties of a single event e which overlaps each vowel slot. However,

---

[13] It has often been observed that what we have called the homogeneous/heterogeneous distinction for events has a parallel in mass/count distinction for objects (e.g. Taylor, 1977, 210f).

consider a sequence $V C V$, where the two Vs harmonise, say, for the feature [+back]. This means, in particular, that a [+back] event overlaps both of the V events. Does it also overlap C? At a phonological level, we do not want to be committed to such a consequence, although it is one which follows on Sagey's account,[14] since the feature [+back] might be either inappropriate or false for the C.

More generally, we are concerned here with a characteristic of events which has been termed 'convexity'. An event e is CONVEX, by definition, if it satisfies the following condition:

(2.39) $convex(e) =_{\text{def}}$
$$\forall x_1 x_2 x_3, x_1 \prec x_2 \prec x_3 \land x_1 \circ e \land x_3 \circ e \rightarrow x_2 \circ e.$$

That is, if e overlaps two events x_1 and x_3, then it also overlaps any other event x_2 which intervenes between x_1 and x_3.

(2.40)

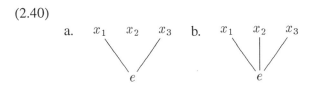

An event not satisfying condition (2.39) will be called NON-CONVEX. We will admit into our framework events of both sorts. Thus, the harmonising Vs in our immediately preceding example may be part of a non-convex [+back] event. This convexity requirement is fundamental to Attribute Value Phonology (Scobbie, 1991a) and it is called the sharing constraint (see §1.5.3).

2.3.7 *Linear ordering and immediate precedence*

Recall that §2.3 began with an illustration of the difference of interpretation between (2.22a) and (2.22b), reproduced below.

---

[14]To see why this is so, consider four intervals x_1, x_2, x_3 and e, where $x_1 \prec x_2$, $x_2 \prec x_3$, $x_1 \circ e$, and $x_3 \circ e$. From (2.35b) we know there are points $p_1 \in x_1$ and $q_1 \in e$ such that $p_1 = q_1$. Now from (2.35a), $\forall p_2 \in x_2, q_1 < p_2$. By a similar argument, $\exists q_3 \in x_3, p_2 < q_3$. Therefore $p_2 \in e$, and so $x_2 \circ e$.

(2.22)

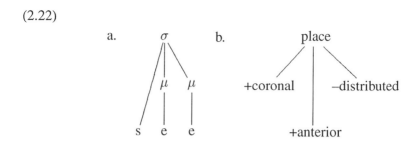

This difference of interpretation lies in the identity of the nodes themselves. If distinct nodes have the same sort then one must precede the other. In a prosodic tree it tends to be the case that all daughters of a node share the same label and are linearly ordered. In a sub-segmental tree it is more usual for all daughters of a node to have distinct labels and to be temporally coincident (or coarticulated). However, sub-segmental structures do not exclusively involve coarticulation. For example, (2.41a) is a (partial) manner subtree for [s] and (2.41b) is a (partial) manner subtree for an affricate (Sagey 1986b, 28; Hayes 1990, 60).

(2.41)   a.

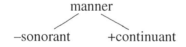

         b.

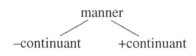

In (2.41a) the daughters are coarticulated and left-to-right ordering is insignificant. However, in (2.41b) the daughters are not coarticulated; the part of an utterance corresponding to the left daughter precedes that corresponding to the right daughter. Again, this difference of interpretation is accompanied by a difference in the patterning of sorts. In (2.41a) neither daughter shares a common sort, whereas in (2.41b) both daughters have the sort *continuant*. This view is compatible with Sagey's discussion; she states that 'it is only branchings to specifications on a single tier that are phonologically ordered' (Sagey, 1986, 28).

The temporal relations $\prec$ and $\circ$ will be used between sister constituents of a node. For (2.41), suppose a is the node at the end of the left branch and b is the node at the end of the right branch. For (2.41a) we have the constraint $a \circ b$ while for (2.41b) we have the constraint $a \prec b$. Those constituents which have the same sort will be required to stand in a linear ordering, as formulated in schema (2.42).[15]

(2.42) **Linearity constraint:**

$\forall xy, s(x) \land s(y) \rightarrow x \prec y \lor x = y \lor x \succ y$

If x and y both have sort s then x and y are linearly ordered.

This schema has an important articulatory phonetic basis. It states that a given articulator cannot do two different things simultaneously. The schema says nothing about the fact that constituents having different sorts must overlap, as in (2.41). In the general case, we cannot *require* constituents having different sorts to overlap. For example, consider the following structure.

(2.43)

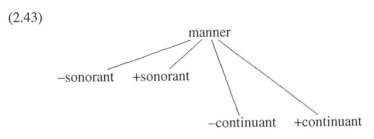

The above linear ordering axioms ensure that the two continuant nodes do not overlap and that the two sonorant nodes do not overlap. If we required nodes having different sorts to overlap then we would have a situation where both continuant nodes overlap both sonorant nodes, a violation of the no-crossing constraint.

Another reason why it is not possible to require that constituents having different sorts must overlap is that [−continuant] and [+continuant] in (2.43) have different sorts, and yet we do not want them overlapping each other. In the absence of a general constraint, requirements for overlap within constituents must be formulated within individual phonological theories.

---

[15]Note that (2.42) is not an axiom but an axiom schema, which stands in place of a number of axioms. In fact, there will be an instance of (2.42) for each sort s.

Since tiers are linearly ordered we can define immediate precedence relations $\prec_0^s$ for each sort s, as shown below.

(2.44) $x \prec_0^s y =_{\text{def}} s(x) \wedge s(y) \wedge x \prec y \wedge (\exists z, x \prec z \prec y \rightarrow \neg s(z))$
        x *immediately precedes* y *on tier* s *iff nothing intervenes between*
        x *and* y *on tier* s.

Now we can give Itô's UNIVERSAL CORE SYLLABLE CONDITION (Itô, 1986, 5), which states that 'the sequence CV must belong to a single syllable'. Here it is modified slightly to take prosodic structure into account.

(2.45) $\forall xyz, P(z) \wedge z\,\delta^\star\, x \wedge z\,\delta^\star\, y \wedge c(x) \wedge v(y) \wedge x \prec_0^{\text{segment}} y$
        $\rightarrow \exists w, syl(w) \wedge w\,\delta^\star\, x \wedge w\,\delta^\star\, y$
        If the sequence CV occurs inside a prosodic constituent P then it
        also occurs within a single syllable.

We shall see an application of the universal core syllable condition in §3.4.

2.3.8   Conclusion

Recall that this section began with a discussion of the diagrams in (2.22), reproduced below:

(2.22)

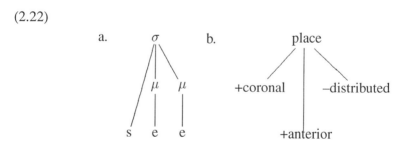

The fact that the leaves of (2.22a) are linearly ordered is stated by the Linearity Constraint (2.42). We are also able to state the desired overlap properties for (2.22b), such as [+coronal] ∘ [+anterior].

Now that we have discussed the temporal relationship between sister constituents, it is natural to wonder what temporal relationship, if any, holds between a parent node and its constituents. At an intuitive level, it is reasonable to suppose that the temporal extent of, say, a phrase is co-extensive with the combined temporal extents of its constituents, since the various levels of hierarchical structure are all located in a single flow of time. However, it is not a trivial matter to add formal content to these intuitions. The next section discusses these issues.

2.4 The interaction of hierarchical and temporal structure

So far in this chapter we have seen the definition and application of sorts, two dominance relations (δ, $\delta^\star$) and two temporal relations ($\prec$, $\circ$) and we have seen interactions between sorts and the dominance relations, and interactions between sorts and the temporal relations. In this section the interactions between the dominance and temporal relations are discussed.

None of the hierarchical structures presented above contained crossing lines. This seems to be a general requirement, even in situations where re-entrancy is employed. However, nothing about the dominance relation currently prevents such a possibility from arising. A simple, intuitive way to prevent this is to add the following constraint.

(2.46) **Locality constraint:**
$\forall xy, x \; \delta^\star \; y \; \rightarrow \; x \circ y$
If x dominates y then x overlaps y

Now, any situation where lines of dominance cross is also a violation of the no-crossing constraint. This constraint has further motivation: for example, the period of time occupied by an utterance of the word 'cat' temporally overlaps the period of time occupied by the utterance of 'c' which forms a part of the utterance of 'cat'. Hayes (1990, 44) has adopted a constraint very similar to (2.46), his 'percolation convention'.

The locality constraint brings dominance and association into a rather close relationship. However, there is good reason not to conflate them, which is what Hammond (1988), Scobbie (1991a, 60) and Wiese (1990) propose. This is because there are numerous cases of overlap between nodes which are not related by dominance, such as in most sub-segmental structures.

The locality constraint has important consequences for the inheritance of precedence. Consider the following structure, resembling the prosodic trees we have seen already.

(2.47)

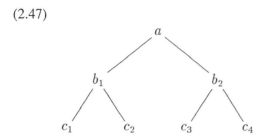

Suppose that each level of this tree consists of nodes having the same sort. Suppose that b_1 and b_2 are distinct. Then the linearity constraint ensures that they cannot overlap. Suppose further that $b_1 \prec b_2$. In a similar fashion, suppose that $c_1 \prec c_2$ and $c_3 \prec c_4$. What, then, is the relationship between the nodes dominated by b_1 and b_2? From the linearity constraint we know that none of the c_i overlap. From the no-crossing constraint, we know that none of the nodes dominated by b_2 precede any of the nodes dominated by b_1 (since both b_1 and b_2 overlap all of their constituents). Therefore, each node dominated by b_1 must either precede or equal each node dominated by b_2. This leaves only two possible arrangements, indicated schematically in (2.48), where the temporal extent of the nodes is indicated explicitly.

(2.48) a.

b.

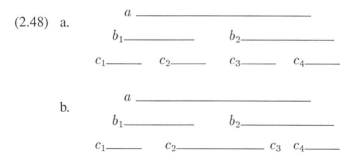

The picture in (2.48a) is intended to show that both c_1 and c_2 completely precede both c_3 and c_4. The picture in (2.48b) is ambiguous between the possibility of c_2 and c_3 overlapping, and the possibility of c_2 and c_3 being identical. Therefore, structure sharing only occurs at the edges of subtrees.

In graphical terms, this is equivalent to the requirement that the lines of dominance cannot cross.

In this section we have seen areas of interaction between hierarchical and temporal structure. Now let us consider a situation where hierarchical, temporal and sort structure all interact. Suppose that the ordering within a constituent is fully predictable from the sorts. An example of this comes from syllable structure, where onsets must precede moras. In this case, we could employ the constraint in (2.49).[16]

(2.49) $\forall xyz, x \, \delta \, y \wedge onset(y) \wedge x \, \delta \, z \wedge mora(z) \rightarrow y \prec z$

This concludes the discussion of the motivation and interaction of sortal, hierarchical and temporal information. We can summarise the current state of affairs in the following diagram. At the corners of the triangle are the fundamental entities in our ontology: sorts (§2.1), hierarchy (§2.2) and time (§2.3).

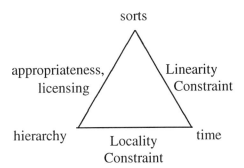

Combining sorts and hierarchy are the appropriateness (§2.2.2) and licensing (§2.2.5, §2.2.6) constraints. Combining sorts and time is the linearity constraint (2.42), and combining hierarchy and time is the locality constraint (2.46). Some constraints, like (2.49) above, combine all three. Now it is time to draw all these strands together and define a formal description language.

---

[16]This constraint has connections with the linear precedence statements of Generalised Phrase Structure Grammar (Gazdar et al., 1985).

2.5   Temporal feature logic

In this section a classical, first-order, function-free theory $\mathcal{L}(V, S)$ is defined.[17] This logic represents an outgrowth of work on temporal logic (van Benthem, 1983) and feature logic (Johnson, 1988).

2.5.1   The syntax of $\mathcal{L}$

We begin by defining the primitive symbols of $\mathcal{L}(X, S)$:

1. A set of individual variables $\mathcal{X}$

2. A finite set of sort symbols $\mathcal{S}$

3. The symbols δ, $\delta^\star$, $\prec$, $\preceq$, $\circ$, $=$, $\neg$, $\vee$, $\wedge$, $\forall$, $\exists$, $\rightarrow$, $\equiv$, $($, $)$, $\top$, $\bot$

Modifying the signature $(\mathcal{X}, \mathcal{S})$ is how we customise $\mathcal{L}$ for a particular phonological theory. However, we shall normally only be explicit about $\mathcal{S}$ in this connection.

The TERMS, or denoting expressions, are just the individual variables. The FORMULAS (wffs) of $\mathcal{L}$ are constructed out of the primitive symbols as follows.

1. An expression consisting of a sort symbol followed by one or two individual variables is a wff

2. $x\,\delta\,y$, $x\,\delta^\star\,y$, $x \prec y$ and $x \circ y$ are wffs for all individual variables x, y

3. If ϕ is a wff then so is $\neg\phi$

4. If ϕ and ψ are wffs, so are $(\phi \vee \psi)$, $(\phi \wedge \psi)$, $(\phi \rightarrow \psi)$, $(\phi \equiv \psi)$

5. If ϕ is a wff, then for each individual variable x, $\forall x, \phi$ and $\exists x, \phi$ are wffs

---

[17] $\mathcal{L}(V, S)$ is classical because the double negation of a formula is always equivalent to the formula. It is first-order because quantification is over individual variables and not predicates. The theory is also function-free, in that the only arguments a predicate can take are variables.

The standard connectives are related as follows:

1. $\phi \wedge \psi$ iff $\neg(\neg\phi \vee \neg\psi)$

2. $\phi \rightarrow \psi$ iff $(\neg\phi) \vee \psi$

3. $\phi \equiv \psi$ iff $(\phi \rightarrow \psi) \wedge (\psi \rightarrow \phi)$

4. $\exists x, \phi$ iff $\neg(\forall x, \neg\phi)$

5. $\forall xy, x \preceq y \equiv x \prec y \vee x = y$

6. $\forall xy, x \, \delta^\star \, y \equiv x \, \delta \, y \vee \exists z(x \, \delta \, z \wedge z \, \delta^\star \, y)$

The default operator M and the default arrow $\overset{d}{\rightarrow}$ are not a part of $\mathcal{L}$ but belong to a metalanguage, $\mathcal{L}'$. This metalanguage – and not $\mathcal{L}$ – is the language in which linguistic descriptions will be couched. However, I shall ignore the distinction between $\mathcal{L}$ and $\mathcal{L}'$ because the precise formulation of defaults is not central to this study.

2.5.2 A model-theoretic semantics for $\mathcal{L}$

A formal semantics for this language is inherited from the standard model theoretic semantics of classical first-order predicate calculus (Boolos and Jeffrey, 1989).

2.5.3 Depicting models

Although models are abstract mathematical objects, we ultimately want to think about expressions in $\mathcal{L}$ as descriptions of sets of utterances. To assist this interpretation, we shall adopt certain graphical conventions for depicting models that make them look more familiar. In particular, we shall use the notation of GESTURAL SCORES (Browman and Goldstein, 1989), exemplified in (2.50) for the word *tense*. This notation is intended to show the orchestration of the articulators of the vocal tract: the tongue tip, tongue body, velum and glottis.[18]

---

[18] A detailed explanation of this diagram is given in §4.2.1.

(2.50)

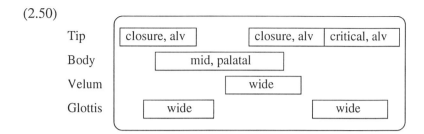

Notice that overlap and precedence relations are clearly represented in (2.50). Since speech is not inherently hierarchically organised, dominance is not depicted in gestural scores. Recall that the tree diagrams we have seen for depicting dominance and precedence relations were initially viewed as the representations we were giving a semantics to. Now that we have an independent syntax and semantics for a phonological description language, these diagrams can be viewed as objects. Thus, gestural scores and tree diagrams will be considered to be *projections* of the temporal and hierarchical aspects of phonological frames.

2.5.4   Validities

The $\circ$, $\prec$ and δ relations must satisfy the following axioms.

(2.51)   a. $\forall x, x \circ x$
                Overlap is reflexive

          b. $\forall xy, x \circ y \rightarrow y \circ x$
                Overlap is symmetric

          c. $\forall xy, x \prec y \rightarrow \neg y \prec x$
                Precedence is asymmetric

          d. $\forall xy, x \prec y \rightarrow \neg x \circ y$
                Precedence is disjoint from overlap

          e. $\forall wxyz, w \prec x \wedge x \circ y \wedge y \prec z \rightarrow w \prec z$
                Precedence is transitive (through overlap)

          f. $\forall xy, x \prec y \vee x \circ y \vee x \succ y$
                Time is linear

g. $\forall xy, x \, \delta^* \, y \;\rightarrow\; x \circ y$
   Locality constraint

h. $\forall x_0 x_1 \cdots x_n, \neg x_0 \, \delta \, x_1 \, \delta \, \cdots \, \delta \, x_n \, \delta \, x_0, (n \geq 0)$
   Acyclicity

i. $\forall xy, s(x) \wedge s(y) \wedge x \circ y \;\rightarrow\; x = y$
   Tiers are linearly ordered (stated for all s)

2.5.5 Some abbreviatory conventions

The formulas provided above tend to be somewhat long-winded. From a programming languages perspective, it is natural to view these formulas as comprising a low-level 'machine language'. We can employ a variety of high level constructs, just so long as they can be compiled away in a reasonable number of steps. This allows descriptions to be more succinct while retaining precision. For the sake of clarity these constructs (or abbreviatory conventions) are defined by example.

The first abbreviatory convention is for stating appropriateness constraints. The unabbreviated formula in (2.52a) is written as (2.52b).

(2.52) **Abbreviatory Convention 1:**

a. $\forall xy, place(x) \wedge x \, \delta \, y \;\rightarrow\; coronal(y) \vee anterior(y) \vee$
   $distributed(y)$

b. place $\Rightarrow$ [coronal, anterior, distributed]

If it is necessary to constrain the amount of branching which is permitted from nodes of a particular sort to nodes of some other sort, the following notation will be used, where the *max* and *min* predicates are defined in (2.12) and (2.13) respectively. The example given in (2.53) states that syllables consist of one or two moras.

(2.53) **Abbreviatory Convention 1′:**

a. max(syl,mora,2) $\wedge$ min(syl,mora,1)

b. syl $\Rightarrow$ [mora(1,2)]

We adopt binary versions of the sort predicates, as stated in (2.54):

(2.54) **Abbreviatory Convention 2:**
$$s(x, y) =_{\text{def}} x \, \delta \, y \wedge s(y)$$

The next convention concerns sorts and subsorts.

(2.55) **Abbreviatory Convention 3:**

    a. $\forall x, nasal(x) \equiv +nasal(x) \vee -nasal(x)$
            $\forall x, +nasal(x) \rightarrow \neg -nasal(x)$

    b. $nasal = \{+nasal, -nasal\}$

The fourth convention is for composing relations of the kind defined in the second convention.

(2.56) **Abbreviatory Convention 4:**
$$f|g(x, z) =_{\text{def}} \exists y, f(x, y) \wedge g(y, z)$$

In general, $f|g(x, z)$ is true just in case there is some y such that $f(x, y)$ and $g(y, z)$.

    The next convention is for sequences. A similar convention will be assumed for sets, using '{' and '}' instead of '⟨' and '⟩'.

(2.57) **Abbreviatory Convention 5:**
$$f(a, \langle b, c, d \rangle) =_{\text{def}} f(a, b) \wedge f(a, c) \wedge f(a, d) \wedge b \prec c \prec d$$

    This concludes the definition of the language $\mathcal{L}$. Now we shall see how $\mathcal{L}$ can be used to represent phonological rules.

2.6   Phonological rules

    Although rules are considered to play a central part in phonological description, the conception of phonological rules in the literature is a good deal less clear than the conception of a phonological representation. In autosegmental phonology some have simply incorporated the autosegmental representation notation into the SPE rule notation (e.g. Hall, 1989). Goldsmith (1990) catalogues a bewildering variety of attested operations, as reviewed by Bird and Ladd (1991). Others have complained that 'standard autosegmental approaches to rules fail because they allow too many unattested rule types' (Archangeli and Pulleyblank, 1987, 32). In this section we see how the language $\mathcal{L}$ can be used for phonological rules.

2.6.1 *Phonological rules and logical implication*

The constraint on rules which arises in a monostratal framework is that the arrow (*i.e.* implication) relates classes of objects which are at the same level rather than on different levels. For example, consider the simple rule in (2.58a), which states that voiceless segments must not be nasal. It is translated into the present formalism as (2.58b). A paraphrase of the rule appears in (2.58c).[19] This is just the standard semantics for implication.

(2.58) a.   [–voice] → [–nasal]

  b. $\forall x, -voice(x) \rightarrow -nasal(x)$

This style of interpretation is equivalent to viewing rules as partial descriptions.[20]

Observe that the constraint in (2.58b) does not involve the dominance relation. However, in a hierarchical structure, two features like [voiced] and [nasal] may be linked to different parts of a tree structure, as in Clements' feature geometry (Figure 2.3). As our descriptions are generally only partial (and so may not be fully specified) the reference to a node which is low in the 'tree' structure necessarily assumes the existence of the intervening nodes.[21] Recall that the composite relation notation (see (2.56)) is ultimately an abbreviation for an expression which has existential quantifiers. Therefore it is only necessary to explicitly state the existence of the leaf node (here, z).

---

[19]This interpretation of the arrow was made explicit in some early generative writings. For example, Schane (1973, 36) states that the arrow 'is to be read as "is also" or "implies" '.

[20]Here is an instance where a purely logical approach to the interpretation of rules has an advantage over the interpretation given in unification based frameworks (see §1.5.3). Suppose a segment s_1 is unspecified for the features [high] and [round]. The rule [+high] → [+round] will instantiate s_1 to [+high,+round]. This property has also been observed by Pierrehumbert (Bird et al., 1992). Responding to this problem, Scobbie (1991a, 53) has suggested that rules should only apply when the rule context subsumes part of the representation the rule is being applied to. Although this does prevent a rule context from further instantiating a representation, it does not give rise to the logical interpretation of rules. For example, under Scobbie's interpretation, the rule [+high,+back] → [+round] will not apply to a segment $s_2 = $ [+high,–round]. However, given the logical interpretation of rules, we ought to be able to infer that s_2 is also [–back].

[21]This proposal connects with the 'Node Activation Condition', discussed by Avery and Rice (1989, 183), who cite unpublished work by Archangeli and Pulleyblank. This condition states that 'a rule or convention assigning some feature or node x to some node b creates a path from x to b'.

(2.59) a. $\forall xy, laryngeal| voice(x, y) \wedge -voice(y)$
               $\rightarrow \exists z, supralaryngeal| manner| nasal(x, z) \wedge -nasal(z)$

        b.

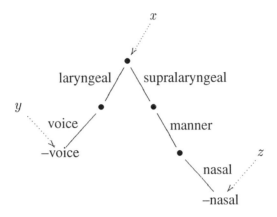

2.6.2 *Default rules*

For some time it has been argued that default rules should play a part in
phonological descriptions (e.g. Stanley (1967), Chomsky and Halle (1968,
382ff)). The generally accepted interpretation of a default rule such as that
in (2.60a) is given in (2.60b).

(2.60) a.   [+low] $\rightarrow$ [+back]

        b.   If a segment is specified as +low and it is not specified as
              −back then assume that it is +back

Generalising from this, the interpretation of a default rule $a \rightarrow b$ is as
follows. If a segment s meets the description a and it is consistent to
assume that b is true of s, then take b to be true.

The difference in interpretation between standard rules and default rules
is not signalled directly in the above notation. An attractive way to signal
this difference formally is to employ Reiter's notation (Reiter, 1980). Reiter
considers that 'inferences sanctioned by default are best viewed as beliefs
which may well be modified or rejected by subsequent observations'.
Although his approach concerns the reasoning about beliefs, there is no

reason to suppose that his approach cannot be equally well applied to other areas of default behaviour. Reiter's approach involves enriching a first-order theory with a collection of metarules which employ a special operator M. $M(\phi)$ is read as 'it is consistent to assume ϕ'. The default rule (2.61a) is expressed as the formula in (2.61b).

(2.61) a. $[+\text{low}] \rightarrow [+\text{back}]$

   b. $\forall x, +low(x) \wedge M +back(x) \rightarrow +back(x)$

Properties which are *required* to be present for a rule to apply are specified in the structural description (*i.e.* rule left hand side) as normal. Properties which only need to be *compatible* with the context are prefixed by the M operator. The expression in (2.62a) is a schematic version of Reiter's format, and the one in (2.62b) is our abbreviated version.

(2.62) a. $\phi \wedge M\psi \rightarrow \psi$

   b. $\phi \xrightarrow{d} \psi$

Conveniently, Reiter's restricted format includes the expressions required for default rules in phonology. It also permits the statement of defaults such as the following:

(2.63) $\forall x, syl(x) \xrightarrow{d} \exists yz, (y \neq z \wedge mora(x, \langle yz \rangle))$
   By default, syllables consist of two moras.

We shall see an application of this kind of constraint in §3.4 for Prince's maximality principle (Prince, 1985).

   Another approach to defaults is to employ a compilation strategy. It has occasionally been noted that the need for default rules can be avoided by enriching the context part of rules (Karttunen et al., 1987; Calder, 1990, 30). When rules are ordered by the elsewhere condition (Kiparsky, 1973), so that rules with more specific contexts can override rules with more general contexts, then the context part of a more general rule can be refined by adding the negations of the contexts of the more specific rules For example, consider the rules in (2.64), where (2.64b) is a default rule.

(2.64) a. $[+\text{back}, +\text{high}] \rightarrow [+\text{round}]$

   b. $[] \rightarrow [-\text{round}]$

The first rule states that high, back segments are also round. The second states that if it is consistent to assume any segment is [–round] then let it be [–round]. The elsewhere principle orders (2.64b) after (2.64a). However, no ordering statement is required if the context of (2.64b) is enriched in either of the following logically equivalent ways.

(2.65)   a.   ¬ [+back, +high] → [–round]

         b.   [–back] ∨ [–high] → [–round]

Not only is ordering not required, there is also no need to make use of the default / non-default distinction. This does not mean to say that default rules such as (2.64b) should be avoided. On the contrary, the above discussion simply reveals their docile nature; they can be viewed as a useful abbreviatory convention.[22]

In this section we have seen two approaches to default rules. There will not be any reason to attempt to choose between them here. Other approaches to defaults in computational phonology were discussed in §1.5.4.

2.7   Conclusion

In this chapter it has been shown how a collection of informally defined diagrammatic conventions can be studied by elucidating the properties of the objects and relations which are encoded in these diagrams. The properties of objects were expressed in terms of sorts, and sorts were structured into a lattice. A number of hierarchical and temporal relations were defined and many aspects of their interaction were explored. A phonological description language was defined, along with a formal syntax and semantics. A first-order predicate logic was used, following van Benthem (1983) and Johnson (1988), since important properties such as soundness, completeness, decidability and compactness do not need to be proven from scratch and reproven each time a modification is made.

---

[22]There is another reason for wishing to retain the default rule notation of (2.64b). Observe that both rules in (2.65) refer to unnatural classes. This is precisely because the default rule (2.64b) applies to an unnatural class. Although the standard notation in (2.64) therefore admits unnatural classes, it does so in a restricted way which cannot be captured if rules like (2.65) are used without any independent restrictions.

Furthermore, there exists a significant body of work on satisfiability algorithms for the formulas, as also pointed out by Johnson (1990, 178). First-order predicate logic also has the useful property of being readily understood and being a generic specification language.

Now that a phonological description language has been defined, the next task is to demonstrate how it can be applied in the analysis of phenomena which have been cited as evidence against the constraint-based approach.

3   A critique of destructive processes

The monostratal view which underlies the constraint-based approach taken here has sometimes been criticised as being insufficiently powerful to enable the expression of observations which demand rule ordering and deletion. It is argued here that observations expressed using rule ordering and deletion are either unfounded or can be expressed in other ways. The chapter begins with a discussion of the mechanism by which prosodic and lexical information can constrain the selection of allophones. The next two sections are devoted to a variety of so-called deletion phenomena. Section 3.4 presents a reconstruction of resyllabification, and this is followed in section 3.5 by reanalyses of the two known examples of so-called feature-changing harmony.

3.1   Conditions on alternations

Most phonological frameworks other than SPE have acknowledged a fundamental split between phonological processes which are sensitive to morphological information and those which are not. In the structuralist tradition a distinction was drawn between morphophonemic and automatic alternations. More recently, the framework of Lexical Phonology (Kiparsky, 1982) has distinguished lexical and post-lexical rules. Here, it will be convenient to distinguish lexical and prosodic generalisations. The primary criteria for this distinction are set out in the following table.

	Lexical generalisation	Prosodic generalisation
Lexical exceptions permitted	yes	no
Applies across words	no	yes
Can refer to word structure	yes	no

In the present model, this distinction is grounded in two hierarchies: a LEXICAL HIERARCHY and a PROSODIC HIERARCHY. We have already seen a prosodic hierarchy in §2.1. The lexical hierarchy is structurally similar, but its nodes are lexical entries and generalisations over those entries. For example, intransitive verbs share the property that they all subcategorise for a single noun phrase and their semantic function has an arity of one. This information will be expressed as a property of a single node *intrans* and all intransitive verbs will inherit from this node (see Pollard and Sag, 1987 for a more detailed presentation of this view of the lexicon).

Phonological properties can also be stated in the lexical hierarchy. As a simple example, consider orthographic *th* in English, pronounced as either [θ] or [ð]. As it happens, [θ] only occurs in open class words (e.g. *think* [θɪŋk]) while [ð] only occurs in closed class words (e.g. *this* [ðɪs]). If we had the lexical types *open* and *closed*, we could simply state that [θ] does not occur in *closed* and [ð] does not occur in *open*, and then the voicing of *th* does not need to be stated in individual lexical entries.

When a generalisation is purely phonological then it is expressed in the prosodic hierarchy. For example, consider the phenomenon of homorganic nasal assimilation, whereby nasals agree in place of articulation with a following consonant, as evident in the following data from English:

(3.1)	Place	Word	Transcription
	dental	tenth	tɛn̪θ
	palatal	inch	ɪɲč
	velar	ink	ɪŋk

In English, this constraint might be expressed as part of the definition of the prosodic phrase, since assimilation generally does not occur across phrase boundaries. So within the sort *phrase* we must rule out all sequences of unassimilated nasal-obstruent clusters.[1]

---

[1] An automaton version of this constraint is discussed in Bird (1992), using the framework of One-Level Phonology (see §1.5.6). A similar approach is taken in Montague Phonology, since phonetic interpretation rules (responsible for assimilations) are tied to specific levels of prosodic structure. See (1.25) for an example.

A direct consequence of adopting the lexical hierarchy and the prosodic hierarchy is that it is now straightforward to introduce prosodic structure into the lexicon. Lexical entries can be partially specified for prosodic structure. Prosodic generalisations, such as the claim that major category words must be minimally bimoraic (see §1.5.7), or the claim that Yoruba nouns exhibit tongue root harmony (Archangeli and Pulleyblank, 1989), can then be located in the lexical hierarchy.

3.2 Deletion as alternation with zero

When a particular segment is manifested in some forms of a morpheme but not in others, a deletion or insertion rule is usually formulated to account for the behaviour. When the identity of the alternating segment is predictable given a certain phonological context, then an insertion rule is normally used. However, when the identity of the segment is unpredictable, the segment is included in the underlying representation and a deletion rule is used to remove it in certain contexts. We shall see some examples of so-called deletion phenomena in Samoan and English in this section. The approach taken, following Hudson (1980), is to reconstruct deletion as 'alternation with zero'. A rule of the form 'delete x in the context ϕ' can be replaced with the generalisation: 'x appears as its zero allophone in the context ϕ'.

3.2.1 Consonant deletion in Samoan

In Samoan, passive verbs formed with the *-ia* suffix give classic evidence for deletion. Consider the data in (3.2), from Marsack (1962).

(3.2)

Active	**Passive**	**Gloss**
mataʔu	mataʔutia	*to fear*
alofa	alofagia	*to love*
utu	utufia	*to draw (water), to fill*
fau	fausia	*to build*
inu	inumia	*to drink*
tau	taulia	*to fight*

One possible analysis of this data posits six allomorphs of the passive suffix (*-tia, -gia, -fia, -sia, -mia, -lia*), and assigns verbs to six different morphosyntactic categories depending on which form of the affix they select. A more plausible analysis (so goes the argument) would represent the active verbs in the lexicon with final consonants. Since Samoan words must end with a vowel, these consonants must be deleted in the unsuffixed form, while remaining untouched in the suffixed form.

This analysis of Samoan can be reconstructed in terms of alternation with zero. We adopt an abbreviatory convention which permits parenthesised segments to be optionally omitted; so *utu(f)* is a shorthand for {*utu, utuf*}. The passive suffix for (3.2) is simply *-ia*. Now, we adopt the constraint that words consist of one or more syllables of the form *(C)V(V)*, but where syllable-initial vowels must also be word-initial.[2] This constraint is stated in the lexicon. The possible active and passive forms of the verbs are displayed below.

Lexical form	Active (with C)	(without C)	Passive (with C)	(without C)
mataʔu(t)	*mataʔut	mataʔu	mataʔutia	*mataʔuia
alofa(g)	*alofag	alofa	alofagia	*alofaia
utu(f)	*utuf	utu	utufia	*utuia
fau(s)	*faus	fau	fausia	*fauia
inu(m)	*inum	inu	inumia	*inuia
tau(l)	*taul	tau	taulia	*tauia

Another approach to this data would be to adopt a parochial constraint on the appearance of particular segments. Let π be the following function:

$$(3.3) \quad \pi(x, y) = \begin{cases} x, & \text{when the next segment is a vowel} \\ y, & \text{when the next segment is a consonant} \end{cases}$$

Using this function, we can state the lexical entry of *fau(s)* where the *(s)* is replaced by $\pi(s, \emptyset)$. Of course, π could not be evaluated until the following context was available. Nevertheless, $\pi(x, y)$ satisfies the requirement for a monostratal framework, since it acts to further specify a disjunction $x \vee y$ once the context is sufficiently specified.

---

[2] The additional stipulation that syllable-initial vowels must also be word-initial, while appearing somewhat *ad hoc*, has been advocated for other (unrelated) languages, e.g. Axininca (Payne, 1981, 72). A similar constraint, which states that word-final syllables must be consonant-final, is adopted for Tagalog (French, 1988, 6).

Perhaps a more interesting way of constraining and being constrained by context is for a lexical representation to place constraints on the prosodic structure in which it occurs. For example, if we lexically specify the alternating consonants in Samoan to be syllable onsets, then they can only appear if there is a syllable nucleus to the right. Crucially, we do not have to refer to that extra material, which is not available to a lexical representation since it resides in a different morpheme. Rather, it is the definition of the syllable that requires an onset be syllabified with a following nucleus. In the lexicon, it is only necessary to say that these alternating consonants are always onsets, and also that lexical words (and not morphemes) must be made up of one or more well-formed syllables.

3.2.2 R-insertion/deletion in English

English manifests an *r*~∅ alternation in many dialects. Here we shall consider the Australian dialect.[3] Consider the following words: *spa/spar*, *tuna/tuner* and *yaw/you're*. The data in (3.4) shows the behaviour of *r* when these words are followed by a consonant.

(3.4) a. The spa   seems to be broken
              [spa]

       b. The spar   seems to be broken
              [spa]

       c. He put the tuna   near the table
              [čunə]

       d. He put the tuner   near the table
              [čunə]

       e. The boat tends to yaw   some
                               [jɔ]

       f. You're somewhat older
           [jɔ]

---

[3]The patterning of *r* in Australian English is similar to Eastern Massachusetts English as described by McCarthy (1991). Here I shall adapt McCarthy's data.

As we can see, whether the orthography manifests *r* or not, the *r* never appears in the pronunciation. Now consider the same words when followed by a vowel, as shown in (3.5).

(3.5) a.   The   spa   is broken
                 [spaɹ]

       b.   The   spar   is broken
                 [spaɹ]

       c.   He put the   tuna   on the table
                          [čunəɹ]

       d.   He put the   tuner   on the table
                          [čunɔɹ]

       e.   The boat tends to   yaw   a little
                                 [jɔɹ]

       f.   You're   a little older
            [jɔɹ]

Here, all forms manifest the *r*. McCarthy (1991) has surveyed a variety of analyses of this data which involve deletion, insertion or both. He points out that an analysis involving the insertion of *r* intervocalically is inadequate since vowel-final function words do not manifest the alternation. Rather, we posit an *r*∼∅ alternation in all 'vowel-final' major category words (and function words ending in an orthographic *r*). Now, we adopt the following two constraints: constraint (3.6a) states that *r* is licensed by the onset and (3.6b) states (of the alternating *r* in the lexicon) that *r* cannot be ambisyllabic.[4]

(3.6) a.   *onset* licenses *r*

       b.   not-shared(*r*)

Consider now the representations for *tuner near* and *tuner on*, given in (3.7).

---

[4]Licensing was introduced in §2.2.5 and defined formally in (2.20). The constraint against sharing in (3.6b) was defined in (2.18).

(3.7)   a.

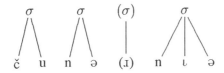

    b.

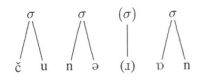

In neither case can the *r* be syllabified with the material to the left. Since these *r*s must not be geminate by (3.6b), and since *r* is licensed by the onset, it can only be syllabified to the right, if at all. However, *r* cannot be syllabified as the first member of a complex onset, since *rC* onset clusters are not permitted in English. Therefore, in (3.7a) the *r* must be omitted. This omission of unsyllabifiable material is sometimes referred to as stray erasure (see §2.2.6) and Steriade (1982) has claimed that all consonant deletion is of this nature. In (3.7b) the *r* can be syllabified with the material to the right.

3.3   Deletion as a phonetic process

In §3.2 we saw deletion reconstructed as alternation with zero. A completely different approach to deletion is available for phenomena which can be construed as phonetic processes.

3.3.1 *Acoustic hiding*

Consider again the phenomenon of homorganic nasal assimilation in English, where nasals agree in place of articulation with the following obstruent. In a generative analysis, the place of articulation specification for a nasal is deleted and the specification for the obstruent is copied to the nasal. Such an analysis runs into at least two problems. First, the assimilation rule is descriptively inadequate, since assimilations are often only partial (Nolan, 1986, 1992). Secondly, attention to articulatory phonetics sometimes reveals that a supposedly deleted gesture is still present, only hidden. As an example of the second situation, consider the gestural score in (3.8) for the utterance *ten pin* [tɛmpʊn].

(3.8)

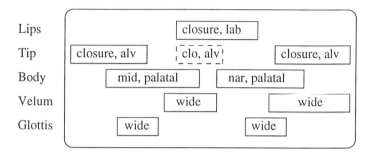

Browman and Goldstein (1989, 215ff) note that utterances like this regularly have a persistent alveolar closure (the dashed box in (3.8)), which fails to manifest itself acoustically because it is *hidden* behind a labial closure.

3.3.2 *Neutralisation*

Dresher (1981), in his criticism of Natural Generative Phonology (see §1.5.1), cited a familiar example from some dialects of North American English, where the voicing contrast of *t* and *d* in *writer* and *rider* is claimed to be manifested only in the length of the preceding vowel. Two rules, lengthening and flapping, were proposed to account for this behaviour.

(3.9)   a.   **Lengthening:**

$$a \rightarrow [\text{+long}] / \text{---} (\upsilon) \begin{bmatrix} C \\ \text{+voice} \end{bmatrix}$$

b.   **Flapping:**

$$\begin{Bmatrix} t \\ d \end{Bmatrix} \rightarrow ɾ / \begin{bmatrix} V \\ \text{+stress} \end{bmatrix} \text{---} \begin{bmatrix} V \\ \text{-stress} \end{bmatrix}$$

In order to produce the correct result, the lengthening rule must apply before the flapping rule.

(3.10)   Underlying form   /raɪtɚ/ 'writer'   /raɪdɚ/ 'rider'
         Lengthening   –   raːɪdɚ
         Flapping   raɪɾɚ   raːɪɾɚ
         Phonetic form   [raɪɾɚ]   [raːɪɾɚ]

However, both rules are descriptively inadequate. The lengthening rule is incorrect for words like *italic* and *idyllic* where the length distinction does not appear (Selkirk, 1982, 372). Chen's (1970) cross-linguistic study of the lengthening phenomena gives a phonetic explanation for lengthening.[5] Furthermore, the flapping rule is a major simplification from the actual data (e.g. Kahn, 1976, 56–61), and the claim that *t* is distinguished from *d* by the property of voicing is controversial.[6]

More generally, Dinnsen (1985, 276) has claimed that 'every genuine phonological distinction has some phonetic reflex, though not necessarily in the segments which are at the seat of the distinction'. This would indicate that a rule which 'copies' an underlying voicing distinction elsewhere (3.9a) and a rule which removes the underlying distinction (3.9b) are more intimately related than the analysis in (3.9) suggests. Analyses based on neutralisation – such as Dresher's and Gussmann's (1980) – clearly stand in need of revision.[7]

Another neutralisation phenomenon, namely final devoicing, has been claimed to exist in several languages such as German, Polish, Catalan and

---

[5] '... it is well known that a voiceless consonant is articulated with open glottis, whereas a voiced one is made with closed glottis. As a result, the intraoral pressure during a voiced consonant closure is relatively low, since the pressure is built up by the air of the mouth cavity *alone*; in the case of a voiceless consonant occlusion, the intraoral pressure is considerably higher, since the volume of air of the mouth *and* lungs is increased. ... the transition from vowel to a voiceless consonant closure would be faster than the transition from vowel to a voiced consonant closure.' (Chen, 1970, 152f)

[6] The 'voicing' of English stop consonants is not generally manifested as phonetic voicing at all, since both varieties of stop are phonetically voiceless (except for the flaps: Kahn (1976, 41); see also Keating (1984) and Lisker (1986)). The difference between *t* and *d* is one of aspiration.

[7] Gussmann's arguments are based on Polish data. However, Slowiaczek and Dinnsen (1985) provide experimental evidence which shows that the underlying contrasts which are said to be neutralised are in fact phonetically preserved. Despite the clear evidence to the contrary, Gussmann (1992, 31) holds to his claim about Polish devoicing, citing only a pronunciation dictionary in support.

Russian. However, it has been shown that these neutralisations are variable and do not support the idea of there being a binary voicing feature:

> The data show that speakers can control the degree of neutralisation depending on pragmatics and that information about the underlying contrast is distributed over much of the word... The data support a scalar valued neutralisation effect in the German voicing rule, and clearly refute a rule using a binary voicing feature. (Port and Crawford, 1989, 257f)

Similar findings have been reported for Catalan (Charles-Luce and Dinnsen, 1987), Polish (Slowiaczek and Dinnsen, 1985; Slowiaczek and Szymanska, 1989) and Russian (Pye, 1986). Even so, some people have presented analysis of final devoicing in constraint-based frameworks: Wiese (1990), Coleman (1991, 367ff) and Wheeler (1988) present analyses of final devoicing in German, Japanese and Russian respectively (see §1.5.3 and §1.5.2).

3.4   Resyllabification

In some languages, segments alternate with respect to the position that they occupy within syllable structure. In particular, a stem-final consonant may be syllabified with a following vowel-initial word, as can be seen in the following data from Turkish, where syllable boundaries are marked with a point, and the segments we are interested in are underlined.[8]

(3.11)   a.   şa.rap 'wine'

         b.   şa.rap .sev.di 'he liked wine'

         c.   şa.ra.p al.dı 'he took wine'

Observe that in (3.11a,b), the *p* is syllabified with the material to the left, while in (3.11c) it is syllabified with the material to the right (in spite of the word boundary). If we follow standard practice and assume that the isolation form of a word is the same as the underlying form, then we are forced to say that the *p* has *moved* from the coda of a syllable into the onset of the following syllable. This movement process is called RESYLLABIFICATION.

---

[8] The transcription in (3.11) employs Turkish orthography, where ş = IPA ʃ and ı = IPA ɨ.

A constraint-based approach to data like (3.11) cannot employ a resyllabification rule since such a rule is inherently destructive. However, it is possible to achieve the syllabifications in (3.11) without recourse to such a rule. Instead, the lexical entry for a word like *şarap* must generalise across all possible surface forms of the word. It is specified in (3.12).

(3.12)

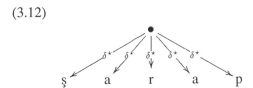

In the presence of appropriateness constraints (see §2.2.2) and the universal core syllable condition (2.45), the structure in (3.12) is constrained to have the form in (3.13). Note that this and subsequent diagrams in this section are interpreted as descriptions; the syllable nodes are not necessarily distinct.

(3.13)

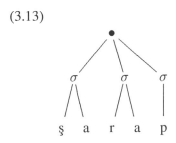

There are at least two ways of forcing the *p* to be syllabified with the preceding syllable. One approach is to adopt the MAXIMALITY PRINCIPLE, which states that 'units are of maximal size, within the other constraints on their form' (Prince, 1985). This principle is formulated in (3.14).

(3.14) **Maximality principle for syllables:**
$\forall xy, syl(x) \wedge syl(y) \stackrel{d}{\to} x = y$
Where possible, identify syllable nodes.

This constraint states that syllable nodes are to be collapsed together wherever possible. When applied to (3.13), the second and third syllables are equated, to produce the structure in (3.15). The dashed line is used to indicate the fact that this association line is only present by default.

(3.15)

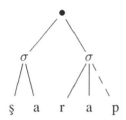

Another way of requiring that the p in (3.13) be syllabified with the preceding syllable is to adopt the following two constraints, which are universal constraints about syllable structure.

(3.16) a. $\forall x, syl(x) \rightarrow \exists y, v(y) \wedge x \, \delta \, y$
              Syllables must have a vowel.

        b. $\forall x, v(x) \rightarrow \text{not-shared}(x)$
              Vowels cannot be ambisyllabic.

Constraint (3.16a) requires that all syllables contain a vowel, and constraint (3.16b) requires that vowels cannot be shared between two syllables.[9]

Returning to the case of resyllabification in Turkish, the syllable node which dominates p must also dominate a vowel (by (3.16a)). However, we cannot have the situation in (3.17) for this violates (3.16b).

(3.17)

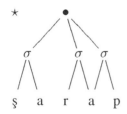

[9] See (2.18) for the definition of *not-shared(x)*.

Consequently, the only possibility is (3.18). This is just like (3.15), except the new association line is *required* to be present, rather than only being present by default.

(3.18)

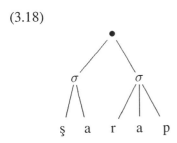

Now consider the representation for *şarap aldı*, once the appropriateness constraints and the Universal Core Syllable Condition have been enforced.

(3.19)

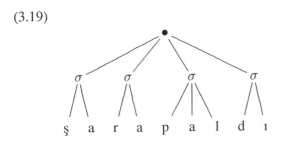

Note that the *p* in (3.19) has now been syllabified with the material to the right as required.[10] Bird and Klein (1994) take a similar approach to syllabification in an analysis of French schwa.

Others who have attempted to come up with a declarative account of resyllabification phenomena include Rice (1989) and Kaye et al. (1990). Rice (1989) employed the notion of EXTRASYLLABICITY in order to avoid having to do structure changing operations. However, although extrasyllabicity is commonly invoked it is seldom rigorously defined. Moreover,

---

[10] We require an independent constraint to ensure that the *l* cannot be syllabified with the material to the right, where it would form a prohibited onset cluster.

as we have seen, it has been possible to simulate the alternations of word-peripheral segments without having recourse to extrasyllabicity. In the framework of Government Phonology, Kaye et al. (1990) propose a model of syllable structure where there are no codas and so the *p* of the Turkish word *şarap* is always an onset. Consequently this framework has no need of destructive resyllabification rules for treating this data.

3.5   Feature changing harmony

In this section two cases of harmony are discussed that have previously been cited as clear evidence for the necessity of feature changing rules. The first section concerns height harmony in the vowel system of a Spanish dialect, and the second section concerns sibilant harmony in Chumash.

3.5.1   *Vowel harmony in Montañes Spanish*

Consider the case of vowel harmony in the Pasiego dialect of Montañes Spanish. This language has a nine-vowel system consisting of five tense vowels and four lax vowels. Our examples will employ the tense vowels only; these are partitioned according to the following table for the purposes of height harmony.

(3.20)

[+high]	i	u
[–high]	e	o
neutral	a	

In the data tabulated in (3.21), the non-low vowels in the verb roots must agree in height with the stressed vowel in the suffix (McCarthy, 1984). Low vowels are transparent to this process. The verb stems are given using the vowels E and O which represent the classes {i, e} and {o, u} respectively.

(3.21)

stem	-áis -ámus	-émus -erémus	-íːs
sEnt-	sintáis	sentémus	sintíːs
bEb-	bebámus	bebémus	bibíːs
kOx-	koxámus	koxerémus	kuxíːs
sal(g)-	salgáis	salémus	salíːs

In the first column, the stressed vowel is *a*, and no harmony occurs; the root vowels are evidently in their 'underlying' forms. In the second column the stressed vowel is [–high], and the root vowels agree on this specification. In the third column the stressed vowel is [+high], and again, the root vowels agree (except for the transparent vowel *a*). McCarthy (1984, 304) claims that a feature changing rule is required, since underlying high vowels can be changed to mid and underlying mid vowels can be changed to high. If non-low vowels are unspecified for height, acquiring it from the application of a spreading rule, then there is no account of the height contrast before low vowels.

A monostratal solution involves the use of morphologically conditioned (or lexically determined) defaults (see §2.6.2). The use of morpheme-specific defaults is undesirable in a model where it is preferable to limit the use of defaults as much as possible. As it happens, Vago (1988, 353) has pointed out that the vowel lowering in *sentémus* is something of an aberration, since verbs like *iskupémus* do not permit lowering (**eskopémus*). On the basis of this and other evidence, Vago concludes that while there is strong support for vowel raising, there is 'no evidence to motivate general vowel lowering'. McCarthy (*pers. comm.*) agrees that the argument presented in McCarthy (1984) for feature changing harmony no longer goes through.

3.5.2   Consonant harmony in Chumash

Another argument for feature changing harmony has been advanced by Poser (1982), citing evidence from Chumash.[11] The data is displayed in (3.22).

(3.22)   ʃapitʃʰolit   /s + api + tʃʰo + it/
            I have a stroke of good luck
        sapitsʰolus   /s + api + tʃʰo + us/
            He has a stroke of good luck
        ʃapitʃʰoluʃwaʃ /s + api + tʃʰo + us + waʃ/
            He has had a stroke of good luck

---

[11]Lieber (1987, 145–50), Steriade (1987, 350f) and Yip (1988, 79f) have proposed similar analyses.

Observe that the sibilants of a word are either all *s* or all ʃ. It is claimed that the rightmost sibilant determines the anteriority (or distributedness) of all other sibilants in the word. Poser argues:

> It is a straightforward matter to demonstrate that this harmony is feature-changing. Since a morpheme containing a sibilant need not be followed by any other such morpheme, it is possible to observe the isolation form of harmonising segments. If Chumash were not feature-changing, we should expect to find that the isolation form of harmonising segments was either /s/ in every case or /ʃ/ in every case, since the specification for the harmony feature of underspecified segments would have to be supplied by a default rule that would necessarily assign the same default value to every harmonising segment. Consequently, if some harmonising segments surface as /s/ when outside the domain of another sibilant, and others surface as /ʃ/ when outside the domain of another sibilant, we must [distinguish] /s/ from /ʃ/, and therefore we must conclude that the harmony process changes these underlying feature specifications. (Poser, 1982, 132)

While we might fashion an account of this harmony using morpheme-specific defaults as was suggested for Montañes (cf. Avery and Rice, 1989, 194), there are good reasons to challenge the empirical basis of the claimed harmony process, as pointed out by Russcll (1993). According to Harrington's study of a dialect of Chumash (Harrington, 1974), there is ample evidence that the assimilation is usually incomplete, and that it is dependent upon speech rate. Moreover, Harrington found that the assimilation was not symmetric, since ʃ triggered a greater amount of harmony than *s*. Accordingly, Chumash harmony would appear to have the same status as the syllable-final devoicing (discussed in §3.3.2), namely that of a phonetic process.

3.6 Conclusion

In this chapter a variety of phenomena have been discussed which underpin classic arguments for rule ordering and feature changing. It has been demonstrated that these arguments carry no weight. In §1.5.1 several attempts by others to rebut these traditional assumptions were also surveyed. This provides vindication for the constraint-based approach and gives grounds for optimism that it can be usefully applied to the full range of phonological phenomena. In the next chapter we shall see how the approach can be applied to a particular model of segmental structure.

4   A theory of segmental structure

For many years it was assumed that the smallest unit which needed to be recognised in phonology was the phoneme. Swadesh, drawing on work by Bloomfield, Jones, Sapir and others, provided the following compact statement about the phoneme:

> The phonemic principle is that there are in each language a limited number of *elemental* types of speech sounds, called phonemes, peculiar to that language; that all sounds produced in the employment of the given language are referable to its set of phonemes; that only its own phonemes are at all significant in the given language. (Swadesh, 1934, 32, *emphasis added*)

Once phonemes were characterised according to the oppositions they entered into, it became clear that these oppositions were not arbitrary but revealed the organisation of phonemes into natural classes. These classes had defining properties, such as voicing or lip rounding, which could be cast in terms of distinctive features (Trubetzkoy, Jakobson and others). A phoneme (or a segment) was viewed as a set of features, and an utterance corresponded to a sequence of these sets, or a two-dimensional array of features.

Although features are properties of phonemes, they can also be regarded as entities in their own right which come together to form phonemes. Chomsky and Halle (1968, 299ff) showed how these features do not all have the same status but can be grouped; there are major class, cavity, manner, source and prosodic features. Some of these groups have subgroups in turn. However, for Chomsky and Halle the purpose of this grouping was only expository. Clements (1985) and others have argued in favour of hierarchical representations of segments which reflect this grouping, as we shall see in §4.1. This enables phonological observations to be stated more succinctly and we have the beginnings of an explanation for why certain groups of features pattern together for the purposes of assimilation and other phenomena. Sagey (1986) provided a detailed study in support of the claim that the feature hierarchy is based on phonetic structure. 'Features are grouped according to the articulator in the vocal tract that they are executed by. Articulators are grouped according to their acoustic effects on the formant structure' (Sagey, 1986, 2). Browman and Goldstein (1989) further explored this phonetic basis of feature hierarchy, making it more explicitly phonetic and providing a model of the causal relation between articulatory and acoustic properties.

When we survey the developments in distinctive feature theory in detail it becomes clear that the lasting and non-controversial categories employed by phonology are those which also have a clear phonetic basis. Those proposed units which lack a phonetic basis – such as Clements' manner and supralaryngeal categories – have increasingly been undermined by new phonological evidence, as we shall see in §4.1. Therefore, one can observe a persistent historical trend towards the view that the basic units recognised by phonology correspond directly to the articulatory gestures which speakers have direct control over. This should not be surprising. On the contrary, paraphrasing Fowler's (1980, 118–19) arguments, it would be surprising if a category arose in evolution or ontogeny which did not bear a close resemblance to the actualisation with which it co-evolved or co-developed; furthermore, such a category (if it existed) would vastly complicate the communication process.

This chapter consists of three main sections. The first section takes a look at the phonological evidence for the hierarchical organisation of features, and the second section proposes an articulatory model and shows how acoustic properties can be viewed as emergent from articulatory configurations. The third section formalises the proposals using the notation of chapter 2.

4.1 The evidence for hierarchical organisation

There have been numerous proposals for the hierarchical organisation of features in the literature.[1] Perhaps the earliest clear statement was made by Lass:

(i) Any phonological/phonetic segment is represented as a two-part matrix, consisting of submatrices labelled [oral] and [laryngeal].

(ii) The notational independence of the two parameters implies that each is a possible proper domain for a phonological rule, in addition to the whole segment being such a domain.

... submatrices as wholes can function in rules; not only in deletions, but also in rules appealing to the notions 'homorganic' and 'identical'. (Lass, 1976, 154f)

Lass's identification of the three functions of his submatrices is still widely assumed today. For example, Yip states that:

three kinds of evidence can be used to argue for a particular constituent structure for distinctive features: (i) constituents spread as units; (ii) constituents delete/detach as units; (iii) constituents are identified as units by rules which compute identity, such as the obligatory contour principle. (Yip, 1989b, 349)

For the remainder of this section a number of feature groupings which have been proposed in the literature are presented and evaluated. We begin with the laryngeal node.

4.1.1 The laryngeal node

Clements (1985) groups the features [spread], [constricted] and [voiced] under the laryngeal node (cf. Figure 2.3), which we may depict schematically as in (4.1).

---

[1] McCarthy (1988) and Broe (1992) have provided excellent surveys of this work.

(4.1)

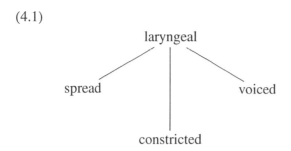

In support of this he cites phenomena from Thai, Klamath and Proto-Indo-Iranian, which indicate that the features [spread], [constricted] and [voiced] behave as a unit in phonological processes. In Thai, syllable-initial stop consonants can be voiced, voiceless aspirated and voiceless unaspirated. Syllable-final stops can only be voiceless unreleased. McCarthy (1988, 90) explains that 'delinking of the laryngeal node in syllable-final position reduces all three categories to just the unmarked one'. Equivalently, we might state that a laryngeal node can only be specified for segments in syllable onsets.[2]   The segments in syllable codas can only receive the default laryngeal node [+spread, –constricted, –voiced].

Evidence for the laryngeal node only motivates a hierarchical structure in conjunction with similar evidence for the independent behaviour of the laryngeal features themselves. In fact, such further evidence is hard to come by, and those who have advocated the laryngeal node have not provided it. Consequently, we shall assume that the laryngeal node is a bundle of features which may only be treated as a group.

The only clear case for the independent functioning of subsets of the laryngeal set concerns tone features. Although the autosegmental approach has its origins in analyses of tone, there has been relatively little discussion of what the relevant distinctive features are.[3]   However, it is clear from the vast array of analyses involving the spreading, delinking and obligatory contour principle effects of tone that the tone features may operate independently of the other laryngeal features. For example, it is uncommon for the spreading of tones to non-adjacent vowels to be hindered

---

[2] Note that this is the same as the behaviour described for *r* in §3.2.2. See in particular (3.6).

[3] Wang (1967), Pulleyblank (1986, 125), Hyman (1986), Yip (1989a) and Snider (1990) have suggested distinctive features for tone.

by the presence of intervening consonants, even when these consonants are distinctively specified for laryngeal features such as [voiced]. Whatever these tone features are, there have been no attempts to locate them in the feature hierarchy (Goldsmith, 1990, 293).

A possible reason for the apparent difficulty in coming up with a phonological geometry to represent the linguistic function of the larynx may be the unusual nature of the larynx itself. Unlike the other members of the vocal tract, the larynx may be involved in INITIATION (for implosives and ejectives), PHONATION (voicing, murmur, creak) and ARTICULATION (for the glottal stop), as discussed by Catford (1988, 23ff, 51ff, 100ff).

4.1.2 The supralaryngeal node

Lass has discussed English consonant reduction to the glottal stop, providing evidence from New York and Scots dialects (Lass, 1976, 149f). He makes the following proposal:

> every segment [is] (at least) 'bi-gestural': there are two relevant articulatory configurations, one laryngeal and the other supralaryngeal... Thus [ʔ] and [h] are defective; their matrices lack defining specifications for features that are purely intra-oral, like 'coronal', 'back' and so forth. They are missing an entire component or parameter that is present in 'normal' segments. (Lass, 1976, 153)

Consonant reduction is then just the deletion of the supralaryngeal gesture from a consonant, concurrently replacing the supralaryngeal closure with a laryngeal one (Lass, 1976, 155).[4]

Evidence from Icelandic has received much attention in the literature on feature hierarchy.[5] Thráinsson (1978) observed that underlying geminate voiceless stops appear as preaspirated: /pp, tt, kk/ → [hp, ht, hk]. He analysed this as involving the spreading of the supralaryngeal node of a preceding vowel onto the first part of the geminate consonant, along with

---

[4]Note that Lass's discussion does not settle the question of the representation of [h]; see Iverson (1989) for further discussion. See §4.2.4 for an analysis of this consonant reduction.

[5]Thráinsson (1978), Clements and Keyser (1983, 79), Clements (1985, 233-4), Árnason (1986), Sagey (1986, 32ff), Iverson (1989), Hayes (1990).

the delinking of the supralaryngeal node for that consonant. Thráinsson's rule is shown in (4.2), where [ ] stands for an arbitrary supralaryngeal node.

(4.2)

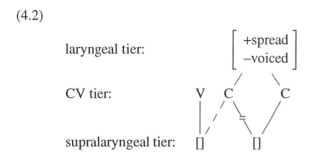

It is as though the supralaryngeal specification of the vowel has extended *rightwards*, pushing the supralaryngeal specification for the consonant further right. However, Árnason (1986, 19) has taken the opposing view that 'we are dealing with a movement of the openness of the glottis connected with the stop towards the nucleus. It is thus an anticipatory opening of the glottis ... [which occurs] when a vowel preceded that did not become long in the [historical] quantity shift.' Similarly Sagey's account involves the *leftwards* realignment of the laryngeal node that was initially part of the geminate (Sagey, 1986, 32ff).

Now we have seen two analyses of preaspiration. In the first, a *supralaryngeal* node is realigned to the right, while in the second a *laryngeal* node is realigned to the left. While is clear that there needs to be a separation between laryngeal and supralaryngeal features, it is not clear that *both* classes need to be able to function independently. The evidence only requires that one of the two classes function independently.[6]

Clements (1985, 234–5) has adduced further support for the existence of a supralaryngeal node from Klamath. However, Iverson (1989, 295ff) argued that a supralaryngeal node is not necessary for Klamath. Another example is from Acoma (Sagey, 1986, 34), where two vowels are normally identical when separated only by a glottal stop. Sagey argued that the

---

[6] These analyses of the Icelandic data rest on independent assumptions about the nature of geminates – the true vs. fake distinction (Hayes, 1986a, 490, 1986b, 341; McCarthy, 1986, 218) – and the assumption that preaspiration affects only geminates, called into question by Árnason (1986, 13).

glottal stop lacks supralaryngeal features and so the vowels on either side can share their supralaryngeal specification.[7]

(4.3)

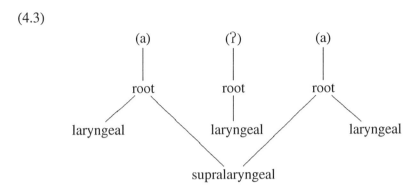

However, as for Klamath, another analysis is conceivable. Sagey's supralaryngeal node dominates the feature nasal and a place node. If nasality is not shared across a glottal stop the Acoma data can equally well be analysed as the sharing of just the place node. This observation accords with McCarthy's remark that 'spreading of the supralaryngeal node, as distinct from spreading of the place node, is known from only one or two examples that are subject to plausible reanalysis' (McCarthy, 1988, 92). As the above evidence is uncompelling we shall follow McCarthy (1988) and Iverson (1989) in eliminating the supralaryngeal node.

4.1.3   The manner node

Although Clements acknowledged that 'there is very little evidence to suggest that the manner tier functions as a unit' (1985, 238) he still employed a hierarchical manner node and grouped underneath it the features [continuant], [consonantal], [nasal], [sonorant], [strident] and [lateral]. Given the absence of evidence for the manner node, Sagey (1986, 45) assumed that these features do not form a constituent. However, she only dealt with the first three manner features, omitting [sonorant], [strident] and [lateral] because, she argued, sonorant corresponds to a

---

[7] See Steriade (1987, 602ff) for other examples of this 'trans-laryngeal' harmony.

disjunction of properties, strident is an acoustic property, and lateral does not fit naturally into her conception of the place node (1986, 280–1). Others have advocated different structural positions for these features, as tabulated in (4.4).[8] Note that [sonorant], [strident] and [lateral] have received little attention in the literature on the feature hierarchy.

(4.4)

Feature	Position	Reference
cont	root	Sagey (1986)
		McCarthy (1988)
		Avery and Rice (1989)
		Paradis and Prunet (1989)
	supralaryngeal	Davis (1989)
cons	root	Sagey (1986)
		Smith (1988)
		Paradis and Prunet (1989)
		Kaisse (1992)
	inside root	McCarthy (1988)
nasal	root	Piggott (1987)
		McCarthy (1988)
		Paradis and Prunet (1989)
	supralaryngeal	Sagey (1986)
		Avery and Rice (1989)
		Smith (1988), Hayes (1990)
son	inside root	McCarthy (1988)
strid	—	—
lateral	place|coronal	McCarthy (1988)
	supra|sonorant	Avery and Rice (1989)

The proposal discussed by McCarthy (1988, 97) differs significantly from the others in that it permits features to be *inside* a node. McCarthy observes that the features [sonorant] and [consonantal] never spread, delink or exhibit OCP effects unless they do so in concert with all the other features. However, if [sonorant] and [consonantal] are represented as normal constituents then there is nothing (principled) which prevents them

---

[8] Note that suggestions to locate all or some of these features under a manner node (Iverson, 1989; Hayes, 1990) are omitted.

from manifesting this unobserved behaviour. McCarthy's solution is to employ the structure in (4.5).[9]

(4.5)

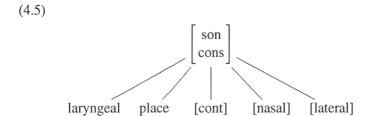

How are we to interpret the conflicting claims represented in table (4.4)? There are a number of possibilities. There seems to be a widely held assumption that there is a single, universal organisation of features, and that, given time, the empirical evidence will mount up sufficiently in favour of one option over all the others. However, from the perspective of so-called universal grammar, there is no reason to assume that phonology is not parametrised. For example, some languages could be specified 'nasal:supralaryngeal' and others as 'nasal:root' to indicate variation in the locus of the feature nasal. Indeed, Piggott (1992) makes such a proposal.

A different response to the problem raised by table (4.4) is to reject the assumption that manner features are represented in the same way as other features. Existing proposals for manner features fail to capture their atypical behaviour. This approach to manner features is developed in §4.2.

4.1.4 The place node

Although the manner features do not function as a unit, there is considerable evidence to suggest that the place features do. The place features include the following: [coronal], [anterior], [distributed], [high], [low], [back], [round] and [labial]. Clements (1985, 235–6) cites the case of place assimilation of /t, d, n/ in English and provides the data in (4.6).

---

[9]Note that the idea of representing features inside hierarchical nodes is familiar from syntax (e.g. Gazdar et al., 1985) and its application to phonology has been suggested by Vincent (1986, 317).

(4.6)

	–[θ]	–[tʃ], –[dʒ]	–[r]
[t]–	eighth	each, cheer	tree
[d]–	hundredth	edge, gem	dream
[n]–	tenth, enthuse	inch, hinge	enrol

Here we can observe that the place of articulation of the stop agrees with that of the following segment. Consider the following data from Kpelle provided by Welmers (1973, 65, 67).[10]

(4.7)   m̀bôlu   'my back'
         ńdǐa   'my taboo'
         ŋ̀gɔ́ɔ   'my foot'
         m̀ŋgbîŋ   'myself'
         ɱ̀véla   'my wages'
         ńǰǔa   'my nose'

Sagey (1986, 37) notes that the nasal prefix (the first person singular marker) assimilates in all and only the place features to the following obstruent. Manner and laryngeal features are not spread onto the nasal, for if they were the nasal preceding a [v] would be a fricative and voiceless. Note that the nasals are syllabic (bearing tone) and are not part of prenasalised stops or fricatives. Therefore the only possible account is regressive homorganic assimilation. Although we shall later have cause to question Sagey's treatment of this data (see §4.2.4), place assimilation is widely attested and the use of a place node is incontrovertible. We now move on to discuss various proposals for the structure below the place node.

4.1.5   Sub-place groupings

Clements' model of the place node has it directly dominating all of the place features. However, Sagey (1986) observed (citing Halle, 1983) that this approach is inadequate for the representation of double and triple (oral) articulations. The relevant passage is reproduced below:

> Consonantal occlusions are thus produced by three distinct active articulators: the lower lip, the front part of the tongue, and the tongue body. Since the position of each of these three articulators is independent of

---

[10] Note that [gb] and [mŋ] denote labio-velar articulations.

the other two it should be possible to produce consonants with more than one occlusion. Since there are three active articulators and since a given articulator can be at exactly one point at a given time there should exist three types of consonants with double occlusion and a single type of consonant with triple occlusion. (Halle, 1983, 99)

Halle provided the data in (4.8), where 'ʇ' denotes the dental click. Although Halle found no example of a triply occluded consonant, Walli-Sagey (1986) has claimed that such a consonant exists in Kinyarwanda,[11] and so this has been included for completeness.

(4.8)	labio-velar	[kp]	Yoruba
		[akpa]	'arm'
	labio-coronal	[pt]	Margi
		[ptel]	'chief'
	corono-velar	[ʇ]	Zulu
		[ʇaʇa]	'climb'
	labio-corono-velar	[tkw]	Kinyarwanda
		[tkwaaŋga]	'we hate'

Sagey showed that previous accounts of sub-place structure such as Clements' are unable to express the fact that these are the only kinds of double or triple articulations that are possible. She made the following proposal:

> The solution to this problem lies in realising that it is really irrelevant to the articulation of the labial closure (*i.e.* to the behaviour of the lips) whether or not there is additional [+coronal] closure. Therefore, a lack of coronal closure should not be part of the universal definition for a labial, indeed its defining characteristic, as it is when we define a labial as [+anterior, –coronal]... In short, the problem with the feature specifications in [Clements' model] is that they define segments, not simply in terms of what constrictions or articulators are involved, but also in terms of what is not involved. (Sagey, 1986, 64f)

Sagey proposed sub-place nodes for each of the three articulators: the nodes 'labial', 'coronal' and 'dorsal'. Second, the appropriateness (see

---

[11] However, *tkw* might just be a cluster of two double articulations, namely *tk* and *w*, or *t* and *kw*. Note that other triple articulations can be found in Shona, according to Sagey (1986, 72).

§2.2.2) of the various place features is restricted to a particular articulator, as shown in (4.9).

(4.9)

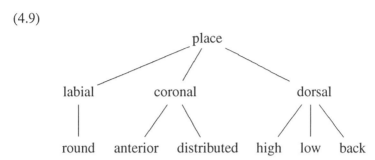

Segments having one (distinctive) place of articulation are only specified for one of these articulator nodes; a doubly articulated segment is specified for two of these nodes, and so on. In other words, the presence of a labial, coronal or dorsal node denotes the active involvement of the corresponding articulator (Sagey, 1986, 67). For languages which only have singly articulated segments we merely need to stipulate that the place node only ever dominates one articulator node.

Now, consider the case of secondary articulations. For example, English coronal and velar consonants are often labialised when followed by a labial vowel. Compare the *k* in [kul] *cool* with that in [kil] *keel.* In Sagey's hierarchy, the labialised *k* might be represented as in (4.10) after a rule supplies the labial specification (omitting the laryngeal and supralaryngeal nodes).

(4.10)

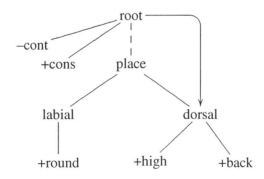

The information that the closure is dorsal and not labial is represented by the arrow from the root node to the dorsal node. This indicates that the manner features [–cont] and [+cons] describe the dorsal articulation. An articulator node at the head of such an arrow is called a MAJOR ARTICULATOR (Sagey, 1986, 203). Double articulations, like the ones in (4.8), have two major articulators and so have two of these arrows. This represents the fact that both articulators have the same degree of closure (Sagey, 1986, 217).[12]

Further arguments for Sagey's model have been advanced by Yip (1989b), who has surveyed the co-occurrence restrictions in homorganic consonant clusters in several languages. Problems remain, however, with the dorsal node. McCarthy has observed 'the feature [dorsal] alone is obviously inadequate to characterise the degrees of freedom of the tongue body, and in particular it is an entirely unsatisfactory account of the interactions and lack of them between vowels and consonants' (McCarthy, 1988, 102). Currently there exists no consensus on the resolution of this problem.

4.1.6 Conclusion

In this section we have examined the evidence for the hierarchical arrangement of subsegmental features for consonants. Several proposals for the incorporation of vowels into feature geometry have been made in the literature,[13] but they are not addressed here. Also omitted is any discussion of pharyngeal features.[14] However, the evidence we have seen would seem to motivate the arrangement of nodes displayed in (4.11), where the manner features inhabit various nodes, as will be made explicit in (4.18).

---

[12] How Sagey intends this proposal to work for the Kinyarwanda *tkw* in (4.8) is unclear, since the degree of closure for *w* is not the same as that for *t* or *k*.

[13] Steriade (1987), Odden (1991), van der Hulst (1988, 1991), Clements (1991).

[14] See Trigo (1991).

(4.11)

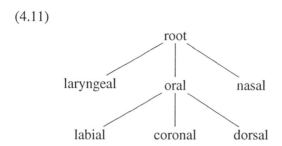

Now we move on to consider an articulatory model of subsegmental feature organisation, and how such a model can be made to fit into a hierarchy like that in (4.11).

4.2   An articulatory model

It has already been claimed above that the structure of the vocal tract provides support for particular feature groupings. Sagey has made an explicit connection between phonetics and feature geometry:

> Greater understanding of phonology, and a more explanatory phonological theory, result from investigating phonology hand in hand with phonetics. In phonetics are often found explanations of why phonology is the way it is. For example 'place of articulation' is a basic, and long-recognised, parameter in phonology. Features dealing with place of articulation form a natural class of features. Is it an accident that those features we refer to as place of articulation features form a class in phonology? Could human language just as easily have grouped the features [constricted glottis], [coronal], and [low] into some parameter? This would be expected if the grouping into place features were purely formal, and not grounded in some way in the physical mechanism of speech. However, the grouping of features into a place constituent is not an accident, but is due to the physical mechanism of speech... Thus phonetics can explain why there is a unit 'place of articulation' in phonology. (Sagey, 1986, 17f)

Sagey's emphasis on the phonetic basis for feature geometry is somewhat unusual in the phonology literature. However, autosegmental phonology began life emphasising the orchestration of articulators as the basis for the organisation of phonology. Goldsmith stated that 'autosegmental phonology is a theory of how the various components of the articulatory apparatus – the tongue, the lips, the larynx, the velum – are coordinated' (Goldsmith, 1976, 16). Despite these phonetic motivations, more recent phonological theorising has sought to distance itself from this position. For example, Clements (1985, 230) states that 'the ultimate justification for a model of phonological features must be drawn from the study of phonological and phonetic processes, and not from *a priori* considerations of vocal tract anatomy or the like'. Similarly, Goldsmith (1990, 10) now believes that 'we must remember that while phonetic reality may motivate a phonological representation, it neither justifies nor ultimately explains it'. For Clements and Goldsmith, the fact that certain groupings are physiologically justified while others are not can only be an irrelevant artifact.

In this section we continue to acknowledge the central role played by phonetic structure, here taking Browman and Goldstein's work as the starting point (Browman and Goldstein, 1989). We begin by presenting the gestural score notation, which we already met in §2.5.3.

4.2.1 The gestural score

The GESTURAL SCORE represents the temporal organisation of articulatory gestures, hiding their hierarchical (phonological) organisation. Here is a gestural score for the word *tense*.

(2.50)

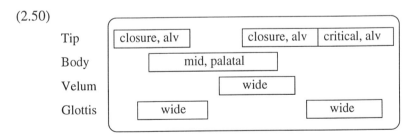

Note that the *absence* of articulations is not specified in (2.50), just as in Sagey's articulator model (see §4.1.5). The initial consonant *t* is formed as a result of the temporal coincidence of the first alveolar closure and the first glottal widening. The widening persists after the end of the closure period, producing a period of aspiration until the onset of voicing, by which time the tongue body is in the mid, palatal position required for the vowel. During this vowel the velum is lowered so that air can escape through the nasal cavity (heard as nasalisation of the vowel). Soon there is alveolar closure again, but this time it is coordinated with the velic gesture (producing the *n*). As the velum is raised (closing off the nasal cavity) and the glottis widens, air pressure builds up behind the tongue tip, which when released is heard as *t* (the so-called intrusive stop). By this time the tongue tip articulation has a critical constriction degree appropriate for *s*.

4.2.2   The hierarchical organisation of articulatory features

The hierarchical organisation to be adopted here – based on (4.11) – is depicted in (4.12). Each node consists of a feature bundle,[15] where [deg] is a (polyvalent) feature for constriction degree, [loc] is a (polyvalent) feature for constriction location and [shp] is a (binary) feature for articulator shape (lip rounding or tongue laterality). Each bundle has a sort which is specified as a subscript, and each leaf node corresponds directly to an articulator.

(4.12)

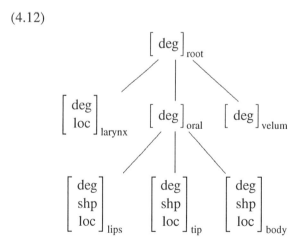

---

[15] Recall from §2.1 that sorts are classifications of nodes. In general, there is no limit to the number of sorts which can be true of a node. When a node has more than one sort, it will often be convenient to depict its sorts using feature bundles.

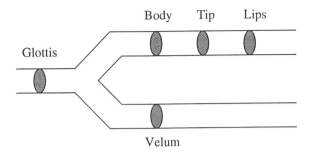

Figure 4.1: Tube geometry

The [deg] feature corresponds roughly to the manner features [continuant], [sonorant], [consonantal] and [nasal], except that it is present on *every* node. The value of this feature is propagated through the tree: its value at a node is constrained by its value at the daughters and the mother of the node. The propagation of constriction degree is best understood in terms of TUBE GEOMETRY (Browman and Goldstein, 1989, 234ff). Imagine the vocal tract as a collection of interconnected tubes along with a number of valves. This can be represented schematically as in Figure 4.1. Each valve will have a number of settings. When a valve is closed, we shall say that the corresponding section of tubing is maximally constricted. This setting will be called 'closure'. The other settings (in order of decreasing constriction) are 'critical', 'narrow', 'mid' and 'wide'. The last of these corresponds to minimal constriction. The constriction degree of a pair of tubes connected in parallel is the minimum of the individual constriction degrees of the two tubes. If the tubes are connected in series then the overall constriction is the maximum of the individual constrictions.[16]

To illustrate this propagation, consider the segment [s]. A representation appears in (4.13), where the double lines specify propagation of constriction degree.

---

[16]This use of maximum and minimum differs from that of Browman and Goldstein (1989, 237), but it is adopted as it seems more natural for a stop to correspond to maximal constriction rather than minimal constriction.

(4.13)

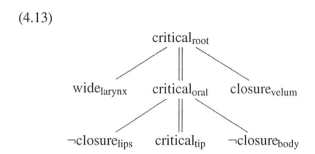

The mnemonic value of the double lines lies in their similarity with the '=' sign. Nodes joined by a double line have equal constriction degrees.

Consider the *oral* node in our feature hierarchy. According to the model in Figure 4.1, the constriction degree of the *oral* node is the maximum of the constriction degree of the three articulator nodes. We can write this constraint as shown in (4.14).

(4.14)   oral:deg = max(lips:deg, tip:deg, body:deg)

However, the representation in (4.13) requires that oral:deg = tip:deg. Therefore, constraint (4.14) requires that the *lips* and *body* nodes do not have a higher constriction degree than the *tip* node. Consequently, the *lips* and *body* nodes do not need to be specified in (4.13); their values are predictable. The constriction degree of the entire vocal tract is computed as follows:

(4.15)   root:deg   =   max(larynx:deg, min(velum:deg, oral:deg))
                    =   max(wide, min(closure, critical))
                    =   max(wide, critical)
                    =   critical

For the segment in (4.13) to be voiceless and non-nasal the constriction degree of the larynx must be *wide* and the velum constriction degree must be *closure* (the default), as specified in (4.17). Now we can give the minimal information necessary to specify an [s] in (4.16).

(4.16)

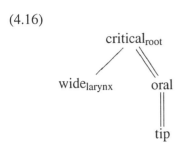

Note that it is only necessary to represent the constriction degree in one node, and the value can propagate up (or down) from that node. The direction of propagation has no formal significance since '=' is an equivalence relation. In (4.16) it is specified in the root, and the oral, lips, tip and body constriction degrees of (4.13) are produced automatically.

We conclude this section by tabulating the values of the [deg] and [loc] features for each node. The unmarked (or default) value of each is shown in boldface.

(4.17)

Node	Constriction Locations	Constriction Degrees
larynx	raised, **lowered**	wide, **critical**, closure
velum	**velic**	wide, **closure**
body	palatal, **velar**, uvular, pharyngeal	**wide**, mid, narrow, critical, closure
tip	labial, dental, **alveolar**, post-alveolar, palatal	**wide**, mid, narrow, critical, closure
lips	protruded, **labial**, dental	**wide**, mid, narrow, critical, closure

4.2.3 Manner features

Browman and Goldstein (1989, 240) have shown how constraints on constriction degree give rise to an elegant account of manner features. Translating their suggestion into the present framework, the following manner features can be expressed: [sonorant], [continuant], [consonantal] and [nasal]. In the following table, the constriction degree 'open' covers for *narrow, mid* and *wide*; '¬open' corresponds to *closure* and *critical*.

(4.18)

Constraint	Feature	Natural Class
open$_{root}$	+son	sonorants (nasals, liquids, glides, vowels)
¬open$_{root}$	−son	obstruents (stops, affricates, fricatives)
closure$_{oral}$	−cont	nasals, stops, affricates
¬closure$_{oral}$	+cont	liquids, glides, vowels, fricatives
open$_{oral}$	−cons	vowels, glides
¬open$_{oral}$	+cons	obstruents, liquids, nasals
open$_{velum}$	+nasal	nasals
closure$_{velum}$	−nasal	orals

The only manner features that this leaves out are [strident] and [lateral]. The feature [strident] distinguishes dental fricatives and affricates from alveolar ones; these are distinguished using the [loc] feature. The feature [lateral] is represented using our (binary) feature [shp] in the *tip* and *body* nodes.

4.2.4 *Spreading constriction degree*

Tying constriction location and degree together at the level of the leaves in these tree structures would appear to go against the abundantly exemplified claim that place and manner features are independent. Consequently, it may seem that the organisation advocated here will not be able to deal appropriately with place assimilation phenomena. There are two ways around this problem. One is to postulate that in certain cases where place features are thought to spread independently of manner features, they actually spread together, but that the spread manner features have a relatively minor acoustic effect. Consider the Kpelle data already discussed in §4.1.4, reproduced below:

(4.7) ḿbôlu   'my back'
       ńdĭa   'my taboo'
       ŋ́gɔ́ɔ   'my foot'
       ḿŋgbîŋ   'myself'
       ŋ́véla   'my wages'
       ńjŭa   'my nose'

Sagey observes that 'only place features, and not manner or laryngeal features, are spread onto the nasal. /v/ conditions a labial nasal stop, not a labial nasal fricative.' However, Catford claims that the labiodental nasal ɱ 'is probably realised most frequently as a nasalised approximant rather than the usual type of nasal, which requires an airtight oral closure' (Catford, 1988, 85). From an aerodynamic point of view, a nasalised fricative clearly requires a relatively narrow velic aperture. If the velic aperture is wide then almost all of the air will be released through the nasal passage. The amount escaping through the narrow oral aperture will not be sufficient to produce turbulence (Poser, *pers. comm.*). Browman and Goldstein (1989, 242) make essentially the same observation, showing how it follows from constriction degree propagation. Given these phonetic facts, Sagey's observation that /v/ conditions a labial nasal stop and not a labial nasal fricative does not justify her conclusion that the manner features must not spread. The required assimilation is expressed in (4.19), exemplified for [ɱv].[17]

(4.19)

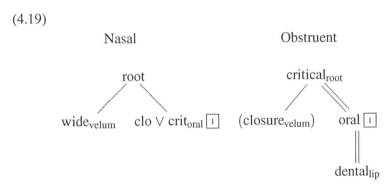

The indices in (4.19) require that the nasal and the obstruent have the same oral gesture. Consequently both segments end up with a constriction degree of *critical* for a labiodental articulation.

In the case of Kpelle assimilation, it has been argued that information about constriction degree and constriction location spread together. This embodies a claim that homorganic nasal assimilation involves both manner and place features. This kind of assimilation has normally been assumed to involve only place features. However, as we have seen, when a nasal

---

[17] For clarity the default constriction degree of the velic gesture is given for the obstruent.

assimilates to a fricative, there are grounds to suspect that the nasal does not involve complete oral closure.[18]

A more convincing case of place/manner independence is found in voiceless consonant reduction to glottal stop in some English dialects (see §4.1.2). Lass (1976, 155) treats this as a two stage process, involving deletion of the oral node along with the transfer of a [–cont] specification from the oral node to the laryngeal node. In the current framework we can analyse consonant reduction by employing the alternation between (4.20a) and (4.20b). The generalisation of these two, shown in (4.20c), will be taken to be the (partial) underlying representation of voiceless stops for these dialects. The structure in (4.20a) is intended to be the default kind of constriction degree propagation, and that in (4.20b) will arise in various phonological environments.

(4.20)

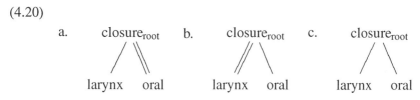

This concludes the discussion of (subsegmental) hierarchical feature structure. In this section I have attempted to combine Sagey's proposals for feature geometry with the tube geometry and gestural scores of Browman and Goldstein. At this point we leave the development of the phonological theory, and turn to its formalisation in terms of the theoretical foundation established in chapter 2 and the language $\mathcal{L}$.

4.3   Formalising the theory

In this section, we shall see how the proposals of the last two sections can be formalised using the language $\mathcal{L}$. The presentation here is rather terse, because the motivation and explanation of each definition or constraint has already been given in detail.

---

[18] The same might be said for nasal assimilation to liquids. Does [ɛn̪ɹoʔ] 'enrol' really involve complete closure for the [n̪] in fluent speech? This question must await further investigation.

The statements in (4.21) define the hierarchical structure. Recall that the parenthesised numbers indicate the permissible degrees of branching.

(4.21) a. root $\Rightarrow$ [oral(0,1), velum(0,1), larynx(0,1)]

      b. oral $\Rightarrow$ [lip(0,1), tip(0,1), body(0,1)]

Each of the (active) articulators has a constriction location.

(4.22) **Constriction Locations:**

    a. lips = {protruded, labial, labiodental}

    b. tip = {linguo-labial, dental, alveolar, post-alveolar, palatal}

    c. body = {dorso-palatal, velar, uvular, pharyngeal}

    d. velum = {velar}

    e. larynx = {raised, lowered}

Sorts will also be used to represent articulator shape distinctions, e.g., for round versus spread lip shape and lateral versus central tongue shape.

(4.23) a. lips = {round_{lips}, spread_{lips}}

      b. tip = {central_{tip}, lateral_{tip}}

      c. body = {central_{body}, lateral_{body}}

All five active articulators have a constriction degree. The hierarchical nodes also have constriction degrees.

(4.24) **Constriction Degrees:**

    a. lips = {closure_{lips}, critical_{lips}, narrow_{lips}, mid_{lips}, wide_{lips}}

    b. tip = {closure_{tip}, critical_{tip}, narrow_{tip}, mid_{tip}, wide_{tip}}

    c. body = {closure_{body}, critical_{body}, narrow_{body}, mid_{body}, wide_{body}}

    d. velum = {closure_{velum}, wide_{velum}}

    e. larynx = {closure_{larynx}, critical_{larynx}, wide_{larynx}}

    f. oral = {closure_{oral}, critical_{oral}, narrow_{oral}, mid_{oral}, wide_{oral}}

    g. root = {closure_{root}, critical_{root}, narrow_{root}, mid_{root}, wide_{root}}

It is convenient to be able to refer to a constriction degree without referring to its location, so we need the following definitions.

(4.25) a.   closure = {closure$_{lips}$, closure$_{tip}$, closure$_{body}$,
                     closure$_{velum}$, closure$_{larynx}$, closure$_{oral}$, closure$_{root}$}

        b.   critical = {critical$_{lips}$, critical$_{tip}$, critical$_{body}$,
                     critical$_{larynx}$, critical$_{oral}$, critical$_{root}$}

        c.   narrow = {narrow$_{lips}$, narrow$_{tip}$, narrow$_{body}$,
                     narrow$_{oral}$, narrow$_{root}$}

        d.   mid = {mid$_{lips}$, mid$_{tip}$, mid$_{body}$, mid$_{oral}$, mid$_{root}$}

        e.   wide = {wide$_{lips}$, wide$_{tip}$, wide$_{body}$, wide$_{velum}$,
                     wide$_{larynx}$, wide$_{oral}$, wide$_{root}$}

Now we can formalise constriction degree propagation. Recall that this is marked by a double line to symbolise the '=' relation. Accordingly, we adopt a new relation $\delta^=$ which has the properties laid out in (4.26).

(4.26) a. $\forall xy, x\delta^=y \;\rightarrow\; x\,\delta\,y$
              $\delta^=$ *is a kind of dominance*

        b.

$$\forall xy, x\delta^=y \;\rightarrow\; \begin{array}{l} closure(x) \leftrightarrow closure(y) \\ \wedge \quad critical(x) \leftrightarrow critical(y) \\ \wedge \quad narrow(x) \leftrightarrow narrow(y) \\ \wedge \quad mid(x) \leftrightarrow mid(y) \\ \wedge \quad wide(x) \leftrightarrow wide(y) \end{array}$$

A further constraint is required in order to prevent a labiodental articulation coinciding with a linguo-labial articulation. This is, in effect, a spatial correlate of the no-crossing constraint (see §2.3.3), for it is physically impossible for the tongue to touch the upper lip at the same time as the lower lip is in contact with the upper teeth.[19]

(4.27) **Oral no-crossing constraint:**
        $\forall xy, x \circ y \;\rightarrow\; (labiodental(x) \rightarrow \neg linguo\text{-}labial(y))$

---

[19] Note that (4.27) is the only such constraint that is necessary, assuming the possible mappings between articulators and constriction locations suggested by Browman and Goldstein (1989, 227).

4.4 Conclusion

In this chapter we have seen an application of the formalism of chapter 2 to a theory of phonological structure. The literature on feature geometry was surveyed, and the connection between the extant proposals for hierarchical organisation of phonological structures and the phonetic structure of the vocal tract was observed. This observation has previously been exploited by Sagey, Browman and Goldstein, and an attempt was made to bring both proposals together by identifying Sagey's arrow notation with Browman and Goldstein's constriction degree propagation mechanism. Finally, this theory was formalised using the framework of chapter 2.

5   Implementation

In chapter 2, a language $\mathcal{L}$ for linguistic description was presented along with a formal syntax and a model-theoretic semantics. We have now seen applications of this description language for representing and reasoning about phonological structures and alternations in chapters 3 and 4. In this chapter we shall endow $\mathcal{L}$ with an OPERATIONAL SEMANTICS, set within the the paradigm of constraint logic programming (Jaffar and Lassez, 1987; Smolka, 1992), and implemented using the programming languages C and Prolog.

The reason for wanting to produce an implementation is to enable the proposals of earlier chapters to be tested automatically. After all, a formal approach was employed to enable phonological theories to be implemented directly, as explained in §1.3.1.

This chapter is divided into four sections. The first section introduces the idea that the consistency of a set of constraints can be checked by constructing a minimal model which satisfies those constraints. The second section gives the internal representation for truth values, predicates and the axioms, and discusses some complexity issues. The final section explains how the C program which implements the constraint engine is synchronised with Prolog's search and backtracking. A detailed example is given to illustrate the Prolog/C interface.

5.1   Model building

The system is responsible for ensuring the consistency of a dynamic set of constraints. In doing this, the system must construct a model which is minimally compatible with the constraints that are currently in force. By minimally compatible, it is meant that the model does not have any properties other than those it is required to have. If, for example, we stated the constraint $a \circ b \circ c$, the system will construct a model in which an event a overlaps another event b, which in turn overlaps another event c. The system will not invent the further requirement that a precedes c, even though a model with such a property would still be compatible with the constraint $a \circ b \circ c$. This is because we do not want the system to prejudge what the model is going to look like, over and above what it has already been told. Such a model is called a MINIMAL MODEL. As the set of constraints is updated, the system must update the model accordingly.

An important formal property of the model building process is that it should be REFUTATION COMPLETE. When a set of constraints is inconsistent, so that there is no model which satisfies them, the model building process produces an empty model (symbolised by $\perp$). Moreover, the process must be CORRECT, in the sense that it only produces $\perp$ for an inconsistent set of constraints.

Each computation step involves an application of an inference rule (such as modus ponens). With each step, further information is inferred. As long as each new piece of information is consistent with the existing information the inferencing process can continue until no more rules of inference can be applied. If a new piece of information contradicts the existing information then the inferencing process cannot continue any further.

This computational technique can be used to test the consistency of an expression of $\mathcal{L}$: we simply compute all of the logical consequences of the expression and check that no contradictions can be derived. We can also use the model building process for automatic theorem proving. If A is a set of axioms and ϕ is a theorem, then we simply check if $A \wedge \neg \phi$ is consistent. If it is *in*consistent then ϕ is valid.

5.2   Internal representation

The internal representation of phonological structures and constraints is in three parts, truth values, predicates and axioms. We deal with these in turn.

5.2.1   Truth values

Atomic formulas, like $syl(a)$ or $a \prec b$, are either true or false. However, at some point of the model building process we may not happen to know whether such formulas are true or not. Accordingly, it is necessary to manage this partial information explicitly. This is done by adopting Belnap's four-valued logic (Belnap, 1977). The four truth values are t (true), f (false), $\top$ (unknown) and $\bot$ (inconsistent). These truth values are related by $\wedge$, $\vee$ and $\neg$ according to the following tables:

(5.1)   a.

$\wedge$	$\top$	t	f	$\bot$
$\top$	$\top$	t	f	$\bot$
t	t	t	$\bot$	$\bot$
f	f	$\bot$	f	$\bot$
$\bot$	$\bot$	$\bot$	$\bot$	$\bot$

b.

$\vee$	$\top$	t	f	$\bot$
$\top$	$\top$	$\top$	$\top$	$\top$
t	$\top$	t	$\top$	t
f	$\top$	$\top$	f	f
$\bot$	$\top$	t	f	$\bot$

c.

	$\top$	t	f	$\bot$
$\neg$	$\bot$	f	t	$\top$

These tables are summed up in the following Hasse diagram:

(5.2)

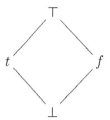

Truth values are stored internally using bit strings. For each truth value there are two bits, the first encoding 'possible truth' and the second encoding 'possible falsehood'. The correspondence between the truth values and the bit strings is shown in (5.3).

(5.3)

Truth Value	Unknown	True	False	Inconsistent
Bit String	11	10	01	00

Now the $\wedge$, $\vee$ and $\neg$ operations we saw in (5.1) correspond to the bitwise logical operators &, | and !.

(5.4) a.

&	11	10	01	00
11	11	10	01	00
10	10	10	00	00
01	01	00	01	00
00	00	00	00	00

b.

|	11	10	01	00
11	11	11	11	11
10	11	10	11	10
01	11	11	01	01
00	11	10	01	00

c.

	11	10	01	00
!	00	01	10	11

5.2.2 Predicates

Information about the sorts, featural and temporal relations is maintained in arrays, indexed by the (finite) set of constant symbols, a strategy also used by Allen (1983) and Schmiedel (1988). For each sort predicate s there is a one-dimensional array A_s, and for each featural and temporal relation r there is a two-dimensional array. An array for a sort predicate syl is shown in (5.5a) and an array for the temporal relation $\prec$ is shown in (5.5b).

(5.5)   a.

syl	x	y	z
	$\top$	t	f

       b.

$\prec$	x	y
x	$\top$	t
y	f	$\perp$

If we begin with the information that $r(a, b)$ is true and later add the information that $r(a, b)$ is false, we do not simply replace 10 with 01. Instead we must perform the bitwise-and operation (see (5.4a)) between the two values, giving the result 00. This is the desired result, because an expression which implies that $r(a, b)$ is simultaneously true and false is inconsistent. More generally, as the system operates we are continually adding further restrictions on truth values, and so there are only two paths that truth values can follow:

(5.6)   a. $\top \rightarrow t \rightarrow \perp$

       b. $\top \rightarrow f \rightarrow \perp$

That is, we must move uphill in terms of diagram (5.2).

5.2.3 *Axioms*

In terms of our internal representation, axioms are to be understood as general constraints holding between the entries of different tables. Each time a table entry is updated, these axioms can be used to update other table entries, and so on. For decidability, the system is restricted to the class of universally-quantified function-free prenex formulas with equality (the Schönfinkel-Bernays class), a class of formulas already advocated for linguistic applications by Johnson (1991). These formulas have the form:

$$\exists x_1 \ldots x_n \forall y_1 \ldots y_n \phi$$

where ϕ contains no function symbols or quantifiers.

We begin by translating each axiom into a formula in conjunctive normal form:

(5.7) $\forall x_1 \cdots x_n, (l_1 \vee \ldots \vee l_m) \wedge \ldots \wedge (l'_1 \vee \ldots \vee l'_m)$

In (5.7), each l is a (possibly negated) predicate (*i.e.* a literal). The next step is to convert each conjunct into a new axiom. Consequently, all axioms have the form in (5.8).

(5.8) $\forall x_1 \cdots x_n, l_1 \vee \ldots \vee l_m$

The final step translates each axiom into a piece of C code, the details of which will not be of any concern here. Now we display the axioms from chapter 2 in the above format.

Background axioms

For all x, y and z:

B1. $x \circ x$

B2. $\neg x \circ y \vee y \circ x$

B3. $\neg x \prec y \vee \neg y \prec x$

B4. $\neg x \prec y \vee \neg x \circ y$

B5. $\neg x \prec y \vee \neg y \prec z \vee x \prec z$

B6. $x \prec y \vee x \circ y \vee x \prec y$

B7. $\neg x \prec y \vee \neg y \circ z \vee \neg z \prec x$

B8. $\neg x \, \delta^\star \, x$

B9. $\neg x \, \delta^\star \, y \vee x \circ y$

B10. $\neg x \, \delta \, y \vee \neg y \, \delta^\star \, z \vee x \, \delta^\star \, z$

General Equality Axioms:

E1. $x = x$

E2. $\neg x = y \vee y = x$

E3. $\neg x = y \lor \neg y = z \lor x = z$

E4. $\neg x = y \lor \neg y \circ z \lor x \circ z$

E5. $\neg x \circ y \lor \neg y = z \lor x \circ z$

E6. $\neg x = y \lor \neg y \prec z \lor x \prec z$

E7. $\neg x \prec y \lor \neg y = z \lor x \prec z$

E8. $\neg x = y \lor \neg y \, \delta \, z \lor x \, \delta \, z$

E9. $\neg x \, \delta \, y \lor \neg y = z \lor x \, \delta \, z$

Linguistic axioms

The following axioms are based on the constraints presented in §4.3. This is not a complete set but an illustrative selection.

L1. $\neg root(x) \lor \neg x \, \delta \, y \lor oral(y) \lor velum(y) \lor larynx(y)$

L2. $\neg oral(x) \lor \neg x \, \delta \, y \lor lips(y) \lor tip(y) \lor body(y)$

L3. $\neg lips(x) \lor protruded(x) \lor labial(x) \lor labio\text{-}dental(x)$

L4. $\neg labial(x) \lor lips(x)$

L5. $\neg lips(x) \lor round(x) \lor spread(x)$

L6. $\neg lips(x) \lor closure_{lips}(x) \lor critical_{lips}(x) \lor narrow_{lips}(x)$
$\qquad \lor mid_{lips}(x) \lor wide_{lips}(x)$

5.2.4 An example

In this section a small example is given to illustrate the internal representation of the temporal relations, and to show how the no-crossing constraint is implemented. Suppose we know that there is some w, x, y and z such that $w \prec x$, $x \circ y$ and $y \prec z$. The following diagram illustrates the situation.

(5.9)

The tables for $\prec$ and $\circ$ are as follows:

(5.10) a.

$\prec$	w	x	y	z
w	T	t	T	T
x	T	T	T	T
y	T	T	T	t
z	T	T	T	T

b.

$\circ$	w	x	y	z
w	T	T	T	T
x	T	T	t	T
y	T	T	T	T
z	T	T	T	T

Using the above axioms, we are able to infer some positive information:

(5.11) a. $w \circ w$ (B1)

     b. $x \circ x$ (B1)

     c. $y \circ y$ (B1)

     d. $z \circ z$ (B1)

     e. $y \circ x$ (B2)

     f. $w \prec z$ (B6, B7)

and a large amount of negative information:

(5.12) a. $\neg w \prec w$ (B3)   b. $\neg x \prec x$ (B3)

c. $\neg y \prec y$ (B3)   d. $\neg z \prec z$ (B3)

e. $\neg x \prec w$ (B3)   f. $\neg x \circ w$ (B4)

g. $\neg w \circ x$ (B4, B2)   h. $\neg x \prec y$ (B4)

i. $\neg y \prec x$ (B4, B3)   j. $\neg z \prec y$ (B3)

k. $\neg z \circ y$ (B4)   l. $\neg y \circ z$ (B4, B2)

m. $\neg y \prec w$ (B6)   n. $\neg z \prec x$ (B6)

o. $\neg z \prec w$ (B6, B7, B3) p. $\neg z \circ w$ (B6, B7, B4)

q. $\neg w \circ z$ (B6, B7, B4, B2)

This results in the tables being updated as follows:

(5.13) a.

$\prec$	w	x	y	z
w	f	t	$\top$	t
x	f	f	f	$\top$
y	f	f	f	t
z	f	f	f	f

b.

$\circ$	w	x	y	z
w	t	f	$\top$	f
x	f	t	t	$\top$
y	$\top$	t	t	f
z	f	$\top$	f	t

Notice that very few table entries now contain $\top$. The cases where $\top$ remains express the following information: w may precede or overlap y, and x may precede or overlap z. Suppose that we now wished to add the information that $w \circ z$, creating the line crossing situation in the following diagram:

(5.14)

The value in the fourth column of the first row of (5.13b) (*i.e.* f) must be updated with the new value (t). These two values must be 'anded' together, with the result being $\perp$. This cell now expresses the information that w both overlaps and does not overlap z, which is inconsistent. Consequently, the attempt to add the information $w \circ z$ fails. In phonological terms, this means that the attempt to create a crossing line situation is blocked.

5.2.5   Complexity issues

Lewis (cited by Johnson, 1991) has demonstrated that the satisfiability problem for Schönfinkel-Bernays formulas has non-polynomial complexity. Nevertheless, the behaviour of the present system for a large axiom set and large phonological representations has turned out to be fast in practice. There are three reasons why this might be so.

First, since the axioms do not involve existential quantifiers, the inferencing process never creates new variables, and so the amount of work that needs to be done is bounded above by the number of variables employed in the user's constraints (*i.e.* the number of nodes in a phonological representation). Second, once the system has been initialised with a set of axioms, this set remains fixed. As the system runs it is given atomic constraints (like $a \prec b$ and $syl(a)$) but never universally quantified constraints like $\forall xy, x \circ y$. The checking done by the axioms is somewhat localised to the new information, much as refining the structure of one part of a phonological representation generally has no effect on remote parts of the representation. Possible exceptions to this, such as vowel harmony, are nevertheless restricted to small domains like individual words. Finally, recall that the range of possible updates that a cell in a table can have is limited to just two, where the second update produces $\perp$ and immediate termination. Therefore, checking the consistency of a formula over n variables will involve at most $u.n + b.n^2$ updates, where u is the number of unary predicates and b is the number of binary predicates.

5.3   Prolog/C interface

The implementation consists of two virtual computing devices, the Prolog engine and the constraint engine. These are connected together according to the architecture depicted in Figure 5.1. The programmer

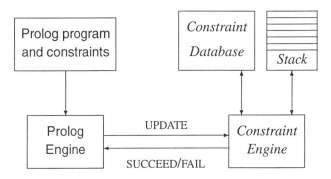

Figure 5.1: System architecture

writes Prolog programs in the normal style, making use of special predicates such as ovlp for ∘ and prec for ≺. The Prolog interpreter passes these to the constraint engine which then accesses internal structures to perform inferences.

The system has been constructed with the following requirements in mind. First, inconsistency should be detected as early as possible. Second, the user should not need to be aware of any implementation details; to the user it appears as if Prolog has a built-in phonological constraint solver, which in effect it has.

This section is divided up as follows. First, Prolog's method of search and backtracking is briefly discussed and the necessity for the constraint engine to maintain a stack is explained. In the second section, the behaviour of the system for a small program is demonstrated. Next we consider a way of overcoming the Schönfinkel-Bernays restriction on formulas. Finally, we look at the problems that arise if one attempts to implement the constraint engine directly in Prolog.

5.3.1 *Prolog search and backtracking*

When a Prolog program executes, it attempts to find an assignment to variables which satisfies all the constraints placed on those variables.

Prolog's search strategy involves BACKTRACKING. The details of back-tracking will not concern us here.[1] For present purposes, it suffices to know that when a particular constellation of constraints is found to be untenable, Prolog is able to undo the effect of adding the constraints and try other avenues as it searches for a solution.

Since the constraint engine is independent of Prolog, it must track Prolog's execution by emulating the backtracking process and restoring the model to an earlier version if necessary. In other words, we must *undo* the changes in the internal representation brought about by the addition of a certain constraint. This task is made significantly easier by the fact that constraints are undone in the opposite order to that in which they were originally applied.

To allow backtracking, the constraint engine incorporates a stack which records all previous states of the model. For space reasons, it does not keep a copy of the entire model each time it is updated, only those particular table entries which were updated. When a table entry is updated, the system pushes its old value, along with information about where that value used to reside, onto the stack. So each stack element is a pair $\langle loc, val \rangle$, consisting of the old value of an entry val and a reference to the location of the entry loc. When an entry $\langle loc, val \rangle$ is popped off the stack, the system overwrites location loc with val.

How then does the constraint engine know when the Prolog engine is backtracking? The solution is to CHAIN the stack pointer through the Prolog program.[2] Consider the Prolog program displayed in (5.15).

(5.15)   p :- a≺b, q, b≺c.
          q :- c≺a; a≺c.

We decorate each predicate with two variables. The first variable indicates the stack pointer's value before the predicate is executed, and the second variable indicates its value afterwards. The program in (5.15) is rewritten as follows:

    p(S0, S) :- prec(a, b, S0, S1), q(S1, S2), prec(b, c, S2, S).
    q(S0, S) :- prec(c, a, S0, S); prec(a, c, S0, S).

---

[1] See any introductory text on Prolog, such as Clocksin and Mellish (1981) or Pereira and Shieber (1987), for an explanation of backtracking.

[2] This solution was suggested to me by Chris Mellish. Chaining is a technique originated by Pereira and Warren (1980), also discussed by Clocksin and Mellish (1981) and Pereira and Shieber (1987).

Observe that the input value (S0) for the first clause is copied to the input value to the subgoal inside the clause. The output value (S1) for the first subgoal is copied to the second subgoal, and so on. Finally, the output (S) of the last subgoal is copied to the output of the whole clause. The second clause is similar except its body is a disjunction, and so the input to the clause is the input to both predicates, and the output of both predicates is the output of the clause.

When a subgoal like prec(a, b, S0, S1) is tried, the constraint engine is passed the stack pointer S0 along with the new information $a \prec b$. Once the inferences have been successfully performed, the constraint engine returns a new stack pointer S1. Crucially, each time the constraint engine is invoked, it pops the stack and restores the internal tables until the input stack pointer is equal to the top of stack value. This enables the constraint engine to remain in lockstep with the Prolog engine.

The precise behaviour of the constraint engine for the program in (5.15) will now be demonstrated.

5.3.2 The Prolog/C interface illustrated

Suppose we have the Prolog program displayed in (5.15) and suppose that we have the goal p. Prolog commences execution by trying to prove the subgoal $a \prec b$. It passes the current stack pointer (initially zero) and the constraint $a \prec b$ to the constraint engine, as shown below. Here, the Prolog code is given on the left (where the current point of execution is boxed) and the internal table for $\prec$ and the stack are given on the right.

$$\boxed{\text{p}} :\text{-} \boxed{a \prec b}, \text{q, } b \prec c. \qquad \xrightarrow{0,a\prec b} \qquad \begin{array}{c|cc} \prec & a & b \\ \hline a & \top & \underline{t} \\ b & \top & \top \end{array} \qquad 0 \boxed{(a,b) \quad \top} \\ tos = 1$$
$$\text{q :- } c \prec a; \ a \prec c.$$

The constraint engine creates rows and columns in its internal tables for a and b and initialises all entries to $\top$. Next, it identifies the (a, b) entry in the $\prec$ table (underlined) and pushes the current entry ($\top$) onto the stack, along with a record of its former location. The tos (top of stack) value is incremented. Storing the location enables the system to restore the table entries to their earlier values. Next, we use axiom (B3), which states that

$\prec$ is irreflexive and asymmetric, to infer that $\neg a \prec a$, $\neg b \prec b$ and $\neg b \prec a$, thereby adding more information to the table.

$$\boxed{p} :\text{-}\; a{\prec}b, \boxed{q}, b{\prec}c.$$
$$\boxed{q} :\text{-}\; c{\prec}a;\; a{\prec}c.$$

$\xleftarrow{4,yes}$

$\prec$	a	b
a	$\underline{f}$	t
b	$\underline{f}$	$\underline{f}$

1	(b,a)	$\top$
2	(a,a)	$\top$
3	(b,b)	$\top$

$$tos = 4$$

Now the constraint engine has successfully processed the constraint $a{\prec}b$. It reports the success back to the Prolog engine and also passes back the current tos value, which is the output stack pointer. Now the Prolog engine moves on to try to prove the goal q. The clause for q consists of a disjunction, and the first disjunct – $c{\prec}a$ – is tried first. The table entry for (c, a) is updated with the value t and the old value ($\top$) is pushed onto the stack.

$$\boxed{p} :\text{-}\; a{\prec}b, \boxed{q}, b{\prec}c.$$
$$\boxed{q} :\text{-}\; \boxed{c{\prec}a};\; a{\prec}c.$$

$\xrightarrow{4,c{\prec}a}$

$\prec$	a	b	c
a	f	t	$\top$
b	f	f	$\top$
c	$\underline{t}$	$\top$	$\top$

4	(c,a)	$\top$

$$tos = 5$$

Since we know $c \prec a$ and $a \prec b$ we can infer that $c \prec b$ from (B5). We also know that $\neg a \prec c$, $\neg b \prec c$ and $\neg c \prec c$ from (B3). So these four new pieces of information are added to the table.

$$\boxed{p} :\text{-}\; a{\prec}b, \boxed{q}, b{\prec}c.$$
$$q :\text{-}\; c{\prec}a;\; a{\prec}c.$$

$\xleftarrow{9,yes}$

$\prec$	a	b	c
a	f	t	$\underline{f}$
b	f	f	$\underline{f}$
c	t	$\underline{t}$	$\underline{f}$

5	(a,c)	$\top$
6	(b,c)	$\top$
7	(c,c)	$\top$
8	(c,b)	$\top$

$$tos = 9$$

Now that q has been proven, Prolog continues to prove p by trying to prove $b{\prec}c$. The (b, c) entry, currently f, is updated with t.

$$\boxed{p} :\text{-}\; a{\prec}b, q, \boxed{b{\prec}c}.$$
$$q :\text{-}\; c{\prec}a;\; a{\prec}c.$$

$\xrightarrow{9,b{\prec}c}$

$\prec$	a	b	c
a	f	t	f
b	f	f	$\perp$
c	t	t	f

9	(b,c)	f

$$tos = 10$$

Given the earlier inference that $c \prec b$, the new information that $b \prec c$ is inconsistent, and this results in the $\bot$ entry in the table at position (b, c).

$\boxed{\text{p}}$:- a$\prec$b, $\boxed{\text{q}}$, b$\prec$c. $\overset{10,no}{\longleftarrow}$ $\boxed{\text{INCONSISTENCY}}$
q :- c$\prec$a; a$\prec$c.

The system tells the Prolog engine that the attempt to prove b$\prec$c has failed. This forces Prolog to backtrack and retry the goal q, this time with the second disjunct a$\prec$c. Prolog passes this new constraint to the constraint engine, but this time the input stack pointer is 4. Note that this value is the same that was used when the first subgoal of q was tried. The constraint engine detects that the input stack pointer is not the same as its internal *tos* value, so it accordingly pops the stack, restoring the table, until *tos* has the required value of 4. Straight away it adds the new information that $a \prec c$, updating the cell (a, c).

$\boxed{\text{p}}$:- a$\prec$b, $\boxed{\text{q}}$, b$\prec$c. $\overset{4,a\prec c}{\longrightarrow}$
$\boxed{\text{q}}$:- c$\prec$a; $\boxed{\text{a}\prec\text{c}}$.

$\prec$	a	b	c
a	f	t	$\underline{t}$
b	f	f	$\top$
c	$\top$	$\top$	$\top$

4   (a, c) $\top$
$tos = 5$

Given that $a \prec c$, the system infers that $\neg c \prec a$. It also knows that $\neg c \prec c$. This leads to two more updates.

$\boxed{\text{p}}$:- a$\prec$b, $\boxed{\text{q}}$, b$\prec$c. $\overset{7,yes}{\longleftarrow}$
$\boxed{\text{q}}$:- c$\prec$a; a$\prec$c.

$\prec$	a	b	c
a	f	t	t
b	f	f	$\top$
c	$\underline{f}$	$\top$	$\underline{f}$

5   (c, a) $\top$
6   (c, c) $\top$
$tos = 7$

Now that q has been successfully retried, Prolog progresses to b$\prec$c for the second time. The (b, c) entry is updated with t and the old value is pushed onto the stack.

$\boxed{\text{p}}$:- a$\prec$b, q, $\boxed{\text{b}\prec\text{c}}$. $\overset{7,b\prec c}{\longrightarrow}$
q :- c$\prec$a; a$\prec$c.

$\prec$	a	b	c
a	f	t	t
b	f	f	$\underline{t}$
c	f	$\top$	f

7   (b, c) $\top$
$tos = 8$

Given that $b \prec c$ the system infers that $\neg c \prec b$ and updates the table, then reporting success back to the Prolog engine.

$\boxed{\text{p}}$:- a≺b, q, b≺c. $\underset{\longleftarrow}{9, yes}$

q :- c≺a; a≺c.

≺	a	b	c
a	f	t	t
b	f	f	t
c	f	f	f

$$8 \boxed{(c, b) \quad \top} \qquad tos = 9$$

At this point, the initial goal p has been proven and execution terminates, reporting that a≺b, b≺c and a≺c. Note that in the table there is now no trace of the information that $c \prec a$, which was present prior to backtracking.

Now that we have seen an example of the operation of the system we shall consider how to deal with the limitation on formulas that is imposed by the system.

5.3.3 *Overcoming the Schönfinkel-Bernays limitation*

Recall that it was necessary to select a subset of first-order predicate logic in order to have a decidable system. We opted for a constraint on formulas which prevents the use of existential quantifiers. This is a potential problem, since in chapter 2 existential quantification was found to be useful on a number of occasions.

Consider the following constraint, which has already appeared as (3.16a). Note that it contains an existential quantifier and so it is not in the Schönfinkel-Bernays class.

(5.16) $\forall x, syl(x) \rightarrow \exists y, v(y) \wedge x \, \delta \, y$
         Syllables must have a vowel.

Such constraints are indispensable, but cannot be formulated as axioms for the constraint engine. Fortunately, there is a solution to this problem, since Prolog has implicit existential quantification.[3] We can write the clause in (5.17).

(5.17)   syllable(X) :- syl(X), vowel(Y), dom(X,Y).

Here, the predicates syl and vowel are sorts interpreted by the constraint engine. The predicate dom is the dominance relation, δ, also interpreted

---

[3] This implicit existential quantification is achieved using a technique known as SKOLE-MISATION (Clocksin and Mellish, 1981).

by the constraint engine. Although clause (5.17) is not logically equivalent to $(5.16)^4$ it expresses enough of (5.16) to be useful.

5.3.4   Why not use Prolog directly?

Given the technical complexity of the constraint engine described above, it is reasonable to wonder if a direct implementation in a constraint logic programming language would do the task just as well. In fact, such an approach was attempted initially, using an extension of Prolog called CLP($\Re$) (Jaffar and Michaylov, 1987). However, this was abandoned for two reasons. First, it was not possible to represent the sorts, the relations and the axioms in an efficient way which reported inconsistency as soon as it arose and hid uninteresting information from the user. Moreover, it proved to be virtually impossible to debug programs as the number of constraints being carried around grew large. A solution to this problem was to get CLP($\Re$) to use its internal mechanisms for consistency checking. This involved employing a point-based approach to temporal relations (c.f. §2.3.4), exploiting the built-in constraint solving for inequalities. To see how this works, consider again diagram (5.14), reproduced below.

(5.14)

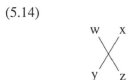

Since each autosegment is represented by a pair of interval endpoints, we can display the diagram as follows.

---

[4]Clause (5.17) does not express the fact that if x is a constituent which lacks a vowel then x cannot be a syllable. This constraint could be expressed as a separate clause.

(5.18)

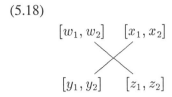

Given the definitions in (2.36), we can write down the following constraints on points:

$$w_1 < w_2 < x_1 < x_2$$
$$y_1 < y_2 < z_1 < z_2$$
$$w_1 < z_2, z_1 < w_2$$
$$y_1 < x_2, x_1 < y_2$$

From this it follows that $w_2 < x_1 < y_2 < z_1 < w_2$, and so $w_2 < w_2$, a contradiction. The information in (5.18) is therefore inconsistent, and so the structure is rejected as illformed.

The problem with this approach is that it is inflexible and unreadable. It is inflexible because it can only be applied to a small subclass of temporal constraints. It is unreadable because the output is stated in terms of points; in a long list of precedence statements it is difficult to get a clear picture of interval relations like overlap.

5.4 Conclusion

In this chapter we have seen an implementation of the phonological description language $\mathcal{L}$ in the paradigm of constraint logic programming. The implementation is a constraint engine which constructs the minimal model which is compatible with the constraints in force at each stage of the execution of a Prolog program. The implementation is flexible since the axioms can be customised by the user. Therefore, it has the potential to encompass a variety of different phonological formalisms. A future development of the system might involve integrating it into an existing grammar formalism for natural language syntax.

6   Conclusion

The goal of this study has been to provide a formal foundation for phonological description that is compatible with existing constraint-based approaches to natural language and with the constraint logic programming paradigm.

In chapter 1, the fundamentals of generative phonology were introduced. Autosegmental phonology was presented and its formal adequacy was investigated and found wanting. Next we turned to computational phonology, surveying the current state of development in this rapidly changing field. A particular approach to computational phonology, namely constraint-based phonology, was introduced. Its defining properties are intensionality, compositionality, monostratality and lexicalism. The final section of chapter 1 showed that the notion of constraint being adopted here has a long history in phonology.

Chapter 2 began with a series of discussions concerning sorts, hierarchy and temporal structure in phonology. It was shown how phonological innovations like feature geometry, prosodic structure, licensing, appropriateness, linearity and locality could be expressed. A formal language was defined, along with a model theoretic semantics and useful abbreviatory conventions. Classical first-order logic was employed because work by van Benthem (1983) on temporal logic and Johnson (1990) on feature logic has shown the fruitfulness of such an approach. Notably, the interaction between temporal and featural predicates was easy to explore in a first-order framework. The chapter concluded with a discussion of how phonological rules can be represented in the language.

In chapter 3 some potential objections to constraint-based phonology were discussed. It was shown how existing arguments in favour of deletion,

153

resyllabification and feature-changing harmony are without substance. In chapter 4 a new model of phonological structure was proposed. Two important recent developments in phonology, one concerning abstract phonology (Sagey, 1986) and the other concerning the phonology-phonetics interface (Browman and Goldstein, 1989), were brought together and shown to be compatible with the framework developed in chapter 2. Finally, chapter 5 described an implementation in the paradigm of constraint logic programming.

This development has a number of consequences for theoretical phonology. First, phonological representations can be described succinctly, without recourse to diagrams or prose, although I do not deny that these latter have their place; indeed the opportunities for visualisation offered by an apt graphical notation are invaluable. Second, inference and consistency checking can be performed directly on representations. Third, abbreviatory conventions can be stated formally, with the consequence that using abbreviated forms is less likely to lead to confusion. Fourth, theoretical claims can be made more explicit if their substantive content is unambiguous, allowing a formal comparison of competing analyses to be made. Finally, the resulting model – being declarative – provides for a non-derivational view of phonology. This, in turn, enables generalisations about linguistic competence to be stated independently of particular performance tasks such as generation or recognition.

There are also consequences for descriptive phonology. The formalism provides a computational representation for phonological descriptions. This development will ultimately enable the automatic checking of the correspondence between an analysis and its target data. Gestural scores – the lowest level of representation employed here – have been used successfully as the basis for automatic speech synthesis (Browman, *pers. comm.*). In elaborating the relationship between articulatory phonetic structure and a particular model of abstract phonology, a practical yet theoretically well-founded view of the phonology-phonetics interface is emerging, one that may ultimately enable the testing of phonological grammars using speech synthesis.

A third set of consequences arise for computational linguistics. Although a variety of constraint-based grammar formalisms have been presented in the literature, they have hitherto been employed mainly for analyses of syntactic and semantic phenomena. Applications to morphological and phonological domains have been severely curtailed because these formalisms have assumed an overly restrictive view of phonological organisation, whereby representations are conceived of as strings over an alphabet. While certain string manipulations can account for a variety of phenomena (e.g. Hoeksema and Janda, 1988), the wholesale conflation of phonology with orthography renders any theory incapable of expressing the observations which have been made in the non-linear phonology literature. Once these formalisms have been suitably enriched, perhaps along the lines of the present proposals, it will be possible to study a wider class of languages, particularly those with complex morphophonology.

This proposal for a constraint-based phonology is certain to have raised many questions which are yet to be addressed. The formality of the approach is no guarantee of linguistic or mathematical correctness, but it should make the theory easier to refute and be replaced by a theory with fewer shortcomings. Such a programme will, it is hoped, ultimately provide us with a theory of phonology that is sufficiently rigorous and precise to be computationally interpretable and testable, an approach to speech technology that is linguistically well-founded and well-integrated with natural language syntax and semantics, and a way of applying grammar formalisms to a significantly broader range of the world's languages than has previously been possible.

Appendix: Logical extensions

A.1 The feature matrix

In this section we shall see how the language $\mathcal{L}$ can be used to define feature matrices.

The kinds of structures we saw in chapter 2 have involved lines between labelled nodes. However, it is sometimes convenient to be able to think of structures as consisting of labelled lines between unlabelled nodes. Of course the most general case is to have a mixture of the two: labelled nodes and labelled lines. Recall abbreviatory convention 2 from (2.54), reproduced below.

(2.54) **Abbreviatory Convention 2:**
$$s(x, y) =_{\text{def}} x \; \delta \; y \wedge s(y)$$

This states that if a *node* has a label 's' then the *lines* of dominance reaching that node from above are also labelled 's'. (These predicates may be viewed as partitions of the δ relation.)

A.1.1 Subsegmental structures

An example for part of Clements' (1985, 248) representation of [s] appears below:

157

(A.1)

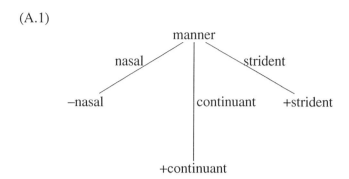

This mapping permits the trees we have seen to be depicted as feature matrices.[1] For example, Clements' representation for [s] in Figure 2.3 can be expressed using the following feature matrix.

(A.2)

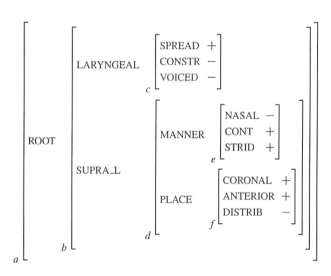

---

[1]For more details about feature matrices, consult Johnson (1988); Kasper and Rounds (1986, 1990); Carpenter (1992). Their use in phonology has been surveyed in §1.5.3. Regarding the mapping discussed above, a minor caveat is necessary. Recall that nodes can be thought of as having more than one label. This is because a node picked out by a sort (say) +*spread* is also picked out by the more general sort *spread*. In this case, the most general label only will become the label of the incoming arc(s).

This matrix notation encodes the same information as Clements' tree diagram. Each pair of brackets and its contents is called a feature matrix. The most deeply nested entities, namely the + and – symbols, are also feature matrices, but of a special kind. They are called ATOMIC FEATURE MATRICES. The + and – symbols will be thought of here as abbreviatory, standing in place of the fuller (redundant) forms such as +spread.

A formula describing both Clements' picture and the above feature matrix is given in (A.3). The indentation is provided to aid visual comparison with (A.2).

(A.3) $c(a) \wedge$

   $root(a, b) \wedge$

      $laryngeal(b, c) \wedge$

         $spread(c, c_1) \wedge +spread(c_1) \wedge$
         $constr(c, c_2) \wedge -constr(c_2) \wedge$
         $voiced(c, c_3) \wedge -voiced(c_3) \wedge$

      $supra\_l(b, d) \wedge$

         $manner(d, e) \wedge$
            $nasal(e, e_1) \wedge -nasal(e_1) \wedge$
            $cont(e, e_2) \wedge +cont(e_2) \wedge$
            $strid(e, e_3) \wedge +strid(e_3) \wedge$

         $place(d, f) \wedge$
            $coronal(f, f_1) \wedge +coronal(f_1) \wedge$
            $anterior(f, f_2) \wedge +anterior(f_2) \wedge$
            $distrib(f, f_3) \wedge -distrib(f_3)$

Rather than considering (A.3) and (A.2) to be notational variants, (A.2) – like the phonological diagrams given earlier – will be viewed as an object in the domain. We shall say that (A.3) *describes* (A.2). More specifically, the denotation of the constant a is the the whole of (A.2), the denotation of the constant b is the outermost-but-one feature matrix in (A.2), and so on. Note that the constants a, b, c, d, e and f are marked in (A.2) as subscripts. The other constants in (A.3) could likewise be marked as subscripts on the individual + and – atomic feature matrices of (A.2). The relationship between a and b is $root(a, b)$, which is equivalent to stating that a dominates b and that b has the sort *root*.

A.1.2   *Prosodic structures*

As a further example, recall the prosodic structure in (2.7), repeated below:

(2.7)

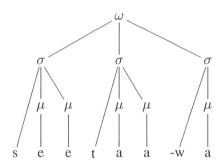

This structure can be represented as the feature matrix in (A.4).

(A.4) $\left[\text{SYL} \; \left\langle \left[\begin{array}{ll} \text{ONSET} & \langle s \rangle \\ \text{MORA} & \langle e\,e \rangle \end{array} \right] \left[\begin{array}{ll} \text{ONSET} & \langle t \rangle \\ \text{MORA} & \langle a\,a \rangle \end{array} \right] \left[\begin{array}{ll} \text{ONSET} & \langle w \rangle \\ \text{MORA} & \langle a \rangle \end{array} \right] \right\rangle \right]$

This matrix introduces a new piece of notation, the angle bracket. (The angle bracket was actually introduced in (2.57).) Angle brackets are used in the representation of sequences (cf. Rounds and Manaster Ramer (1987)). The word *seetaawa* consists of a sequence of three syllables. Each syllable in turn contains an ONSET sequence and a MORA sequence. As there are no complex onsets the onset sequences have only one element. The fact that onsets occur before moras in a syllable may be expressed using the following constraint:

(A.5)   **Onsets Precede Moras:**

$\forall xyz, \text{onset}(x, y) \wedge \text{mora}(x, z) \; \rightarrow \; y \prec z$

The formula describing the above feature matrix (and also describing Pierrehumbert and Beckman's original tree) appears in (A.6).

(A.6) $word(a) \wedge$

$\qquad syl(a, b) \wedge$

$$onset(b, b_1) \wedge s(b_1) \wedge$$
$$mora(b, b_2) \wedge e(b_2) \wedge$$
$$mora(b, b_3) \wedge e(b_3) \wedge$$
$$b_2 \prec b_3 \wedge$$
$$syl(a, c) \wedge$$
$$onset(c, c_1) \wedge t(c_1) \wedge$$
$$mora(c, c_2) \wedge a(c_2) \wedge$$
$$mora(c, c_3) \wedge a(c_3) \wedge$$
$$c_2 \prec c_3 \wedge$$
$$syl(a, d) \wedge$$
$$onset(d, d_1) \wedge w(d_1) \wedge$$
$$mora(d, d_2) \wedge a(d_2) \wedge$$
$$b \prec c \prec d$$

A.1.3 Re-entrant structures

As a final example, consider a structure involving re-entrancy, such as that proposed by McCarthy and Prince (1989), reproduced above, for the word *kattab*. It may be represented in a feature matrix as follows.

$$(A.7) \quad \left[SYL \left\langle \begin{bmatrix} ONSET & \langle k \rangle \\ MORA & \langle a\ t^{\boxed{1}} \rangle \end{bmatrix} \begin{bmatrix} ONSET & \langle t^{\boxed{1}} \rangle \\ MORA & \langle a\ b \rangle \end{bmatrix} \right\rangle \right]$$

The boxed index $\boxed{1}$ indicates that the two *t*s are in fact just one token. Given the index, it is only necessary to mention the *t* once, as in (A.8), and it does not matter which place it is mentioned in.

$$(A.8) \quad \left[SYL \left\langle \begin{bmatrix} ONSET & \langle k \rangle \\ MORA & \langle a\ t^{\boxed{1}} \rangle \end{bmatrix} \begin{bmatrix} ONSET & \langle \boxed{1} \rangle \\ MORA & \langle a\ b \rangle \end{bmatrix} \right\rangle \right]$$

Now that we have sequences, it is necessary to be able to depict constraints on their alignment. The standard notation for autosegmental association can be carried over directly into the feature matrix notation. The overlap statements in (A.9a) will be depicted using lines as in (A.9b).

(A.9)   a. $a \circ d \wedge b \circ d \wedge c \circ e \wedge c \circ f$

   b. $$\begin{bmatrix} \text{F} & \langle \text{a' b' c'} \rangle \\ & \\ \text{G} & \langle \text{d' e' f'} \rangle \end{bmatrix}$$

A.2   A modal language for phonological description

In this section we show how the tense logical approach investigated by Blackburn (1993) can be used to encode hierarchical and temporal phonological information of the kind explored in chapter 2.[2] We employ the same phonological frames as presented in §2.5.2, but linked to a modal language $\mathcal{L}_M$ rather than the language $\mathcal{L}$.

A.2.1   Logical framework

Interval based tense logics are calculi of temporal reasoning in which propositions are assigned truth values over extended periods of time.[3] Three operators F (future), P (past) and O (overlaps) are introduced: $F\phi$ means 'ϕ will be the case (at least once)', $P\phi$ means 'ϕ was the case (at least once)' and $O\phi$ means 'ϕ is the case at some overlapping interval (at least once)'. O corresponds to what phonologists call 'association'. Typically sentences are true at some intervals and not at others. (This is obviously the case, for example, if ϕ encodes the proposition 'the sun is shining'.) Blackburn (1993) has explored the effects of adding a new type of symbol, called *nominals*, to tense logic. Unlike ordinary propositions, nominals are only ever true once. In a sense, a nominal is a 'name' (or a 'temporal indexical') for that unique period of time at which it is true. Certain observations about time can only be expressed in a theory which employs

---

[2]This section presents joint work with Patrick Blackburn, and it is adapted from Bird and Blackburn (1991). For an introduction to modal logic, see Hughes and Cresswell (1968).

[3]See van Benthem (1983) for an introduction to this field and a survey of a variety of possible formulations of temporal structure.

nominals. For example, $i \rightarrow \neg Fi$ picks out precisely the irreflexive time flows, whereas no formula containing only propositional variables can do this. Nominals have been employed in the analysis of temporal reference in linguistic semantics. Here we present an application of nominals to a very different domain, namely phonology. In addition to F, P and O, we shall employ the modality $\Diamond$ to represent dominance.

Syntax

Let $X = \{p, q, r, \ldots\}$ be the propositional variables and let $N = \{i, j, k, \ldots\}$ be the nominals of $\mathcal{L}_M$. Then $\mathcal{L}_M$ is the smallest set such that all of the following hold, where $\phi, \psi \in \mathcal{L}_M$.

$$
\begin{aligned}
\top, \bot &\in \mathcal{L}_M \\
X, N &\subset \mathcal{L}_M \\
\Diamond\phi, F\phi, P\phi, O\phi &\in \mathcal{L}_M \\
\phi \vee \psi, \neg\phi &\in \mathcal{L}_M
\end{aligned}
$$

We define $\rightarrow$, $\leftrightarrow$ and $\wedge$ as usual. We also define the duals of our modal operators in the usual fashion:

$$
\begin{aligned}
G\phi &\equiv \neg F\neg\phi && (\phi \text{ is always } going \text{ to be the case}) \\
H\phi &\equiv \neg P\neg\phi && (\phi \text{ always } has \text{ been the case}) \\
C\phi &\equiv \neg O\neg\phi && (\phi \text{ holds at all overlapping intervals}) \\
\Box\phi &\equiv \neg\Diamond\neg\phi && (\phi \text{ is true at all 'daughter' intervals})
\end{aligned}
$$

Additionally, we define some abbreviations as follows.

$$
\begin{aligned}
M\phi &\equiv P\phi \vee O\phi \vee F\phi && (\phi \text{ holds at some time}) \\
L\phi &\equiv \neg M\neg\phi && (\phi \text{ holds at all times}) \\
\langle p\rangle\phi &\equiv \Diamond(p \wedge \phi) \\
\langle p_1 \cdots p_n\rangle\phi &\equiv \langle p_1\rangle \cdots \langle p_n\rangle\phi
\end{aligned}
$$

$$[p]\phi \;\equiv\; \Box(p \to \phi)$$
$$[p_1 \cdots p_n]\phi \;\equiv\; [p_1] \cdots [p_n]\phi$$
$$\Diamond^n \phi \;\equiv\; \underbrace{\Diamond \cdots \Diamond}_{n} \phi, n > 0$$
$$\Box^n \phi \;\equiv\; \underbrace{\Box \cdots \Box}_{n} \phi, n > 0$$

Semantics

Suppose we have a set of individuals, $\mathcal{E}$, which we shall call events. Let $\mathcal{S}$ be a set of unary relations on $\mathcal{E}$ and let $\prec$, $\circ$ and δ bc binary relations on $\mathcal{E}$. As $\prec$ models temporal precedence, it must be irreflexive and transitive. The $\circ$ relation models temporal overlap and so it is associative and symmetric. The $\prec$ and $\circ$ relations interact as follows:

1. $\prec$ and $\circ$ are disjoint

2. For all $e_1 e_2 e_3 e_4 \in E$, if $e_1 \prec e_2 \circ e_3 \prec e_4$ then $e_1 \prec e_4$

3. For all $e_1 e_2 \in E$, $e_1 \prec e_2$ or $e_1 \circ e_2$ or $e_1 \succ e_2$.

Note that the triple $\langle \mathcal{E}, \prec, \circ \rangle$ is known in temporal logic as an INTERVAL STRUCTURE. The remaining relation, immediate dominance (δ), is acyclic and is contained in the $\circ$ relation. A phonological frame $\mathcal{F}$ is the four-tuple $\langle \mathcal{E}, \prec, \circ, \delta \rangle$.

Here we show how $\mathcal{L}_M$ can be linked with such structures. A valuation $\mathcal{V}$ is a function $(X \cup N) \to 2^T$ that obeys three constraints. First, it must assign a singleton set to each nominal. Second, for each $t \in T$, there is an $i \in N$ such that $\mathcal{V}(i) = \{t\}$. Third, if $t_1, t_2 \in \mathcal{V}(p)$ where $p \in X$ then $t_1 \circ t_2 \to t_1 = t_2$. In short, valuations are functions which ensure nominals act as names, where all intervals are named, and valuations capture the idea that phonological 'tiers' are linearly ordered. A model for $\mathcal{L}_M$ is a pair $\langle \mathcal{F}, \mathcal{V} \rangle$.

Satisfaction

Let $\mathcal{M} = \langle \mathcal{F}, \mathcal{V} \rangle$, $t \in T$, $a \in X \cup N$. Then:

$\mathcal{M} \models_t \top$

$\mathcal{M} \not\models_t \bot$

$\mathcal{M} \models_t a$ iff $t \in \mathcal{V}(a)$

$\mathcal{M} \models_t \neg\phi$ iff $\mathcal{M} \not\models_t \phi$

$\mathcal{M} \models_t \phi \vee \psi$ iff $\mathcal{M} \models_t \phi$ or $\mathcal{M} \models_t \psi$

$\mathcal{M} \models_t \Diamond\phi$ iff $\exists t' : t \delta t'$ and $\mathcal{M} \models_{t'} \phi$

$\mathcal{M} \models_t O\phi$ iff $\exists t' : t \circ t'$ and $\mathcal{M} \models_{t'} \phi$

$\mathcal{M} \models_t F\phi$ iff $\exists t' : t < t'$ and $\mathcal{M} \models_{t'} \phi$

$\mathcal{M} \models_t P\phi$ iff $\exists t' : t' < t$ and $\mathcal{M} \models_{t'} \phi$

If $\mathcal{M} \models_t \phi$ then we say that ϕ is *true* in $\mathcal{M}$ at t.

Validities

If $\langle \mathcal{F}, \mathcal{V} \rangle \models_t \phi$ for all frames $\mathcal{F}$, for all valuations $\mathcal{V}$ on $\mathcal{F}$, and all $t \in T$, then we say ϕ is a *validity*. The following are some examples of validities. The first group concerns the interval structure.

(T1) $i \rightarrow \neg Fi$. *Precedence is irreflexive.*

(T2) $\phi \rightarrow O\phi$. *Overlap is reflexive.*

(T3) $\phi \rightarrow CO\phi$. *Overlap is symmetric.*

(T4) $Fi \rightarrow \neg Oi$. $Pi \rightarrow \neg Oi$.
Precedence and overlap are disjoint.

(T5) $FOF\phi \rightarrow F\phi$. *Precedence is transitive through overlap.*

(T6) $F\phi \wedge F\psi \rightarrow F(\phi \wedge F\psi) \vee F(\psi \wedge F\phi) \vee F(\phi \wedge O\psi)$.
Time is semi-linear.[4]

---

[4]The mirror image of this formula, obtained by replacing all Fs with Ps, is also valid.

The next three validities concern the dominance relation and its interaction with the interval structure.

(D1) $\Diamond^n \phi \rightarrow O\phi$. *The transitive closure of dominance is included in the overlap relation.*

(D2) $i \rightarrow \neg\Diamond^n i$. *Dominance is acyclic.*

(D3) $M(i \wedge L(\neg i \wedge \phi) \rightarrow \Diamond^n \phi)$ *Structures are rooted.*

The next group of validities reflect the constraints we have placed on valuations.

(FORCE)

   Mi. *Each nominal names at least one interval.*

(NOM)

   $i \wedge M(i \wedge \phi) \rightarrow \phi$. *Each nominal names at most one interval.*

(PLIN)

   $p \wedge O(p \wedge \phi) \rightarrow \phi$. *Phonological tiers are linearly ordered.*

Proof theory

   Blackburn (1990) has given techniques for constructing a proof theory and obtaining decidability results.

A.2.2   Expressing phonological constraints

Feature matrices

   $\mathcal{L}_M$ can be used for describing feature matrices (cf. §A.1). For example, consider the matrix below.

$$\left[\text{PHON} \quad \langle \textit{Kay, pats, Blackie} \,\rangle \right]$$

A possible description of this matrix is:

$$\langle \text{PHON} \rangle (Kay \wedge Fi)$$
$$\wedge \quad \langle \text{PHON} \rangle (pats \wedge i)$$
$$\wedge \quad \langle \text{PHON} \rangle (Blackie \wedge Pi)$$

This representation of sequences enables the expression of partial ordering constraints which are widely required in phonological descriptions. Note that all instances of the following variant of the NOM schema are valid. E and E' are strings of modal operators from $\{\Diamond, F, P, O\}$.

(NOM$_\mathcal{E}$)

$Ei \wedge E'(i \wedge \phi) \leftrightarrow E(i \wedge \phi) \wedge E'i.$

Formulas may be transferred between different paths to the same interval.

This schema expresses a familiar equivalence on feature matrices. For example:

$$\begin{bmatrix} \text{SUBJ}|\text{AGR} & \boxed{1}\,pl \\ \text{PRED}|\text{AGR} & \boxed{1} \end{bmatrix} \equiv \begin{bmatrix} \text{SUBJ}|\text{AGR} & \boxed{1} \\ \text{PRED}|\text{AGR} & \boxed{1}\,pl \end{bmatrix}$$

That is, nominals may be used in the representation of re-entrancy, in modal logic.

Sort lattices

Node labels in phonological diagrams can be thought of as classifications. For example, we can think of $\sigma \in X$ as denoting a certain class of nodes in a phonological structure (the *syllable* nodes). Syllables may be further classified into *open syllables* and *closed syllables*, which are written as σ_o and σ_c respectively. The relationship between σ, σ_o and σ_c can then be expressed using the following formulas:

$$L(\sigma \leftrightarrow \sigma_o \vee \sigma_c)$$

$$L(\sigma_o \wedge \sigma_c \leftrightarrow \bot)$$

Such constraints are Boolean constraints. For example, a simple Boolean lattice validating the two formulas concerning moras above is

$\langle\, \{\mu, \mu_o, \mu_c, \perp\}\, ;\ \mu_o \sqcap \mu_c\ =\ \perp,\ \mu_o \sqcup \mu_c\ =\ \mu\,\rangle$. This is depicted as the following Hasse diagram:

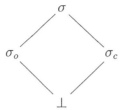

For convenience, constraints on node classifications can be depicted using lattice diagrams of the above form. Trading on the fact that $\mathcal{L}_M$ contains propositional calculus, Boolean constraints can be uniformly expressed in $\mathcal{L}_M$ as follows:

(i) $p \sqcap q = r$ becomes $L(p \wedge q \leftrightarrow r)$

(ii) $p \sqcup q = r$ becomes $L(p \vee q \leftrightarrow r)$

Appropriateness constraints

As we saw in §2.2.2, the hierarchical prosodic structures of phonology are highly constrained: the constituents of a node must be APPROPRIATE for that node. These restrictions on dominance are expressed using an appropriateness graph (Figure 2.6, §2.2.2). We can express in $\mathcal{L}_M$ the constraints captured by such appropriateness graphs. For example, $L(p \rightarrow \neg\Diamond q)$ expresses the fact that a node with sort p cannot dominate a node with sort q. We can also use $\mathcal{L}_M$ to express stronger constraints. For example, $L(p \rightarrow \Diamond q)$ expresses the fact that a node of sort p must dominate at least one node of sort q. In short, the $\Diamond$ operator allows us to express graphical constraints.

Licensing and sharing

An interesting extension is to add an operator $\Diamond^{-1}$ that looks backwards along the dominance relation. That is, $\Diamond^{-1}$ is to $\Diamond$ as P is to F.

Autosegmental licensing (see §2.2.5) can then be expressed as in (A.10a). Prosodic licensing (see §2.2.6) can be expressed as in (A.10b).

(A.10) a. **Autosegmental Licensing:**
$$s_1 \text{ licenses } s_2 =_{\text{def}} L(s_2 \rightarrow \Diamond^{-n} s_1)$$

b. **Prosodic Licensing:**
$$L(\neg phrase \rightarrow \Diamond^{-1} \top)$$

Another application of $\Diamond^{-1}$ is for the constraint that certain kinds of nodes cannot be shared (see §2.2.4).

(A.11) $not\text{-}shared(x) =_{\text{def}} L(x \wedge \Diamond^{-1}\phi \rightarrow \Box^{-1}\phi)$

A.2.3 Conclusion

In this section an alternative language $\mathcal{L}_M$ has been presented. It is a modal language, and gives a different perspective on phonological structure from the language $\mathcal{L}$ that was presented in §2.5. The primary advantage of $\mathcal{L}_M$ over $\mathcal{L}$ is that its formulas are often more compact. For example, in $\mathcal{L}$ we must write (A.12a) for one of the axioms about precedence. In $\mathcal{L}_M$ we write (A.12b).

(A.12) a. $\forall wxyz, w \prec x \wedge x \circ y \wedge y \prec z \rightarrow w \prec z$

b. $FOF\phi \rightarrow F\phi$

However, the advantage that $\mathcal{L}$ has over $\mathcal{L}_M$ is that it has been possible to implement part of $\mathcal{L}$ (see chapter 5). It is less clear how to proceed with an implementation of $\mathcal{L}_M$.

References

Albro, D. M. (1994). 'AMAR: A Computational Model of Autosegmental Phonology'. B.S. Thesis, Dept. of Electrical Engineering and Computer Science, Massachusetts Institute of Technology.

Allen, J., Hunnicutt, S., and Klatt, D. (1987). *From Text to Speech: The MITalk System*. Cambridge University Press.

Allen, J. F. (1983). Maintaining knowledge about temporal intervals. *Communications of the ACM*, 26, 832–43.

Anderson, J. M. and Durand, J. (eds.) (1987). *Explorations in Dependency Phonology*. Dordrecht: Foris.

Anderson, S. R. (1985). *Phonology in the Twentieth Century: Theories of Rules and Theories of Representations*. The University of Chicago Press.

Anderson, S. R. (1989). Johnson-Laird: The computer and the mind. *Language*, 65, 800–11.

Antworth, E. (1990). PC-KIMMO: *A Two-Level Processor for Morphological Analysis*. Dallas: SIL.

Archangeli, D. (1988). Aspects of underspecification theory. *Phonology*, 5, 183–207.

Archangeli, D. and Pulleyblank, D. (1987). Maximal and minimal rules: effects of tier scansion. In McDonough, J. and Plunkett, B. (eds.), *Proceedings of the Seventeenth Meeting of the North East Linguistic Society*, pages 16–35. Graduate Linguistic Student Association, University of Massachusetts at Amherst.

Archangeli, D. and Pulleyblank, D. (1989). Yoruba vowel harmony. *Linguistic Inquiry*, 20, 173–217.

Árnason, K. (1986). The segmental and suprasegmental status of preaspiration in Modern Icelandic. *Nordic Journal of Linguistics*, 9, 1–23.

Avery, P. and Rice, K. (1989). Segment structure and coronal underspecification. *Phonology*, 6, 179–200.

Bach, E. (1976). An extension of classical transformational grammar. In *Problems in Linguistic Metatheory, Proceedings of the 1976 Conference at Michigan State University*, pages 183–224. Michigan State University.

171

Bach, E. (1983). On the relationship between word-grammar and phrase-grammar. *Natural Language and Linguistic Theory*, 1, 65–89.

Bach, E. and Wheeler, D. W. (1981). Montague phonology: a first approximation. In Chao, W. and Wheeler, D. W. (eds.), *University of Massachusetts Occasional Papers in Linguistics*, volume 7 pages 27–45. Graduate Linguistics Student Association, University of Massachusetts.

Batóg, T. (1967). *The Axiomatic Method in Phonology*. London: Routledge & Kegan Paul.

Bear, J. (1990). Backwards phonology. In Karlgren, H. (ed.), *Proceedings of the Thirteenth International Conference on Computational Linguistics*, volume 3, pages 13–20. International Committee on Computational Linguistics.

Bellgard, M. I. (1993). 'Machine Learning of Temporal Sequences: Applications of the Effective Boltzmann Machine'. PhD thesis, University of Western Australia.

Belnap, N. D. (1977). A useful four-valued logic. In Dunn, J. M. and Epstein, G. (eds.), *Modern Uses of Multiple-Valued Logic*, volume 2 of *Episteme* pages 8–37. D. Reidel Publishing Company.

Bennett, M. and Partee, B. H. (1972). *Toward the Logic of Tense and Aspect in English*. Indiana University Linguistics Club.

Bird, S. (1991a). Feature structures and indices. *Phonology*, 8, 137–44.

Bird, S. (1991b). Focus and phrasing in Unification Categorial Grammar. In Bird, S. (ed.), *Declarative Perspectives on Phonology*, pages 139–66. University of Edinburgh.

Bird, S. (1992). Finite-state phonology in HPSG. In *Proceedings of the Fifteenth International Conference on Computational Linguistics*, pages 74–80. International Committee on Computational Linguistics.

Bird, S. (1994a). Automated tone transcription. In *Proceedings of the First Meeting of the ACL Special Interest Group in Computational Phonology*, pages 1–12. Association for Computational Linguistics.

Bird, S. (1994b). Introduction to computational phonology. *Computational Linguistics*, *20*(3), iii–ix.

Bird, S. and Blackburn, P. (1991). A logical approach to Arabic phonology. In *Proceedings of the Fifth Meeting of the European Chapter of the Association for Computational Linguistics*, pages 89–94. Association for Computational Linguistics.

Bird, S., Coleman, J. S., Pierrehumbert, J. B., and Scobbie, J. M. (1992). Declarative phonology. In Crochetière, A., Boulanger, J.-C., and Ouellon, C. (eds.), *Proceedings of the Fifteenth International Conference of Linguists*. Quebec: Presses de l'Université Laval.

Bird, S. and Ellison, T. M. (1994). One level phonology: autosegmental representations and rules as finite automata. *Computational Linguistics*, 20, 55–90.

Bird, S. and Klein, E. (1990). Phonological events. *Journal of Linguistics*, 26, 33–56.

Bird, S. and Klein, E. (1994). Phonological analysis in typed feature systems. *Computational Linguistics*, 20, 455–91.

Bird, S. and Ladd, D. R. (1991). Presenting autosegmental phonology. *Journal of Linguistics*, 27, 193–210.

Blackburn, P. (1990). 'Nominal Tense Logic and other Sorted Intensional Frameworks'. PhD thesis, University of Edinburgh.

Blackburn, P. (1993). Nominal Tense Logic. *Notre Dame Journal of Formal Logic*, 34, 56–83.

Bloch, B. (1948). A set of postulates for phonemic analysis. *Language*, 24, 3–46.

Bloomfield, L. (1926). A set of postulates for the science of language. *Language*, 2, 153–64. Reprinted in M. Joos (ed.) (1957), *Readings in Linguistics I: The Development of Descriptive Linguistics in America, 1925–56*, pages 26–31. The University of Chicago Press.

Bloomfield, L. (1933). *Language*. London: Allen & Unwin. (Reprinted 1976).

Bobrow, D. G. and Fraser, J. B. (1968). A phonological rule tester. *Communications of the ACM*, 11, 766–72.

Bobrow, R. and Webber, B. (1980). Knowledge representation for syntactic/semantic processing. In *Proceedings of AAAI-80*, pages 316–23. American Association for Artificial Intelligence.

Boley, H. (1991). Declarative and procedural paradigms – do they really compete? In Boley, H. and Richter, M. M. (eds.), *International Workshop on Processing Declarative Knowledge*, pages 383–5. Springer Verlag.

Boolos, G. S. and Jeffrey, R. C. (1989). *Computability and Logic* (third ed.). Cambridge University Press.

Bouma, G. (1991). A logical reconstruction of digital phonology. In Bird, S. (ed.), *Declarative Perspectives on Phonology*, pages 93–105. University of Edinburgh.

Brandon, F. R. (1991). *Fonol – Phonological Programming Language*. User Manual, version 4.0.

Broe, M. (1991a). Paradox lost: a non-derivational approach to Grassmann's Law. In Bird, S. (ed.), *Declarative Perspectives on Phonology*, pages 45–63. University of Edinburgh.

Broe, M. (1991b). A unification-based approach to prosodic analysis. In Bird, S. (ed.), *Declarative Perspectives on Phonology*, pages 27–44. University of Edinburgh. Also appeared in G. Docherty, J. Miller & L. Stirling (eds.) *Work in Progress*, 21, 63–82, 1988. Department of Linguistics, University of Edinburgh.

Broe, M. (1992). An introduction to feature geometry. In Docherty, G. J. and Ladd, D. R. (eds.), *Papers in Laboratory Phonology II: Gesture, Segment, Prosody*, pages 149–65. Cambridge University Press.

Broe, M. (1993). 'Specification Theory: the Treatment of Redundancy in Generative Phonology'. PhD thesis, University of Edinburgh.

Bromberger, S. and Halle, M. (1989). Why phonology is different. *Linguistic Inquiry*, 20, 51–70.

Browman, C. and Goldstein, L. (1989). Articulatory gestures as phonological units. *Phonology*, 6, 201–51.

Bruck, A., Fox, R. A., and La Galy, M. W. (eds.) (1974). *Papers from the Parasession on Natural Phonology*. Chicago Linguistic Society.

Cahill, L. J. (1989). 'Syllable-Based Morphology for Natural Language Processing'. PhD thesis, University of Sussex.

Cahill, L. J. (1990). Syllable-based morphology. In Karlgren, H. (ed.), *Proceedings of the Thirteenth International Conference on Computational Linguistics*, volume 3, pages 48–53. International Committee on Computational Linguistics.

Calder, J. (1990). 'An Interpretation of Paradigmatic Morphology'. PhD thesis, University of Edinburgh.

Calder, J. and Bird, S. (1991). Defaults in underspecification phonology. In Bird, S. (ed.), *Declarative Perspectives on Phonology*, pages 107–25. University of Edinburgh.

Calder, J., Klein, E., and Zeevat, H. (1988). Unification Categorial Grammar: A concise, extendable grammar for natural language processing. In *Proceedings of the Twelfth International Conference on Computational Linguistics*, pages 83–6. International Committee on Computational Linguistics.

Carpenter, B. (1992). *The Logic of Typed Feature Structures*, volume 32 of *Cambridge Tracts in Theoretical Computer Science*. Cambridge University Press.

Carson, J. (1988). Unification and transduction in computational phonology. In *Proceedings of the Twelfth International Conference on Computational Linguistics*, pages 106–11. International Committee on Computational Linguistics.

Cartwright, T. A. and Brent, M. R. (1994). Segmenting speech without a lexicon: the roles of phonotactics and speech source. In *Proceedings of the First Meeting of the ACL Special Interest Group in Computational Phonology*, pages 83–90. Association for Computational Linguistics.

Catford, J. C. (1988). *Practical Introduction to Phonetics*. Oxford: Clarendon Press.

Charles-Luce, J. and Dinnsen, D. A. (1987). A reanalysis of Catalan voicing. *Journal of Phonetics*, 15, 187–90.

Chen, M. (1970). Vowel length variation as a function of the voicing of the consonant environment. *Phonetica*, 22, 129–59.

Chomsky, N. (1965). *Aspects of the Theory of Syntax*. Cambridge, MA: The MIT Press.

Chomsky, N. (1970). Remarks on nominalization. In Jacobs, R. A. and Rosenbaum, P. S. (eds.), *Readings in English Transformational Grammar*, pages 184–221. Waltham, Massachusetts: Blaisdell.

Chomsky, N. (1981). *Lectures on Government and Binding*. Dordrecht: Foris.

Chomsky, N. and Halle, M. (1968). *The Sound Pattern of English*. New York: Harper and Row.

Chung, H.-S. (1990). A phonological knowledge base system using unification-based formalism – a case study of Korean phonology. In Karlgren, H. (ed.), *Proceedings of the Thirteenth International Conference on Computational Linguistics*, volume 3, pages 76–8. International Committee on Computational Linguistics.

Church, K. W. (1987). *Phonological Parsing in Speech Recognition*. Kluwer.

Clements, G. N. (1985). The geometry of phonological features. In Ewen, C. and Anderson, J. (eds.), *Phonology Yearbook 2*, pages 225–52. Cambridge University Press.

Clements, G. N. (1991). Place of articulation in consonants and vowels: a unified theory. In Clements, G. N. and Hume, E. (eds.), *Phonetic and Phonological Studies on Vowel Features*, pages 77–123. Phonetics Laboratory, Cornell University.

Clements, G. N. and Keyser, S. J. (1983). *CV Phonology: A Generative Theory of the Syllable*. Cambridge, MA: The MIT Press.

Clocksin, W. F. and Mellish, C. S. (1981). *Programming in Prolog*. Springer-Verlag.

Cohn, A. C. (1989). Stress in Indonesian and bracketing paradoxes. *Natural Language and Linguistic Theory*, 7, 167–216.

Coleman, J. S. (1990). Unification phonology: another look at 'synthesis-by-rule'. In Karlgren, H. (ed.), *Proceedings of the Thirteenth International Conference on Computational Linguistics*, volume 3, pages 79–84. International Committee on Computational Linguistics.

Coleman, J. S. (1991). 'Phonological Representations – Their Names, Forms and Powers'. PhD thesis, University of York.

Coleman, J. S. (1992a). The phonetic interpretation of headed phonological structures containing overlapping constituents. *Phonology*, 9, 1–44.

Coleman, J. S. (1992b). 'Synthesis-by-rule' without segments or rewrite-rules. In Bailly, G., Benoît, C., and Sawallis, T. R. (eds.), *Talking Machines: Theories, Models, and Designs*, pages 43–60. Elsevier.

Coleman, J. S. (1993a). Declarative lexical phonology. In Katamba, F. and Durand, J. (eds.), *Frontiers of Phonology: Primitives, Architectures and Derivations*. London: Longman.

Coleman, J. S. (1993b). English word-stress in Unification-based Grammar. In Ellison, T. M. and Scobbie, J. M. (eds.), *Computational Phonology*, pages 97–106. Centre for Cognitive Science. Presented at the Fifteenth International Conference on Computational Linguistics, 1992, but omitted from the proceedings.

Coleman, J. S. and Local, J. (1991). The 'no crossing constraint' in autosegmental phonology. *Linguistics and Philosophy*, 14, 295–338.

Corina, D. P. (1991). 'Towards an Understanding of the Syllable: Evidence from Linguistic, Psychological, and Connectionist Investigations of Syllable Structure'. PhD thesis, University of California, San Diego.

Daelemans, W. (1987). 'Studies in Language Technology: An Object-Oriented Computer Model of Morphophonological Aspects of Dutch'. PhD thesis, University of Leuven.

Daelemans, W., Gillis, S., and Durieux, G. (1994). The acquisition of stress: a data-oriented approach. *Computational Linguistics*, 20, 421–51.

Davis, S. (1989). [Continuant] in feature geometry. *Lingua*, 78, 1–22.

Dennett, D. C. (1987). *The Intensional Stance*. Cambridge, MA: The MIT Press.

Dinnsen, D. A. (1985). A re-examination of phonological neutralization. *Journal of Linguistics*, 21, 265–79.

Dirksen, A. (1992). Accenting and deaccenting: a declarative approach. In *Proceedings of the Fifteenth International Conference on Computational Linguistics*, volume 3, pages 865–9. International Committee on Computational Linguistics.

Dirksen, A. (1993). Phrase structure phonology. In Ellison, T. M. and Scobbie, J. M. (eds.), *Computational Phonology*, pages 81–96. Centre for Cognitive Science.

Dogil, G. (1984). On the evaluation measure for prosodic phonology. *Linguistics*, 22, 281–311.

Dowty, D. R., Wall, R. E., and Peters, S. (1981). *Introduction to Montague Semantics*, volume 11 of *Studies in Linguistics and Philosophy*. Dordrecht: Reidel.

Dresher, B. E. (1981). Abstractness and explanation in phonology. In Hornstein, N. and Lightfoot, D. (eds.), *Explanation in Linguistics: The Logical Problem of Language Acquisition*. London: Longman.

Dresher, B. E. and Kaye, J. (1990). A computational learning model for metrical phonology. *Cognition*, 32, 137–95.

Eastlack, C. L. (1977). Iberochange: a program to simulate systematic sound change in Ibero-Romance. *Computers and the Humanities*, 11, 81–8.

Ellison, T. M. (1992a). Discovering vowel harmony. In Daelemans, W. and Powers, D. (eds.), *Background and Experiments in Machine Learning of Natural Language*, pages 131–6. Institute for Language Technology and Artificial Intelligence, Tilburg University.

Ellison, T. M. (1992b). 'Machine Learning of Phonological Structure'. PhD thesis, University of Western Australia.

Ellison, T. M. (1994a). Constraints, exceptions and representations. In *Proceedings of the First Meeting of the ACL Special Interest Group in Computational Phonology*, pages 25–32. Association for Computational Linguistics.

Ellison, T. M. (1994b). Phonological derivation in optimality theory. In *Proceedings of the Fifteenth International Conference on Computational Linguistics*, pages 1007–13. International Committee on Computational Linguistics.

Evans, R. and Gazdar, G. (1989a). Inference in DATR. In *Proceedings of the Fourth Meeting of the European Chapter of the Association for Computational Linguistics*, pages 66–71. Association for Computational Linguistics.

Evans, R. and Gazdar, G. (1989b). The semantics of DATR. In Cohn, A. C. (ed.), *Proceedings of the Seventh Conference of the Society for the Study of Artificial Intelligence and Simulation of Behaviour*, pages 79–87. London:Pitman.

Evans, R. and Gazdar, G. (eds.) (1990). *The DATR Papers: February 1990*. Cognitive Science Research Reports. University of Sussex.

Fenstad, J. E., Halvorsen, P.-K., Langholm, T., and van Benthem, J. (1987). *Situations, Language and Logic*, volume 34 of *Studies in Linguistics and Philosophy*. Reidel.

Firth, J. R. (1948). Sounds and prosodies. In *Papers in Linguistics 1934–1951*. London: Oxford University Press (1957).

Flickenger, D., Pollard, C., and Wasow, T. (1986). Structure-sharing in lexical representation. In *Proceedings of the Twenty-Third Annual Meeting of the Association for Computational Linguistics*, pages 262–7. Association for Computational Linguistics.

Foley, J. (1977). *Foundations of Theoretical Phonology*. Cambridge University Press.

Fowler, C. (1980). Coarticulation and theories of extrinsic timing. *Journal of Phonetics*, 8, 113–33.

Frege, G. (1892). On sense and reference. Reprinted in Geach, P. T. and Black, M. (eds.), *Translations from the Philosophical Writings of Gottlob Frege*. Oxford: Blackwell.

French, K. M. (1988). *Insights into Tagalog*, volume 84 of *Publications in Linguistics*. Summer Institute of Linguistics and University of Texas at Arlington.

Friedman, J. and Morin, Y. (1971). *Phonological Grammar Tester: Description*. Technical Report Natural Language Studies No. 9, University of Michigan Phonetics Laboratory.

Gasser, M. (1992a). Learning distributed representations for syllables. In *Proceedings of the Fourteenth Annual Conference of the Cognitive Science Society*, pages 396–401. Hillsdale NJ: Lawrence Erlbaum Associates.

Gasser, M. (1992b). Phonology as a byproduct of learning to recognize and produce words: a connectionist model. In *Proceedings of the Second International Conference on Spoken Language Processing*, pages 277–80. University of Alberta.

Gasser, M. and Lee, C.-D. (1989). *Networks that Learn Phonology*. Technical Report 300, Department of Computer Science, Indiana University.

Gasser, M. and Lee, C.-D. (1990). Networks that learn about phonological feature persistence. *Connection Science*, 2, 265–78.

Gasser, M. and Lee, C.-D. (1991). A short-term memory architecture for the learning of morphophonemic rules. In Lippmann, R. P., Moody, J. E., and Touretzky, D. S. (eds.), *Advances in Neural Information Processing Systems 3: The Collected Papers of the 1990 IEEE Conference on Neural Information Processing Systems*, pages 605–11. Morgan Kaufmann.

Gazdar, G. (1985). Review article: finite state morphology. *Linguistics*, 23, 597–607.

Gazdar, G., Klein, E. H., Pullum, G. K., and Sag, I. A. (1985). *Generalized Phrase Structure Grammar*. Oxford: Blackwell.

Gibbon, D. (1990). Prosodic association by template inheritance. In *International Workshop on Inheritance and Natural Language Processing*. Institute for Language Technology and AI, Tilburg University.

Gilbers, D. G. (1992). *Phonological Networks: A Theory of Segment Representation*, volume 3 of *Groningen Dissertations in Linguistics*. University of Groningen.

Goldsmith, J. A. (1976). 'Autosegmental Phonology'. PhD thesis, Massachusetts Institute of Technology. New York: Garland Publishing. (1979).

Goldsmith, J. A. (1989). Licensing, inalterability and harmonic rule application. In Wiltshire, C., Graczyk, R., and Music, B. (eds.), *Papers from the 25th Regional Meeting of the Chicago Linguistic Society*, pages 145–56. Chicago Linguistic Society.

Goldsmith, J. A. (1990). *Autosegmental and Metrical Phonology*. Oxford: Basil Blackwell.

Goldsmith, J. A. (1991). Phonology as an intelligent system. In Napoli, D. J. and Kegl, J. (eds.), *Bridge between Psychology and Linguistics: A Swarthmore Festschrift for Lila Gleitman*, pages 247–67. Lawrence Erlbaum.

Goldsmith, J. A. (1992). Grammar within a neural network. In *The Reality of Linguistic Rules, Proceedings of the Twenty-First Annual Linguistic Symposium*, University of Wisconsin, Milwaukee. To be published by Benjamins.

Goldsmith, J. A. (1993a). A dynamic computational theory of accent systems. In Kisseberth, C. W. and Cole, J. S. (eds.), *Perspectives in Phonology*. Center for the Study of Language and Information, Stanford University.

Goldsmith, J. A. (1993b). Harmonic phonology. In Goldsmith, J. A. (ed.), *The Last Phonological Rule: Reflections on Constraints and Derivations*, pages 21–60. The University of Chicago Press.

Goldsmith, J. A. (1993c). Local modelling in phonology. In Davis, S. (ed.), *Connectionism: Theory and Practice*, chapter 7, pages 229–46. Oxford University Press.

Goldsmith, J. A. and Larson, G. N. (1990). Local modeling and syllabification. In Ziolkowsky, M., Noske, M., and Deaton, K. (eds.), *Papers from the 26th Regional Meeting of the Chicago Linguistic Society, Volume 2: The Parasession on the Syllable in Phonetics and Phonology*, pages 129–41. Chicago Linguistic Society.

Goldsmith, J. A. and Larson, G. N. (1992). Using networks in a harmonic phonology. In Canakis, C., Chan, G., and Denton, J. (eds.), *Papers from the 28th Regional Meeting of the Chicago Linguistic Society*.

Greenberg, J. H. (1959). An axiomatization of the phonologic aspect of language. In Gross, L. (ed.), *Symposium on Sociological Theory*, pages 437–80. New York: Evanston.

Griffin, T. D. (1985). *Aspects of Dynamic Phonology*, volume 37 of *Amsterdam Studies in the Theory and History of Linguistic Science, Series IV, Current Issues in Linguistic Theory*. John Benjamins.

Griswold, W. (1992). The classic 10 multilingual computing problems. *Notes on Computing*, 11(5), 1–7. Summer Institute of Linguistics.

Gupta, P. and Touretzky, D. S. (1991). What a perceptron reveals about metrical phonology. In *Proceedings of the Thirteenth Annual Conference of the Cognitive Science Society*, pages 334–9. Hillsdale NJ: Lawrence Erlbaum Associates.

Gupta, P. and Touretzky, D. S. (1992). A connectionist learning approach to analyzing linguistic stress. In Moody, J., Hanson, S. J., and Lippmann, R. P. (eds.), *Advances in Neural Information Processing Systems 4*, pages 225–32. Morgan Kaufmann.

Gupta, P. and Touretzky, D. S. (1994). Connectionist models and linguistic theory: investigations of stress systems in language. *Cognitive Science*, 18, 1–50.

Gussmann, E. (1980). *Studies in Abstract Phonology*. Linguistic Inquiry Monograph Four. Cambridge MA: The MIT Press.

Gussmann, E. (1992). Resyllabification and delinking: the case of Polish devoicing. *Linguistic Inquiry*, 23, 29–56.

Hall, T. A. (1989). Lexical Phonology and the distribution of German [ç] and [x]. *Phonology*, 6, 1–17.

Halle, M. (1983). On distinctive features and their articulatory implementation. *Natural Language and Linguistic Theory*, 1, 91–105.

Halle, M. and Clements, G. N. (1983). *Problem Book in Phonology*. Cambridge MA: The MIT Press.

Hammond, M. (1988). On deriving the well-formedness condition. *Linguistic Inquiry*, 19, 319–25.

Hare, M. (1990). The role of similarity in Hungarian vowel harmony: a connectionist account. *Connection Science*, 2, 123–50.

Harrington, J. P. (1974). Sibilants in Ventureño. *International Journal of American Linguistics*, 40, 1–9.

Harris, J. (1978). Two theories of nonautomatic morphophonological alternations. *Language*, 54, 41–60.

Harris, Z. (1944). Simultaneous components in phonology. *Language*, 20, 181–205. Reprinted in M. Joos (ed.) (1957), *Readings in LinguisticsI : The Development of Descriptive Linguistics in America, 1925–56*, pages 124–38. The University of Chicago Press.

Hartman, S. L. (1981). A universal alphabet for experiments in comparative phonology. *Computers and the Humanities*, 15, 75–82.

Hayes, B. (1986a). Assimilation as spreading in Toba Batak. *Linguistic Inquiry*, 17, 467–99.

Hayes, B. (1986b). Inalterability in CV phonology. *Language*, 62, 321–51.

Hayes, B. (1989). Compensatory lengthening in moraic phonology. *Linguistic Inquiry*, 20, 253–306.

Hayes, B. (1990). Diphthongization and coindexing. *Phonology*, 7, 31–71.

Hertz, S. R. (1990). The Delta programming language: an integrated approach to nonlinear phonology, phonetics, and speech synthesis. In Kingston, J. and Beckman, M. E. (eds.), *Papers in Laboratory Phonology I: Between the Grammar and Physics of Speech*, chapter 13, pages 215–57. Cambridge University Press.

Hewson, J. (1974). Comparative reconstruction on the computer. In Anderson, J. M. and Jones, C. (eds.), *Proceedings of the First International Conference on Historical Linguistics*, pages 191–7. North Holland.

Hewson, J. (1989). Computer-aided research in comparative and historical linguistics. In Batori, I. S., Lenders, W., and Putschke, W. (eds.), *Computational Linguistics: An International Handbook on Computer Oriented Language Research and Applications*, pages 576–80. Berlin: de Gruyter.

Hockett, C. F. (1954). Two models of grammatical description. *Word*, 10, 210–31. (Reprinted in M. Joos (ed.) (1957), *Readings in Linguistics I: The Development of Descriptive Linguistics in America, 1925–56*, pages 386–99. The University of Chicago Press.

Hockett, C. F. (1955). *A Manual of Phonology*. Baltimore: Waverly Press.

Hoeksema, J. (1985). *Categorial Morphology*. New York: Garland Publishing.

Hoeksema, J. and Janda, R. (1988). Implications of process morphology for categorial grammar. In Oehrle, R. T., Bach, E., and Wheeler, D. W. (eds.), *Categorial Grammars and Natural Language Structures*, pages 199–247. Dordrecht: Reidel.

Hoekstra, T., van der Hulst, H., and Moortgat, M. (1980). Introduction. In Hoekstra, T., van der Hulst, H., and Moortgat, M. (eds.), *Lexical Grammar*, pages 1–48. Dordrecht: Foris.

Hooper, J. (1976). *An Introduction to Natural Generative Phonology*. New York: Academic Press.

Hudson, G. (1980). Automatic alternations in non-transformational phonology. *Language*, 56, 94–125.

Hughes, G. E. and Cresswell, M. J. (1968). *An Introduction to Modal Logic*. London: Methuen.

Hyman, L. M. (1986). The representation of multiple tone heights. In Bogers, K., van der Hulst, H., and Mous, M. (eds.), *The Phonological Representation of Suprasegmentals*, pages 109–52. Dordrecht: Foris.

Inkelas, S. (1989). 'Prosodic Constituency in the Lexicon'. PhD thesis, Stanford University.

Itô, J. (1986). 'Syllable Theory in Prosodic Phonology'. PhD thesis, University of Massachusetts. New York: Garland Publishing. (1988).

Itô, J. (1989). A prosodic theory of epenthesis. *Natural Language and Linguistic Theory*, 7, 217–59.

Iverson, G. K. (1989). On the category supralaryngeal. *Phonology*, 6, 285–303.

Jackendoff, R. (1975). Morphological and semantic regularities in the lexicon. *Language*, 51, 639–71.

Jaffar, J. and Lassez, J.-L. (1987). Constraint logic programming. In *Conference Record of the Fourteenth ACM Symposium on Principles of Programming Languages*, pages 111–19. Association for Computing Machinery.

Jaffar, J. and Michaylov, S. (1987). Methodology and implementation of a CLP system. In Lassez, J.-L. (ed.), *Logic Programming: Proceedings of the Fourth International Conference, Volume 1*, pages 196–218. Cambridge MA: The MIT Press.

Jensen, J. T. (1978). Review of J. Hooper (1976), *An Introduction to Generative Phonology*. *Language*, 54, 667–74.

Johnson, C. D. (1972). *Formal Aspects of Phonological Description*. The Hague: Mouton.

Johnson, M. (1984). A discovery procedure for certain phonological rules. In *Proceedings of the Tenth International Conference on Computational Linguistics/Twenty-Second Annual Conference of the Association for Computational Linguistics*, pages 344–7. Association for Computational Linguistics.

Johnson, M. (1988). *Attribute-Value Logic and the Theory of Grammar*, volume 16 of *CSLI Lecture Notes*. Center for the Study of Language and Information, Stanford University.

Johnson, M. (1990). Expressing disjunctive and negative feature constraints with classical first-order logic. In *Proceedings of the Twenty-Eighth Annual Meeting of the Association for Computational Linguistics*, pages 173–9. Association for Computational Linguistics.

Johnson, M. (1991). Features and formulae. *Computational Linguistics*, 17, 131–51.

Johnson, M. (1993). The complexity of inducing a rule from data. In *Proceedings of the West Coast Conference on Formal Linguistics*, pages 289–97. Stanford Linguistics Association.

Kahn, D. (1976). 'Syllable-Based Generalizations in English Phonology'. PhD thesis, University of Massachusetts. Reproduced by the Indiana University Linguistics Club.

Kaisse, E. M. (1992). Can [consonantal] spread? *Language*, 68, 313–32.

Kanerva, J. M. (1989). 'Focus and Phrasing in Chicheŵa Phonology'. PhD thesis, Stanford University.

Kaplan, R. M. and Bresnan, J. (1982). Lexical-Functional Grammar: A formal system for grammatical representation. In Bresnan, J. (ed.), *The Mental Representation of Grammatical Relations*, pages 173–281. Cambridge MA: The MIT Press.

Kaplan, R. M. and Kay, M. (1994). Regular models of phonological rule systems. *Computational Linguistics*, 20, 331–78.

Karttunen, L. (1986). *Radical Lexicalism*. Technical Report CSLI–86–68, Center for the Study of Language and Information, Stanford University.

Karttunen, L., Koskenniemi, K., and Kaplan, R. M. (1987). *A Compiler for Two-Level Phonological Rules*. Technical Report CSLI–87–108, Center for the Study of Language and Information, Stanford University.

Kasper, R. T. and Rounds, W. C. (1986). A logical semantics for feature structures. In *Proceedings of the Twenty-Fourth Annual Meeting of the Association for Computational Linguistics*, pages 257–66. Association for Computational Linguistics.

Kasper, R. T. and Rounds, W. C. (1990). The logic of unification in grammar. *Linguistics and Philosophy*, 13, 35–58.

Kay, M. (1983). When meta-rules are not meta-rules. In Sparck Jones, K. and Wilks, Y. (eds.), *Automatic Natural Language Parsing*, pages 94–116. Chichester: Ellis Horwood.

Kay, M. (1987). Nonconcatenative finite-state morphology. In *Proceedings of the Third Meeting of the European Chapter of the Association for Computational Linguistics*, pages 2–10. Association for Computational Linguistics.

Kaye, J. (1989). *Phonology: A Cognitive View*. New York: Erlbaum.

Kaye, J., Lowenstamm, J., and Vergnaud, J.-R. (1990). Constituent structure and government in phonology. *Phonology*, 7, 193–231.

Keating, P. (1984). Phonetic and phonological representation of stop consonant voicing. *Language*, 60, 286–319.

Keating, P. (1990). Phonetic representations in a generative grammar. *Journal of Phonetics*, 18, 321–34.

Kiparsky, P. (1968). Linguistic universals and linguistic change. In Bach, E. and Harms, R. (eds.), *Universals in Linguistic Theory*, pages 170–210. New York: Holt, Rinehart & Winston.

Kiparsky, P. (1973). Elsewhere in phonology. In Anderson, S. and Kiparsky, P. (eds.), *A Festschrift for Morris Halle*, pages 93–106. New York: Holt, Rinehart & Winston.

Kiparsky, P. (1982). From cyclic to lexical phonology. In van der Hulst, H. and Smith, N. (eds.), *The Structure of Phonological Representations*, volume 1 pages 131–75. Dordrecht: Foris.

Kisseberth, C. W. (1970). On the functional unity of phonological rules. *Linguistic Inquiry*, 1, 291–306.

Klein, E. (1991). Phonological data types. In Klein, E. and Veltman, F. (eds.), *Natural Language and Speech*, Basic Research Series. Springer-Verlag. Also appeared in S. Bird (ed), *Declarative Perspectives on Phonology*, pages 127–38, University of Edinburgh.

Klein, E. (1992). Data types in computational phonology. In *Proceedings of the Fifteenth International Conference on Computational Linguistics*, pages 149–55. International Committee on Computational Linguistics.

Kornai, A. (1991). 'Formal Phonology'. PhD thesis, Stanford University. To be published by Garland Publishing.

Koskenniemi, K. (1983a). Two-level model for morphological analysis. In *Proceedings of the Eighth International Joint Conference on Artificial Intelligence*, pages 683–5. Morgan Kaufmann.

Koskenniemi, K. (1983b). 'Two-Level Morphology: A General Computational Model for Word-Form Recognition and Production'. PhD thesis, University of Helsinki.

Koskenniemi, K. (1984). A general computational model for word-form recognition and production. In *Proceedings of the Tenth International Conference on Computational Linguistics/Twenty-Second Annual Conference of the Association for Computational Linguistics*, pages 178–81. Association for Computational Linguistics.

Koskenniemi, K. (1985). Compilation of automata from morphological two-level rules. In *Papers from the Fifth Scandinavian Conference of Computational Linguistics*, pages 143–9. University of Helsinki. Publication 15.

Koutsoudas, A. (1972). The strict order fallacy. *Language*, 48, 88–96.

Koutsoudas, A., Sanders, G., and Noll, C. (1974). The application of phonological rules. *Language*, 50, 1–28.

Laks, B. (1995). A connectionist account of French syllabification. *Lingua*. Forthcoming in Special Issue edited by J. Durand.

Larson, G. N. (1990). Local computational networks and the distribution of segments in the Spanish syllable. In Ziolkowsky, M., Noske, M., and Deaton, K. (eds.), *Papers from the 26th Regional Meeting of the Chicago Linguistic Society, Volume 2: The Parasession on the Syllable in Phonetics and Phonology*, pages 257–72. Chicago Linguistic Society.

Larson, G. N. (1992). 'Dynamic Computational Networks and the Representation of Phonological Information'. PhD thesis, University of Chicago.

Lass, R. (1976). *English Phonology and Phonological Theory, Synchronic and Diachronic Studies.* Cambridge University Press.

Lathroum, A. (1989). Feature encoding by neural nets. *Phonology*, 6, 305–16.

Leben, W. R. (1973). 'Suprasegmental Phonology'. PhD thesis, Massachusetts Institute of Technology.

Liberman, M. Y. (1994). Commentary on Kaplan and Kay. *Computational Linguistics*, 20, 379.

Lieber, R. (1987). *An Integrated Theory of Autosegmental Processes.* SUNY Series in Linguistics. State University of New York Press.

Lifschitz, V. (1984). Some results on circumscription. In *Proceedings of the Non-Monotonic Reasoning Workshop*, pages 151–64. American Association for Artificial Intelligence.

Lisker, L. (1986). "Voicing" in English: a catalogue of acoustic features signaling /b/ versus /p/ in trochees. *Language and Speech*, 29, 3–11.

Lodge, K. (1992). Assimilation, deletion paths and underspecification. *Journal of Linguistics*, 28, 13–52.

Lowe, J. B. and Mazaudon, M. (1989). Computerized tools for reconstructions in Tibeto-Burman. In *Proceedings of the Fifteenth Annual Meeting of the Berkeley Linguistics Society*, pages 367–78. Berkeley Linguistics Society, University of California at Berkeley.

Lowe, J. B. and Mazaudon, M. (1994). The Reconstruction Engine: a computer implementation of the comparative method. *Computational Linguistics*, 20, 381–417.

Marsack, C. C. (1962). *Samoan, A Complete Introductory Course.* Hodder and Stoughton.

Mastroianni, M. (1993). *Attribute Logic Phonology.* CMU-LCL 93-4, Carnegie Mellon University.

Mastroianni, M. and Carpenter, B. (1994). Constraint-based morpho-phonology. In *Proceedings of the First Meeting of the ACL Special Interest Group in Computational Phonology*, pages 13–24.

Maxwell, M. (1991). Phonological analysis and opaque rule orders. In *Proceedings of the Second International Workshop on Parsing Technologies*, pages 110–16. Computer Science Department, Carnegie Mellon University.

Maxwell, M. (1994). Parsing using linearly ordered phonological rules. In *Proceedings of the First Meeting of the ACL Special Interest Group in Computational Phonology*, pages 59–70. Association for Computational Linguistics.

McCarthy, J. (1984). Theoretical consequences of Montañes vowel harmony. *Linguistic Inquiry*, 15, 291–318.

McCarthy, J. (1986). OCP effects: gemination and antigemination. *Linguistic Inquiry*, 17, 207–63.

McCarthy, J. (1988). Feature geometry and dependency: a review. *Phonetica*, 43, 84–108.

McCarthy, J. (1991). Synchronic rule inversion. In *Proceedings of the Seventeenth Annual Meeting of the Berkeley Linguistics Society*, pages 192–207. Berkeley Linguistics Society, University of California at Berkeley.

McCarthy, J. and Prince, A. (1989). Prosodic morphology and templatic morphology. In Eid, M. and McCarthy, J. (eds.), *Proceedings of the Second Annual Symposium on Arabic Linguistics*, pages 1–54. Amsterdam: John Benjamins.

Minker, J. (1987). *Foundations of Deductive Databases and Logic Programming*. Kaufmann.

Moortgat, M. (1988). 'Categorial Investigations: Logical and Linguistic Aspects of the Lambek Calculus'. PhD thesis, Amsterdam University.

Moortgat, M. and Morrill, G. (1993). Heads and phrases, type calculus for dependency and constituent structure. Submitted to *Journal of Logic, Language and Information*.

Nolan, F. (1986). The implications of partial assimilation and incomplete neutralisation. In Hawkins, S. (ed.), *Cambridge Papers in Phonetics and Experimental Linguistics*, volume 5. University of Cambridge, Department of Linguistics.

Nolan, F. (1992). The descriptive role of segments: evidence from assimilation. In Docherty, G. J. and Ladd, D. R. (eds.), *Papers in Laboratory Phonology II: Gesture, Segment, Prosody*, chapter 10, pages 261–80. Cambridge University Press.

Odden, D. (1991). Vowel geometry. *Phonology*, 8, 261–89.

Oehrle, R. T. (1991). Prosodic constraints on dynamic grammatical analysis. In Bird, S. (ed.), *Declarative Perspectives on Phonology*, pages 167–95. University of Edinburgh.

Oehrle, R. T., Bach, E., and Wheeler, D. W. (eds.) (1988). *Categorial Grammars and Natural Language Structures*, volume 32 of *Studies in Linguistics and Philosophy*. Dordrecht: Reidel.

Orgun, C. O. (1993). Monotonic cyclicity and optimality theory. In *Proceedings of the Twenty-Fourth Meeting of the North East Linguistic Society*. Graduate Linguistic Student Association, University of Massachusetts at Amherst.

Paradis, C. (1988). On constraints and repair strategies. *The Linguistic Review*, 6, 71–97.

Paradis, C. and Prunet, J.-F. (1989). On coronal transparency. *Phonology*, 6, 317–48.

Partee, B. H. (1979). Montague grammar and the well-formedness constraint. In Heny, F. and Schnelle, H. (eds.), *Syntax and Semantics 10: Selections from the Third Groningen Round Table*, pages 275–313. New York: Academic Press.

Payne, D. L. (1981). *The Phonology and Morphology of Axininca Campa*, volume 66 of *Summer Institute of Linguistics Publications in Linguistics*. Summer Institute of Linguistics and University of Texas at Arlington.

Penn, G. and Thomason, R. (1994). Default finite state machines and finite state phonology. In *Proceedings of the First Meeting of the ACL Special Interest Group in Computational Phonology*, pages 33–41. Association for Computational Linguistics.

Pereira, F. C. N. and Shieber, S. M. (1987). *Prolog and Natural Language Analysis*, volume 10 of *CSLI Lecture Notes*. Center for the Study of Language and Information, Stanford University.

Pereira, F. C. N. and Warren, D. H. D. (1980). Definite Clause Grammars for language analysis – a survey of the formalism and a comparison with Augmented Transition Grammars. *Artificial Intelligence*, 13, 231–78.

Pierrehumbert, J. B. (1990). Phonological and phonetic representation. *Journal of Phonetics*, 18, 375–94.

Pierrehumbert, J. B. and Beckman, M. E. (1988). *Japanese Tone Structure*. Linguistic Inquiry Monograph Fifteen. Cambridge MA: The MIT Press.

Piggott, G. L. (1980). Implications of linguistic change for concrete phonology. *Canadian Journal of Linguistics*, 25, 1–19.

Piggott, G. L. (1987). On the autonomy of the feature nasal. In Bosch, A., Need, B., and Schiller, E. (eds.), *23rd Annual Regional Meeting of the Chicago Linguistics Society. Part Two: Parasession on Autosegmental and Metrical Phonology*, pages 223–38. Chicago Linguistic Society.

Piggott, G. L. (1992). Variability in feature dependency: the case of nasality. *Natural Language and Linguistic Theory*, 10, 33–77.

Pike, K. L. and Pike, E. V. (1947). Immediate constituents of Mazateco syllables. *International Journal of American Linguistics*, 13, 78–91.

Pollard, C. and Sag, I. (1987). *Information-Based Syntax and Semantics*, volume 13 of *CSLI Lecture Notes*. Center for the Study of Language and Information, Stanford University.

Port, R. and Crawford, P. (1989). Incomplete neutralization and pragmatics in German. *Journal of Phonetics*, 17, 257–82.

Poser, W. (1982). Phonological representation and action-at-a-distance. In van der Hulst, H. and Smith, N. (eds.), *The Structure of Phonological Representations*, volume 2 pages 121–58. Dordrecht: Foris.

Powers, D. M. W. (1991). How far can self-organization go? Results in unsupervised language learning. In Powers, D. M. W. and Reeker, L. (eds.), *Working Notes, AAAI Spring Symposium on the Machine Learning of Natural Language and Ontology*, pages 131–6. American Association for Artificial Intelligence.

Prince, A. S. (1985). Improving tree theory. In Niepokuj, M., van Clay, M., Nikiforidou, V., and Feder, D. (eds.), *Proceedings of the Eleventh Annual Meeting of the Berkeley Linguistics Society*, pages 471–90. Berkeley Linguistics Society, University of California at Berkeley.

Prince, A. S. (1990). Quantitative consequences of rhythmic organization. In Ziolkowsky, M., Noske, M., and Deaton, K. (eds.), *Papers from the 26th Regional Meeting of the Chicago Linguistic Society, Volume 2: The Parasession on the Syllable in Phonetics and Phonology*, pages 355–98. Chicago Linguistic Society.

Prince, A. S. (1993). *In Defense of the Number i: Anatomy of a Linear Dynamical Model of Linguistic Generalizations*. Technical Report 1, Center for Cognitive Science, Rutgers University.

Prince, A. S. and Smolensky, P. (1993). *Optimality Theory: Constraint Interaction in Generative Grammar*. Technical Report 2, Center for Cognitive Science, Rutgers University. To appear, Cambridge MA: The MIT Press.

Pulleyblank, D. (1986). *Tone in Lexical Phonology*. Studies in Natural Language and Linguistic Theory. Dordrecht: Reidel.

Pullum, G. K. (1976). *Rule Interaction and the Organization of a Grammar*. New York: Garland Publishing.

Pulman, S. G. and Hepple, M. R. (1993). A feature-based formalism for two-level phonology: a description and implementation. *Computer Speech and Language*, 7, 333–58.

Pye, S. (1986). Word-final devoicing of obstruents in Russian. In Hawkins, S. (ed.), *Cambridge Papers in Phonetics and Experimental Linguistics*, volume 5. University of Cambridge, Department of Linguistics.

Reinhard, S. and Gibbon, D. (1991). Prosodic inheritance and morphological generalizations. In *Proceedings of the Fifth Conference of the European Chapter of the Association for Computational Linguistics*, pages 131–6. Association for Computational Linguistics.

Reiter, R. (1980). A logic for default reasoning. *Artificial Intelligence*, 13, 81–132.

Rice, K. (1989). On eliminating resyllabification into onsets. *Proceedings of the West Coast Conference on Formal Linguistics*, 8, 331–46.

Ringen, C. (1972). On arguments for rule ordering. *Foundations of Language*, 8, 266–73.

Ristad, E. S. (1990). Computational structure of generative phonology and its relation to language comprehension. In *Proceedings of the Twenty Eighth Annual Meeting of the Association for Computational Linguistics*, pages 235–42. Association for Computational Linguistics.

Ristad, E. S. (1992). *Complexity of the Simplified Segmental Phonology*. Technical Report CS-388-92, Princeton University.

Ritchie, G. D. (1992). Languages generated by two-level morphological rules. *Computational Linguistics*, 18, 41–59.

Ritchie, G. D., Russell, G. J., Black, A. W., and Pulman, S. G. (1992). *Computational Morphology: Practical Mechanisms for the English Lexicon*. Cambridge MA: The MIT Press.

Roosen-Runge, P. H. and Kaye, J. (1973). *A User's Guide to the Phonological Calculator*. Technical Report Linguistic Series No. 2, Center for Linguistic Studies, University of Toronto.

Rounds, W. C. and Manaster Ramer, A. (1987). A logical version of functional grammar. In *Proceedings of the Twenty-Fifth Annual Meeting of the Association for Computational Linguistics*, pages 89–96. Association for Computational Linguistics.

Russell, K. (1993). 'A Constraint-Based Approach to Phonology'. PhD thesis, University of Southern California.

Ryle, G. (1949). *The Concept of Mind*. London: Hutchinson.

Sagey, E. (1986). 'The Representation of Features and Relations in Non-Linear Phonology'. PhD thesis, Massachusetts Institute of Technology.

Sagey, E. (1988). On the ill-formedness of crossing association lines. *Linguistic Inquiry*, 19, 109–18.

Schane, S. A. (1973). *Generative Phonology*. Foundations of Modern Linguistics. Englewood Cliffs, NJ: Prentice Hall.

Schein, B. and Steriade, D. (1986). On geminates. *Linguistic Inquiry*, 17, 691–744.

Schmerling, S. (1983). Montague morphophonemics. In Richardson, J. F., Marks, M., and Chukerman, A. (eds.), *Papers from the Parasession on the Interplay of Phonology, Morphology and Syntax*, pages 222–37. Chicago Linguistic Society.

Schmiedel, A. (1988). *Temporal Constraint Networks*. KIT–Report 69, Technical University, Berlin.

Scobbie, J. M. (1991a). 'Attribute-Value Phonology'. PhD thesis, University of Edinburgh.

Scobbie, J. M. (1991b). Towards declarative phonology. In Bird, S. (ed.), *Declarative Perspectives on Phonology*, pages 1–26. University of Edinburgh.

Scobbie, J. M. (1993a). Constraint violation and conflict from the perspective of declarative phonology. *Canadian Journal of Linguistics*, 38, 155–67.

Scobbie, J. M. (1993b). Formal geminate integrity: an OCP approach. In *Proceedings of the Fourth Western Conference on Linguistics*. Simon Fraser University.

Scobbie, J. M. (1993c). Licensing and inalterability in Tiberian Hebrew. In Canakis, C., Chan, G., and Denton, J. (eds.), *Proceedings of the Twenty-Eighth Annual Regional Meeting of the Chicago Linguistic Society*, pages 457–71. Chicago Linguistic Society.

Selkirk, E. O. (1982). The syllable. In van der Hulst, H. and Smith, N. (eds.), *The Structure of Phonological Representations*, volume 2 pages 337–83. Dordrecht: Foris.

Selkirk, E. O. (1984). *Phonology and Syntax*. Cambridge MA: The MIT Press.

Shibatani, M. (1973). The role of surface phonetic constraints in generative phonology. *Language*, 49, 87–106.

Shieber, S. (1986). *An Introduction to Unification-Based Approaches to Grammar*, volume 4 of *CSLI Lecture Notes*. Center for the Study of Language and Information, Stanford University.

Shieber, S., Uszkoreit, H., Pereira, F. C. N., Robinson, J. J., and Tyson, M. (1983). The formalism and implementation of PATR-II. In Grosz, B. and Stickel, M. E. (eds.), *Research on Interactive Acquisition and Use of Knowledge*, pages 39–79. SRI International.

Shillcock, R., Levy, J., Lindsey, G., Cairns, P., and Chater, N. (1993). Connectionist modelling of phonological space. In Ellison, T. M. and Scobbie, J. M. (eds.), *Computational Phonology*, pages 157–78. Centre for Cognitive Science.

Shillcock, R., Lindsey, G., Levy, J., and Chater, N. (1992). A phonologically motivated input representation for the modelling of auditory word perception in continuous speech. In *Proceedings of the Fourteenth Annual Conference of the Cognitive Science Society*, pages 408–13., Bloomington. Hillsdale NJ: Lawrence Erlbaum Associates.

Slowiaczek, L. M. and Dinnsen, D. A. (1985). On the neutralizing status of Polish word-final devoicing. *Journal of Phonetics*, 13, 325–41.

Slowiaczek, L. M. and Szymanska, H. J. (1989). Perception of word-final devoicing in Polish. *Journal of Phonetics*, 17, 205–12.

Smith, N. (1988). Consonant place features. In van der Hulst, H. and Smith, N. (eds.), *Features, Segmental Structure and Harmony Processes*, volume 1 pages 209–35. Dordrecht: Foris.

Smolka, G. (1992). Feature constraint logics for unification grammars. *Journal of Logic Programming*, 12, 51–87.

Snider, K. L. (1990). Tonal upstep in Krachi: evidence for a register tier. *Language*, 66, 453–74.

Sprigg, R. (1965). Prosodic analysis and Burmese syllable-initial features. *Anthropological Linguistics*, 7, 59–81.

Sproat, R. (1992). *Morphology and Computation*. Natural Language Processing. Cambridge MA: The MIT Press.

Stanley, R. (1967). Redundancy rules in phonology. *Language*, 43, 393–436.

Steedman, M. (1990). Intonation and structure in spoken language understanding. In *Proceedings of the Twenty-Eighth Annual Meeting of the Association for Computational Linguistics*, pages 9–16. Association for Computational Linguistics.

Steedman, M. (1991). Structure and intonation. *Language*, 67, 260–96.

Steriade, D. (1982). 'Greek Prosodies and the Nature of Syllabification'. PhD thesis, Massachusetts Institute of Technology.

Steriade, D. (1987). Locality conditions and feature geometry. In McDonough, J. and Plunkett, B. (eds.), *Proceedings of the Seventeenth Meeting of the North East Linguistic Society*, pages 595–617. Graduate Linguistic Student Association, University of Massachusetts at Amherst.

Steriade, D. (1988). Greek accent: a case for preserving structure. *Linguistic Inquiry*, 19, 271–314.

Stethem, S. E. (1991). Explanation-based learning from rule-governed features in phonological representations. In Powers, D. M. W. and Reeker, L. (eds.), *Working Notes, AAAI Spring Symposium on The Machine Learning of Natural Language and Ontology*, pages 169–73. American Association for Artificial Intelligence.

Swadesh, M. (1934). The phonemic principle. *Language*, 10, 117–29. Reprinted in M. Joos (ed.) (1957), *Readings in Linguistics I: The Development of Descriptive Linguistics in America, 1925–56*, pages 32–7. The University of Chicago Press.

Taylor, B. (1977). Tense and continuity. *Linguistics and Philosophy*, 1, 199–220.

Thráinsson, H. (1978). On the phonology of Icelandic preaspiration. *Nordic Journal of Linguistics*, 1, 3–54.

Tjong Kim Sang, E. F. (1993). Acquiring digital phonology. In Sijtsma, W. and Zweekhorst, O. (eds.), *Computational Linguistics in the Netherlands*, pages 121–32. Institute for Language Technology and Artificial Intelligence, Tilburg University.

Touretzky, D. S. (1989). *Rules and Maps in Connectionist Symbol Processing.* Technical Report CMU-CS-89-158, Carnegie Mellon University.

Touretzky, D. S. and Wheeler, D. W. (1990). A computational basis for phonology. In Touretzky, D. S. (ed.), *Advances in Neural Information Processing Systems 2: The Collected Papers of the 1989 IEEE Conference on Neural Information Processing Systems*, pages 372–9. Morgan Kaufmann.

Touretzky, D. S. and Wheeler, D. W. (1991). Sequence manipulation using parallel mapping networks. *Neural Computation*, 3, 98–109.

Touretzky, D. S., Wheeler, D. W., and Elvgren, G. (1990a). *Rules and Maps II: Recent Progress in Connectionist Symbol Processing.* Technical Report CMU-CS-90-112, Carnegie-Mellon University.

Touretzky, D. S., Wheeler, D. W., and Elvgren, G. (1990b). *Rules and Maps III: Further Progress in Connectionist Phonology.* Technical Report CMU-CS-90-138, Carnegie-Mellon University.

Trigo, L. (1991). On pharynx-larynx interactions. *Phonology*, 8, 113–36.

Uszkoreit, H. (1986). Categorial unification grammars. In *Proceedings of the Eleventh International Conference on Computational Linguistics*, pages 187–94. International Committee on Computational Linguistics.

Vago, R. M. (1988). Underspecification in the height harmony system of Pasiego. *Phonology*, 5, 343–62.

van Benthem, J. (1983). *The Logic of Time: A Model-Theoretic Investigation into the Varieties of Temporal Ontology and Temporal Discourse*, volume 156 of *Synthese Library*. Dordrecht: Reidel.

van Benthem, J. (1988). *A Manual of Intensional Logic (Second Edition).* Center for the Study of Language and Information, Stanford University.

van der Hulst, H. (1988). The geometry of vocalic features. In van der Hulst, H. and Smith, N. (eds.), *Features, Segmental Structure and Harmony Processes*, volume 2 pages 77–125. Dordrecht: Foris.

van der Hulst, H. (1991). *The Molecular Structure of Phonological Segments.* Department of Linguistics, University of Leiden.

van der Linden, E.-J. (1991). Accent placement and focus in categorial logic. In Bird, S. (ed.), *Declarative Perspectives on Phonology*, pages 197–217. University of Edinburgh.

Vennemann, T. (1972). Phonological uniqueness in natural generative grammar. *Glossa*, 6, 105–16.

Vennemann, T. (1974). Words and syllables in natural generative grammar. In Bruck, A., Fox, R. A., and La Galy, M. W. (eds.), *Papers from the Parasession on Natural Phonology*, pages 346–74. Chicago Linguistic Society.

Vennemann, T. (1988). *Preference Laws for Syllable Structure and the Explanation of Sound Change.* Berlin: Mouton de Gruyter.

Vincent, N. (1986). Constituency and syllable structure. In Durand, J. (ed.), *Dependency and Non-Linear Phonology*, pages 305–18. London: Croom Helm.

Waksler, R. (1990). 'A formal account of glide/vowel alternations in prosodic theory'. PhD thesis, Harvard University.

Walli-Sagey, E. (1986). On the representation of complex segments and their formation in Kinyarwanda. In Wetzels, L. and Sezer, E. (eds.), *Studies in Compensatory Lengthening*, pages 251–95. Dordrecht: Foris.

Walther, M. (1992). 'Deklarative Silbifizierung in einem Constraintbasierten Grammatikformalismus'. Master's thesis, University of Stuttgart.

Walther, M. (1993). Declarative syllabification with applications to German. In Ellison, T. M. and Scobbie, J. M. (eds.), *Computational Phonology*, pages 55–79. University of Edinburgh.

Wang, W. (1967). Phonological features of tone. *International Journal of American Linguistics*, 33, 93–105.

Welmers, W. E. (1973). *African Language Structures*. University of California Press.

Wheeler, D. W. (1981). 'Aspects of a Categorial Theory of Phonology'. PhD thesis, University of Massachusetts at Amherst.

Wheeler, D. W. (1988). Consequences of some categorially motivated phonological assumptions. In Oehrle, R. T., Bach, E., and Wheeler, D. W. (eds.), *Categorial Grammars and Natural Language Structures*, pages 467–88. Dordrecht: Reidel.

Wheeler, D. W. and Touretzky, D. (1990). From syllables to stress: a cognitively plausible model. In Ziolkowsky, M., Noske, M., and Deaton, K. (eds.), *Papers from the 26th Regional Meeting of the Chicago Linguistic Society, Volume 2: The Parasession on the Syllable in Phonetics and Phonology*, pages 413–27. Chicago Linguistic Society.

Wheeler, D. W. and Touretzky, D. (1993). A connectionist implementation of cognitive phonology. In Goldsmith, J. A. (ed.), *The Last Phonological Rule: Reflections on Constraints and Derivations*, pages 146–72. The University of Chicago Press.

Wiebe, B. (1992). 'Modelling Autosegmental Phonology with Multi-Tape Finite State Transducers'. Master's thesis, Simon Fraser University.

Wiese, R. (1990). Towards a unification-based phonology. In Karlgren, H. (ed.), *Proceedings of the Thirteenth International Conference on Computational Linguistics*, volume 3, pages 283–6. International Committee on Computational Linguistics.

Williams, S. M. (1991). *Lexical Phonology: a Computational System*. Technical Report CS-91-03, Department of Computer Science, University of Sheffield.

Williams, S. M. (1993). 'LexPhon: A Computational Implementation of Lexical Phonology'. PhD thesis, University of Reading.

Williams, S. M. (1994). Lexical phonology and speech style: using a model to test a theory. In *Proceedings of the First Meeting of the ACL Special Interest Group in Computational Phonology*, pages 43–57.

Williams, S. M., Biggs, C., and Brasington, R. W. P. (1989). A computational implementation of aspects of lexical phonology. *Communication & Cognition – Artificial Intelligence*, 6, 27–33.

Winograd, T. (1975). Frame representations and the declarative/procedural controversy. In Bobrow, D. G. and Collins, A. (eds.), *Representation and Understanding – Studies in Cognitive Science*, pages 185–210. New York: Academic Press.

Withgott, M. M. and Chen, F. R. (1993). *Computational Models of American Speech*, volume 32 of *CSLI Lecture Notes*. Center for the Study of Language and Information, Stanford University.

Yip, M. (1988). The Obligatory Contour Principle and phonological rules: a loss of identity. *Linguistic Inquiry*, 19, 65–100.

Yip, M. (1989a). Contour tones. *Phonology*, 6, 149–74.

Yip, M. (1989b). Feature geometry and cooccurrence restrictions. *Phonology*, 6, 349–74.

Language index

Acoma (Western Keres Pueblo; New Mexico, USA), 114f
Arabic (Semitic, Afro-Asiatic), 45, 161
Axininca (Arawakan; Peru), 94
Catalan (Romance, Indo-European; Spain), 99f
Chicheŵa (Bantu; Malawi, Zambia, Zimbabwe), 48
Chumash (Hokan; California, USA; extinct in 1965), 104–6
Dutch (Western Germanic, Indo-European), 45
English (Western Germanic, Indo-European), 4–7, 15, 42, 92, 95, 97–9, 113, 117, 120, 130
Finnish (Uralic), 15
French (Romance, Indo-European), 103
Fula (West Atlantic, Niger-Congo; West Africa), 62
German (Western Germanic, Indo-European), 45, 99f
Hāṛautī (Rajasthani, Indo-Aryan; India), 44
Icelandic (Scandinavian, Germanic; Iceland), 113f
Indonesian (Indonesian, Austronesian; Indonesia), 20
Japanese, 53, 100
Kikuyu (Bantu; Kenya), 45
Kinyarwanda (Bantu; Rwanda, Uganda, Zaire, Tanzania), 119, 121
Klamath (Penutian; USA), 2, 112, 114f
Korean, 42
Kpelle (Mande; Liberia, Guinea), 118, 128f
Margi (Chadic; Nigeria), 119
Polish (Slavic, Indo-European), 99f
Proto-Indo-Iranian, 112
Russian (Slavic, Indo-European), 42, 100
Samoan (Polynesian, Austronesian; Samoa, New Zealand, Hawaii), 93–5
Sierra Miwok (USA; probably extinct), 48
Spanish (Romance, Indo-European), 104f
Tagalog (Indonesian, Austronesian; Philippines, Guam), 94
Thai (Sino-Tibetan; Thailand, Singapore), 112
Turkish (Altaic), 7–10, 15–17, 24, 38, 100–4
Yoruba (Kwa; Nigeria, Benin, Togo), 36, 93, 119
Zulu (Bantu; South Africa), 119

Name index

Albro, Daniel M., 27
Allen, James F., 15, 68, 139
Anderson, John M., 10
Anderson, Stephen R., 1f, 37, 39
Antworth, Evan, 16f
Archangeli, Diana, 27, 36, 45, 84f, 93
Árnason, Kristján, 113f
Avery, Peter, 85, 106, 116

Bach, Emmon, 2, 32, 34, 40ff
Batóg, Tadeusz, 52
Bear, John, 2
Beckman, Mary E., 52, 57, 160
Bellgard, Matthew I., 24
Belnap, N.D., 137
Bennett, M., 71
Biggs, C., 26
Bird, Steven G., 3, 14, 18, 26, 31f, 42, 45f, 48, 51, 63, 84f, 92, 162
Black, Alan W., 16
Blackburn, Patrick, 45, 162, 166
Bloch, Bernard, 52
Bloomfield, Leonard, 36, 52, 109
Bobrow, Robert, 14f, 35
Boley, Harold, 29
Boolos, George S., 81
Bouma, Gosse, 27, 45
Brandon, Frank R., 26f
Bresnan, Joan, 35
Broe, Michael, 44, 65, 111
Bromberger, Sylvain, 29
Browman, Catherine, 4, 81, 98, 110, 123, 125, 127ff, 154
Bruck, Anthony, 37

Cahill, Lynne J., 45

Calder, Jonathan, 3, 29, 45, 87
Carpenter, Bob, 29, 60, 158
Carson, Julie, 44
Catford, John C., 113, 129
Charles-Luce, Jan, 100
Chater, Nicholas, 22
Chen, Matthew, 18, 99
Chomsky, Noam, 1, 32f, 35, 37, 86, 109
Chung, Hee-Sung, 44
Church, Kenneth W., 26
Clements, George N., 2, 55, 57, 62, 66, 109ff, 121, 123, 157
Clocksin, William F., 146, 150
Cohn, Abigail C., 20
Coleman, John S., 26, 32, 44, 63, 65, 70, 85, 100
Crawford, Penny, 100
Cresswell, Max J., 162

Daelemans, Walter, 26, 45
Davis, Stuart, 116
Dennett, Daniel C., 33
Dinnsen, Daniel A., 99f
Dogil, Grzegorz, 42
Dowty, David R., 40
Dresher, B. Elan., 26, 39, 98f
Durand, Jacques, 10

Eastlack, Charles L., 26
Ellison, T. Mark, 18, 21, 24ff, 36, 46, 48
Evans, Roger, 45

Fenstad, Jens Erik, 30
Firth, John Rupert, 10
Flickenger, Dan, 35

Foley, J., 5
Fowler, Carol, 110
Fox, Robert A., 37
Fraser, J. Bruce, 14f
Frege, Gottlob, 32
French, Koleen Matsuda, 94
Friedman, J., 14

Gasser, Michael, 22–4
Gazdar, Gerald, 3, 15, 29, 35, 45, 79, 117
Gibbon, Dafydd, 45
Gilbers, Dirk G., 27
Goldsmith, John A., 10, 12, 19–21, 25, 48, 61, 63, 84, 113, 123
Goldstein, Louis, 4, 81, 98, 110, 123, 125, 127ff, 154
Greenberg, Joseph H., 52
Griffin, Toby D., 10
Griswold, William, 14
Gupta, Prahlad, 24
Gussmann, Edmund, 39, 99

Hall, Tracy Alan, 84
Halle, Morris, 1f, 29, 32, 37, 86, 109, 118f
Halvorsen, Per-Kristian, 30
Hammond, Michael, 71, 77
Hare, Mary, 22
Harrington, John P., 106
Harris, James, 39
Harris, Zellig, 10
Hartman, Steven Lee, 26
Hayes, Bruce, 44, 56, 59, 63, 74, 77, 113ff
Hepple, Mark R., 16, 44
Hertz, Susan R., 26, 70
Hewson, John, 26
Hockett, Charles F., 10, 31, 40
Hoeksema, Jack, 36, 40, 42, 155
Hoekstra, Teun, 35
Hooper, Joan, 2, 39
Hudson, Grover, 39, 93
Hughes, G. E., 162
Hyman, Larry M., 112

Inkelas, Sharon, 31

Itô, Junko, 63f, 76
Iverson, Gregory K., 113ff

Jackendoff, Ray, 35f
Jaffar, Joxan, 135, 151
Jakobson, Roman, 109
Janda, Richard, 40, 42, 155
Jeffrey, Richard C., 81
Jensen, John T., 39
Johnson, C. Douglas, 16
Johnson, Mark, 26, 29, 51, 80, 88f, 139, 144, 153, 158
Jones, Daniel, 109

Kahn, Daniel, 99
Kaisse, Ellen M., 116
Kanerva, Jonni Miikka, 48
Kaplan, Ronald M., 16, 26, 35, 87
Karttunen, Lauri, 35, 87
Kasper, Robert T., 158
Kay, Martin, 16, 18, 26
Kaye, Jonathan, 10, 15, 22, 26, 48, 103f
Keating, Patricia, 32f, 99
Keyser, S. J., 62, 113
Kiparsky, Paul, 16, 26, 44, 48, 87, 91
Kisseberth, Charles W., 31
Klein, Ewan H., 3, 29, 35, 45f, 51, 79, 117
Kornai, Andr'as, 15, 18, 26
Koskenniemi, Kimmo, 16, 46, 87
Koutsoudas, Andreas, 2, 38

La Galy, Michael W., 37
Ladd, D. Robert, 14, 84
Laks, Bernard, 19
Langholm, Tore, 30
Larson, Gary N., 19, 21
Lass, Roger, 111, 113, 130
Lassez, Jean-Louis, 135
Lathroum, Amanda, 22
Leben, William R., 11f
Lee, Chan-Do, 22
Levy, Joe, 22
Liberman, Mark Y., 18
Lieber, Rochelle, 105
Lifschitz, Vladimir, 24
Lindsey, Geoff, 22

Lisker, Leigh, 99
Local, John, 32
Lodge, Ken, 48
Lowe, John B., 26
Lowenstamm, Jean, 10, 22, 48, 103f

Manaster Ramer, Alexis, 160
Marsack, C.C., 93
Mastroianni, Michael, 45
Maxwell, Michael, 27
Mazaudon, Martine, 26
McCarthy, John, 12, 48, 95f, 104f, 111ff, 121, 161
Mellish, Chris, 146, 150
Michaylov, Spiro, 151
Minker, Jack, 35
Moortgat, Michael, 35, 42, 45
Morin, Yves, 14
Morrill, Glyn, 42, 45

Nolan, Francis, 98
Noll, Craig, 2, 38

Odden, David, 121
Oehrle, Richard T., 35, 39f, 42, 45
Orgun, Cemil Orhan, 24

Paradis, Carole, 31, 34, 62, 116
Partee, Barbara H., 34, 71
Payne, David L., 94
Pereira, Fernando, 35, 146
Peters, Stanley, 40
Pierrehumbert, Janet B., 32, 52, 57, 85, 160
Piggott, Glyn L., 39, 116f
Pike, E. V., 10
Pike, Kenneth L., 10
Pollard, Carl, 3, 29, 35, 92
Port, Robert, 100
Poser, William, 105f, 129
Powers, David, 26
Prince, Alan, 19, 21, 24, 48, 87, 101, 161
Prunet, Jean-François, 62, 116
Pulleyblank, Douglas, 36, 84f, 93, 112
Pullum, Geoffrey K., 3, 29, 35, 38, 79, 117
Pulman, Stephen, 16, 44

Pye, Susan, 100

Reinhard, Sabine, 45
Reiter, R., 86f
Rice, Keren, 48, 85, 103, 106, 116
Ringen, Catherine, 38
Ritchie, Graeme D., 16, 26
Robinson, Orrin W., 35
Roosen-Runge, P.H., 14
Rounds, William C., 158, 160
Russell, Graham J., 16
Russell, Kevin, 45, 106
Ryle, Gilbert, 33

Sag, Ivan A., 3, 29, 35, 79, 92, 117
Sagey, Elizabeth, 4, 56, 58, 67, 69ff, 110, 113ff, 118ff, 129f, 133, 154
Sanders, Gerald, 2, 38
Sapir, Edward, 109
Saussure, Ferdinand de, 29f
Schane, Sanford A., 85
Schein, Barry, 44
Schmerling, Susan, 40
Schmiedel, Albrecht, 68, 139
Scobbie, James M., 24, 32, 42f, 49, 63ff, 73, 77, 85
Selkirk, Elisabeth O., 58, 99
Shibatani, Masayoshi, 31, 38
Shieber, Stuart, 29, 35, 146
Shillcock, Richard, 22
Slowiaczek, Louisa M., 99f
Smith, Norval, 116
Smolensky, Paul, 24
Smolka, Gert, 135
Snider, Keith, 112
Sprigg, R., 37
Sproat, Richard W., 16
Stanley, Richard, 38f, 86
Steedman, Mark, 42
Steriade, Donca, 44, 48, 64, 97, 105, 115, 121
Stethem, Scott E., 26
Swadesh, Morris, 109
Szymanska, Helena J., 100

Taylor, Barry, 72
Thráinsson, Höskuldur, 113f

Tjong Kim Sang, Erik F., 27
Touretzky, David S., 24
Trigo, Loren, 121
Trubetzkoy, N., 109
Tyson, Mabrys, 35

Uszkoreit, Hans, 3, 29, 35

Vago, Robert M., 105
van Benthem, Johan, 30, 32, 51, 68, 72,
   80, 88, 153, 162
van der Hulst, Harry, 35, 121
van der Linden, Erik-Jan, 42, 45
Vennemann, Theo, 19, 38f
Vergnaud, Jean-Roger, 10, 22, 48, 103f
Vincent, Nigel, 117

Waksler, Rochelle, 44
Wall, Robert E., 40
Walli-Sagey, Elisabeth, 119, *See also*
   Sagey
Walther, Markus, 44, 70
Wang, William, 112
Warren, David H. D., 146
Wasow, Tom, 35
Webber, Bonnie, 35
Welmers, William E., 118
Wheeler, Deirdre W., 2, 24, 32, 34, 36,
   40ff, 100
Wiebe, Bruce, 18, 26
Wiese, Richard, 44, 77, 100
Williams, Sheila M., 26
Winograd, Terry, 28
Withgott, M. Margaret, 18

Yip, Moira, 11f, 105, 111f, 121

Zeevat, Henk, 3, 29

Subject index

abstract specification, 28, 45
abstractness, 37
acoustic hiding, 98
activation, 19, 21
alternation, 6
    with zero, 64, 93, 94f
ambisyllabicity, 62
appropriateness, 58–60, 103
    axiomatised, 58
    abbreviatory convention, 83
    depicted graphically, 60
    in modal logic, 168
Appropriateness Constraint, 58
archiphoneme, 37f
assimilation, 6, 17
    nasal, 92
    place of articulation, 117, 128
    voicing, 4ff
    See also harmony
association,
    attribute-value formulation, 43
    defined, 10f, 65ff
    finite-state formulation, 46f
Attribute Value Phonology, 42–4
    See also feature matrix
autosegment, 10
Autosegmental Phonology, 10
    criticised, 12ff
    introduced, 9–11
    not axiomatised, 52
    rule, 84
axiomatic method, 51
axiomatisation,
    flexible, 152
    normal form, 139–41

    of appropriateness, 58
    of branching degree, 61f
    of convexity, 73
    of dominance, 57, 83, 140
    of equality, 140f
    of immediate precedence, 76
    of inclusion, 72
    of licensing, 63f
    of linearity, 75, 82f
    of locality, 77, 83
    of no-crossing constraint, 69
    of overlap, 66f, 82, 140
    of points, 71
    of precedence, 67, 82, 140
    of sorts, 54f

backtracking, 146, 149f
bitwise operations, 138f
bleeding order, 16
branching degree, 61f
    abbreviatory convention, 83

categorial,
    grammar, 35, 39
    logic, 45
    phonology, 39ff
    See also Montague Phonology
chart, 10
coda, 23, 63
Coda Filter, 63
co-indexing, 43f
combinatorial optimisation, 26
completeness, 88, 136
complexity, 144
compositionality, 34ff

computational phonology,
    motivated, 14f
    surveyed, 16ff
connectionism, 19ff, 27
    activation, 19, 21
    perceptron, 24
    recurrent network, 22ff
    simulating segmental rules, 24
consonant reduction, 113, 130
constraint, 31
    appropriateness, 58
    -based grammar, 3, 29ff, 39, 154
    -based phonology,
        criticised, 91
        defined, 27ff
        introduced, 3
    Linearity, 76
    Linking, 63
    Locality, 77ff, 83
    logic programming, 3, 29, 31, 151f
    morpheme structure, 31, 36
    no-crossing,   *See*   no-crossing
  constraint
    in phonology, 31f
    phonotactic, 37
    pool of, 30, 42
    surface phonetic, 38
    surface structure, 31, 36
    violation, 31
constriction degree, 124, 131f
    for manner features, 127f
    propagation, 125ff
    values, 125ff
constriction location, 124, 131
    values, 127
convexity, 72f

decidability, 88
declarative,
    phonology, 44
    vs. procedural, 28
deductive database, 35
defaults, 8, 86, 103, 105, 127
    prioritised, 24
    See also inheritance; Maximality
  Principle
deletion, 17

calls for, 91ff
    eliminated, 48, 91ff
denotation, 3, 28, 34
Dependency Phonology, 10
description, 32
    combining, 33
    language,
        models, 81f
        rules, 84
        semantics, 81, 164
        syntax, 80f, 163f
        validities, 82
    vs. object, 3, 32f
devoicing, final, 42, 99f
diachronic phonology, 26
distinctive feature, 7, 22, 109ff
dominance, 57f, 83, 157
    immediate, 57, 59f, 164
    in modal logic, 163
    vs. association, 77
double articulation, 119ff
Dynamic Phonology, 10

Elsewhere Principle, 44, 88
evaluation metric, 25f
event, 51
extrasyllabicity, 103

feature, distinctive, 7, 22, 109ff
feature changing rule,
    avoided, 48
    calls for, 98ff
    empirical problems, 105f
feature hierarchy, 25, 111ff
    articulator nodes, 118ff
    laryngeal node, 111ff
    manner node, 115ff
    phonetic basis, 110, 122f
    phonetic basis challenged, 123
    place node, 117f
    place/manner independence, 128ff
        questioned, 129
    supralaryngeal node, 110, 113ff
feature logic, 80
feature matrix, 42ff, 157ff, 166f
    for prosodic structure, 160f
    for subsegmental structure, 157ff

in modal logic, 166
feeding order, 16
finite state machines, 16ff, 46ff
    transducers, 16ff
        criticised, 17f
        extensions, 18
        extensions non-regular, 18
Firthian prosodic analysis, 37, 44
first-order logic, 27, 45, 80
    advantages, 88f
formalism,
    advantages of, 1, 51f, 154
    questioned, 1
Free Element Condition, 48

geminate, 17, 44, 48, 113f
    inalterability, 25, 44
    integrity, 44
    true vs. fake, 114
Generative Phonology, 4ff, 31, 37
    becoming declarative, 48f
    implemented, 14f, 26f
gestural score, 81f, 123f
Government Phonology, 10, 22, 45, 104
grammar formalisms, 3, 29, 35, 79
    DATR, 45
    sign-based, 46
Grassmann's Law, 44
Great Vowel Shift, 44

harmony,
    consonant, 105f
    trans-laryngeal, 115
    vowel, 8ff, 16f, 25, 36, 38, 93, 104f
hierarchy,
    inheritance, 44
    prosodic, 25, 31, 92f
    lexical, 31, 35
homogeneity, 72
heterogeneity, 72

inalterability, 25, 44
inclusion, 72
infixation, 17, 42
inheritance, 35, 44f
insertion, 17, 96
instance-based learning, 26

integrity, 25
intensionality, 32f
interval structure, 164
intonation, 42

larynx, 111ff, 118, 129f
lattice, 54ff
    FOPL representation, 54f
    modal representation, 167f
    for prosodic structure, 54, 59
    for subsegmental structure, 56
learning, 19, 25f
lexical, 35ff
    generalisations, 91
    hierarchy, 92f
    information measure, 36
    rules, 36
    symbol, 16
Lexical Phonology, 91
    implemented, 26
Lexicalist Programme, 35
licensing, 25, 96
    autosegmental, 63f
    in modal logic, 168
    prosodic, 64
linear ordering, 73ff, 83
Linearity Constraint, 75ff
Linking Constraint, 63
Locality Constraint, 77ff, 83
logic,
    categorial, 45
    feature, 80
    four-valued, 137
    modal, 45, 162ff
    programming, 3, 29, 31, 151f
    temporal, 80, 162

major articulator, 121
manner of articulation, 109f, 116, 121, 125ff
markedness, 8, 42, 127
Markov Model, 26
Maximality Principle, 101
metathesis, 17, 42
Metrical Phonology, 10, 42
modal logic, 45, 162ff
model,

building, 136f
minimal, 136
pictures, 81f
theory, 81
monostratal, 2, 34f, 91
Montague Grammar, 2, 40
Montague Phonology, 40, 42
compared with NGP, 42
morpheme structure constraint, 31,
36
mora, 53f, 59, 65, 79, 83, 87, 160

natural class, 109, 122
Natural Generative Phonology, 35, 38f
Natural Phonology, 37
neural networks, *See* connectionism
neutralisation, 39, 42, 98ff
phonetic evidence against, 100
no-crossing constraint, 10ff, 44, 75, 78,
141, 144
derived, 68f
for dominance, 77
for mouth, 132
No-Ordering Condition, 39
nucleus, 102

object-oriented programming, 29, 35, 45
Obligatory Contour Principle, 11f, 111
onset, 63, 65f, 79, 160
Optimality Theory, 24f
overlap, 64–78, 82, 164
in modal logic, 162

palatalisation, 41
parameter setting, 117
partiality, 33, 36, 41f, 85, 139, 167
perceptron, 24
phoneme, 109
phonetic interpretation, 40, 42, 44
phonotactic constraint, 36f, 40f
place of articulation, 115ff, 128ff
points, 69ff
criticised, 70f
defined using inclusion, 71
vs intervals, 69
preaspiration, 113f
precedence, 66ff, 78, 82, 164

immediate, 73, 76
in modal logic, 162
Principle of Compositionality, 34
Prolog, 135, 144ff
prosodic hierarchy, 25, 31, 92f

recurrent network, 22ff
reduplication, 17, 42
re-entrancy, 62f, 161, 167
prohibited, 62f, 102, 169
repair strategies, 12f, 31, 34
resyllabification, 100ff
rule,
autosegmental, 10
compilation, 16, 87
conspiracy, 31
default, 86ff
feature filling, 41, 48
lexical, 91
ordering,
bleeding, 16
blocking, 12f
calls for, 91
extrinsic, 2
feeding, 16
impossible, 33, 37, 42
undesirable, 38
unnecessary, 88
phonological, 5f, 98
post-lexical, 91
viewed as a description, 33, 85f
vs. representation, 34
Rule-to-rule Hypothesis, 34, 41

satisfaction, 3, 164
satisfiability, 89
Schönfinkel-Bernays class, 139, 144f,
150
secondary articulation, 120
Segmental Phonology, 4ff
criticised, 9
implemented, 14f, 26f
semantics,
automaton, 46
declarative, 2
denotational, 3, 28, 34
graphical, 51, 81

    modal logic, 164
    operational, 28, 135
    procedural, 2
    temporal, 46, 65ff
sequences, 160, 167
simultaneity, 72
skolemisation, 150
sorts, 52
    abbreviatory convention, 84
    prosodic, 52ff
    subsegmental, 55ff
soundness, 88
speech processing, 1, 3, 15, 26, 32, 44, 154f
spreading, 128
Stray Erasure, 64, 97
stress, 20f, 24, 42
Strict Cycle Condition, 48
Strict Layer Hypothesis, 58
Structure Preservation, 25
syllable structure, 52, 58ff, 62, 76, 100
    coda, 23, 63
    connectionist model, 22ff
    mora, 53f, 59, 65, 79, 83, 87, 160
    nucleus, 102
    onset, 63, 65f, 79, 160

temporal logic, 80, 162
tier, 10, 43f, 53ff, 60, 74, 83
    linear ordering, 67, 75
tone, 112, 118
True Generalisation Condition, 35, 39
Tube Geometry, 125
Two level morphology, 16ff

underspecification, 34, 42, 48
Underspecification Phonology, 27, 45
unification, 16, 29, 42ff
Universal Core Syllable Condition, 76, 101, 103

validities, 165f

Well-Formedness Condition, 14
Well-Formedness Constraint, 34
well-formedness, degress of, 19